IAN CRUISE

20 YEARS OF

talkSPORT

Behind the scenes of the UK's favourite Sports Radio Station

www.talksport.com

talkSPORT Limited
1 London Bridge Street
London SE1 9GF

www.talksport.com

First published by talkSPORT in 2019

3 5 7 9 10 8 6 4 2

Cover design by Steve Leard
Interior design by Jacqui Caulton

A catalogue record for this book is
available from the British Library

ISBN 978-0-9563284-1-0

Printed and bound by
CPI Group (UK) Ltd, Croydon, CR0 4YY

All photographs supplied courtesy of talkSPORT Limited with
the exception of the following: Junior Roberts (plate 1, bottom);
RadioToday.co.uk (plate 3, top); Kathryn Anastasi (plate 4,
bottom; plate 5, middle and bottom); David Richards (plate 5,
top); Jon Norman (plate 6, top and bottom); News Group
Newspapers (plate 7, top and bottom).

Contents

Acknowledgements

A huge thanks to the following people:

Alan Brazil, Mark Saggers, Richard Keys, Andy Gray, Gareth Batty, Ian 'The Moose' Abrahams, Ally McCoist, Darren Gough, Paul Hawksbee, Adrian Durham, Andy Jacobs, Dennie Morris, Sam Allardyce, Steve Harmison, Laurie Palacio, Laura Woods, Lauren Webster, Dave Walker, 'Barman' Dave Richards, Mike Bovill, Tom Bellwood, Georgie Bingham, Lee Clayton, Liam Fisher, Andy Goldstein, Rufus Gordon, Mike Graham, Moz Dee, Sal Ahmad, Kathryn Anastasi, Sam Ellard, Kurt Edwards, Rob Tomalin, Matt Holland, Ray Parlour, Jim White, Steve Morgan, Dean Saunders, Tom Hughes, Bill Ridley, Matt Smith, Scott Taunton, Jon Norman, Matt Davis, David Williams, Scott Richards, Tom Rennie, Ian Morris, Calum Macaulay, Kathryn Hughes, Piers Collins, Laura Cork, Ian Danter, Fiona Macaulay, Emma De Smith, Neil Dowden, John Cadigan, Simon Heilbron, Owain Jones and Jo Kingsbury.

Chapter 1 ⚽

talkSPORT Kicks Off

talkSPORT was born out of chaos and chaos has never been far from the station in the 20 years since its tricky birth on 17 January 2000.

On that winter's morning, sound engineers were still building the studio desks moments before the breakfast show was due to go on air at 6am. There was barely any furniture in the building and no one really knew yet what the name of the first show was to be called.

In those madcap early days as the speech and current affairs station Talk Radio was hastily rebranded as a sports station, talkSPORT, presenters and producers were seemingly hired and fired on a whim by then owner and ex-*Sun* editor Kelvin MacKenzie. The existing speech station as it was had already begun to make forays into sport. But the name change from Talk Radio to talkSPORT saw a raft of producers and presenters axed including David Banks and Nick Ferrari of the *Big Boys Breakfast*. And while it may have been a new station, the old calamity and chaos never seemed to be too far away.

From those humble beginnings, however, talkSPORT has grown into a broadcasting beast and is now one of the most recognisable media brands in the UK.

At the 2018 World Cup finals in Russia, talkSPORT commentary teams travelled the length and breadth of that huge country to bring the nation the best possible coverage of England's glorious run to the semi-finals. It was a far cry from their first real foray into live broadcasting from a major football tournament, namely the 2000 European Championship finals in Holland. Back then, a team of just six people was forced to transmit match coverage from a hotel room in Amsterdam with sound effects coming from the studios back in London, because the station was refused permission to bid for the rights.

And that was only the tip of the iceberg of the issues at that tournament. Following the upholding of a legal complaint from the BBC about the 'off-tube' coverage (meaning they were watching the games on a TV and not actually inside the ground), talkSPORT's commentary team had to announce, every 15 minutes, that they were not live at the stadium and that the crowd noises were sound effects. All the while a young Dutch lawyer was sat next to them to ensure they stayed on message from a legal standpoint.

Despite those difficulties, however, the future was bright. The listening public warmed to the station's unconventional coverage and the tournament was an undoubted success. Unless you were an England fan. Or Phil Neville, who even now must rue his clumsy challenge that handed Romania a last-gasp penalty which they converted to beat England 3-2 and knock them out of the tournament.

But few people back then would have imagined that within two decades talkSPORT would have weekly audiences of over three million adults, would be the proud recipient of the much-coveted Station of the Year prize at the annual Sony radio industry awards, would be the global audio partner of the English Premier League, broadcasting to 69 countries in five different languages and would be the jewel in the crown of a radio group purchased for £220 million by Rupert Murdoch's News Corporation in 2016.

talkSPORT is now a major player, a far cry from those fledgling days under MacKenzie when the milk in the office kitchen sometimes lasted longer than members of staff and there was the constant threat from Mackenzie that he'd turn the lift off to save money.

MacKenzie had decided to rebrand the radio station he owned, Talk Radio, as talkSPORT in late 1999, and he had decided to do it pretty much straight away. He wanted his new all-sports station, a first for the UK, to be up and running within a couple of months, and not only that but he wanted it relocated to new premises.

It sounds crazy now, and clearly it was then as well, but while Talk Radio was broadcasting from its Oxford Street studios, with staff totally in the dark about the planned new venture, a handful of senior personnel were busy devising new formats, new shows and essentially building a new radio station from scratch.

At this stage, they still had to find studios within weeks and eventually a building near London's South Bank, on a road named Hatfields, was located and deemed the most suitable. But it remained a mad, breakneck plan to try to get the new studios up and running in time to re-launch Talk Radio as talkSPORT in early January 2000.

When current drive-time presenter, and one of the longest serving on the station, Adrian Durham visited the studios just a few days before launch to check out the facilities and rehearse for the following week's initial broadcasts, he found there was no furniture in the newly acquired building. There was a makeshift studio nowhere near completion, minus even a chair on which he could sit. It was mayhem.

"It was a mess," says Durham. "Apart from no furniture, there were no clocks on the walls [vital for a radio station], no computers, no nothing. The test run was a joke because we didn't have the facilities to even do that. So I was dubious we'd launch on time, but it actually happened. And the engineer responsible worked night and day for weeks. Evidently he must have been traumatised by the experience because he was never seen at talkSPORT again."

As the days ticked down to hours before the launch, contractors were still crashing and banging around, while engineers were desperately trying to complete the construction of the studio. All the while, in the middle of the madness, producers were working on dummy shows in an attempt to be ready for the off. And even when the 'off' did happen and talkSPORT was broadcasting live to the nation, there was still an engineer underneath the presenter's desk screwing in the final bolts.

How they managed is the stuff of legend and still talked about today by those involved. But manage it they did and a new station burst on to the airwaves on the 1089/1053 medium wave frequency at 6am on 17 January 2000.

However, the name of the breakfast show was still undecided just moments before they were due to be live on air. The production staff in the building were insistent it should be *The Sports Breakfast with Adrian Durham and Gary Newbon* but, as Newbon was due to utter the first words on the new station, he changed it to *The Sports Breakfast with Gary Newbon and Adrian Durham*. It was that kind of anarchic environment.

Owner Kelvin MacKenzie would occasionally go on air and, in one rant, caned the England and Wales Cricket Board over cricket rights and generally made enemies left, right and centre. So for a long time talkSPORT was seen as the runt of the litter, the annoying little brother, and to an extent the station was stigmatised in the industry. BBC Radio 5 Live's Alan Green called talkSPORT "lamentable" in his book that was published in 2000.

MacKenzie was not only rattling cages in the wider world, he was similarly prone to doing so internally, leading to staff coining a memorable phrase that endures to this day, the 'talkSPORT holiday'.

Durham explains: "If you stood up to MacKenzie, it was easy enough to work for him. He would bark in your face and be demanding to the point of ridiculousness, but that was about him and his ego, and in that era there were plenty like him in the media industry. People went on what we called 'talkSPORT holidays'. In other words, they would book a holiday, get back, and find someone else had taken their job. It was chaotic to say the least."

But out of the bedlam came some success with the rebranded station attracting more upmarket male listeners. And the commercial team had a very clear message to sell to potential advertisers both in terms of what the output was like and what the audience was like. The first set of audience figures reported for the new sports station showed that 70% of the audience was male, and what's more 53% were in the coveted upmarket ABC1 demographic – in newspaper terms, more *Daily Telegraph* than *Daily Star.*

Durham says: "Those early days were incredible. They felt under-resourced, badly planned, and ill-equipped and you had to watch out for the ego minefield that had suddenly appeared with some 'so-called' big names brought in to boost the profile of the new station. What you find with some (not all) of those big names is that they're in it for themselves and really don't care about the radio station. Outside of the launch there was very little marketing of talkSPORT so we had an uphill battle."

The then Marketing Director Calum Macaulay recalls: "We'd spent a lot of money supporting the launch of the new sports station and brought in a younger male audience, but not fast enough to replace many of the existing Talk Radio audience who wondered where their diet of current affairs and news content had gone. A whole swathe of them just disappeared overnight. So the audience actually tumbled and in Kelvin's words I'd 'pissed £2 million up the wall'. At that time I was known as Calum Macaulay G.B.C. – Gone by Christmas."

Durham adds: "Those early days were tough but our audience began to build and helped us make it. Alan Brazil and Mike Parry on breakfast were unmissable, mainly for their hilarious absurdity, which made very entertaining radio – perfect for breakfast. Hawksbee and Jacobs are legends of talkSPORT who don't get the recognition they deserve from the industry and they have brought consistent quality from day one. The solid authentic football feel of the Saturday afternoon show gave the radio station a credible cornerstone every week, and a show called *Football First in Europe* with Guillem Balague, Gab Marcotti and myself on Monday evenings really gave us gravitas. We're all still good friends, and listeners still message me about that show. It was brilliant."

The station was up and running in every sense and, although MacKenzie could often still be seen and heard issuing withering warnings to staff, be they presenters or producers, there can be little doubt his frustrations came from a desire to succeed.

Right from the beginning he had been determined to take on the BBC front and centre and he did just that, focusing on the battle for live sports rights. But when it came to football rights he met the familiar Beeb brick wall. They owned the rights to the Premier League, World Cup finals, European Championship finals, the whole shooting match. And, at that time, it was pretty much a closed shop.

talkSPORT did have very limited rights to Premier League coverage involving certain teams in certain areas of the country, but it was nowhere near enough to gain attention on a national level.

They also broadcast live cricket, having won the rights for England's overseas tour of South Africa from the BBC in 1999–2000 when they were still plain old Talk Radio, and they delivered live coverage of The Open golf championship from St Andrews later that same summer.

But the football market proved a ridiculously tough nut to crack, and that situation wasn't to change until after MacKenzie's departure.

There were plenty of bumps in the road along the way in those first few years, of course, including some high-profile exits. And almost exits …

Ebullient breakfast show host and ex-Ipswich, Manchester United and Scotland player Alan Brazil was sacked in March 2004 after going AWOL during the Cheltenham Festival (more of that later), only to be reinstated three weeks later following a furious backlash from his talkSPORT audience. Popular presenters James Whale and Jon Gaunt were both axed following on-air controversies – Whale for flouting Ofcom rules on impartiality during election periods and championing the cause for Boris Johnson to be elected as London's Mayor, and Gaunt for calling Redbridge councillor Michael Stark a "Nazi" in a row over whether smokers should be allowed to foster children in the borough.

MacKenzie himself was forced out in May 2005 when, following a failed management buyout, Northern Irish TV company UTV bought the Wireless Group for £98.2 million. talkSPORT was MacKenzie's baby, but it was losing money. MacKenzie's title was actually Chairman and Chief Executive of Wireless Group, with he himself owning 6.4% of the company. The majority shareholders were Rupert Murdoch's News International, which owned 24.5%, and US company Liberty Media, which owned 26.7%.

As well as Talk Radio, Wireless Group had also acquired two major UK companies in 1999 – the Radio Partnership and its six regional stations, plus the Independent Radio Group and its five stations. But by the end of 2004 the company continued to lose money and, Murdoch and Liberty Media Chairman John Malone had chosen to dispose of their UK radio asset.

MacKenzie attempted to take sole control of the company with a management buyout, but was unable to raise the necessary capital. Eventually the Wireless Group board retained the services of investment bankers Goldman Sachs to instigate a sale and UTV bought the company for £98.2 million. And that was set to be the real game-changer for talkSPORT.

Australian-born Scott Taunton was named as the man in charge of the UTV radio operation and he would take day-to-day control of talkSPORT from its London offices, relocating from Belfast. And he arrived in England with a very clear sense of the direction the station needed to take.

He says: "If you think back to 2005 when UTV acquired talkSPORT along with the rest of Wireless Group, talkSPORT had lost £84 million cumulatively at that point. And it had done it mostly because it had attempted to do programming in a relatively cheap fashion and expected advertisers to step up to the plate and to back that lesser-quality product. And it just doesn't work in that way.

"So one of the things I was keen to change from very early on was that anything we did, we did properly. So if we were going to broadcast a football match we were going to have the rights to do that, we weren't going to have an unofficial commentary. And we were going to bring in sponsors to support that."

The first step on this road was acquiring the rights to be an official radio broadcaster of the 2006 FIFA World Cup in

Germany. And the station broadcast the tournament with aplomb, including releasing a 'road-trip' video following the exploits of Rodney Marsh, Adrian Durham, Alvin Martin, Gary Stevens, Mike Parry and the team as they weaved their way across Germany. England would eventually crash out of the tournament in the quarter-finals to Portugal following a penalty shoot-out. As had Wayne Rooney for an earlier indiscretion.

But the real sea-change moment for talkSPORT came in October of that year when they were awarded live English Premier League commentary rights for the first time, so breaking the BBC's monopoly on the coverage.

Admittedly, the Beeb retained six of the seven packages on offer, with talkSPORT claiming the second choice 3pm Saturday kick-off.

Just having that badge, "Official UK Broadcast Radio Partner" of the English Premier League, alongside their sales collateral made a big difference to talkSPORT. And that was enhanced in 2010 when talkSPORT announced it had signed a deal to win further Premier League rights from their rivals at BBC Radio 5 Live from the start of the 2010/11 season. This meant that, for the next three years at least, the station would broadcast two live matches every weekend – the Saturday 5.30pm kick-off and the Sunday lunchtime match. So going from 32 matches a season to over 60. It would lead to significant growth in the station's audience.

That decision left the top brass at the BBC livid, and talkSPORT CEO Scott Taunton delighted. He said at the time to the media press: "It's a great day for talkSPORT and commercial radio in the UK. To have won the rights to broadcast live and exclusive Barclays Premier League football on both a Saturday and Sunday, when no other national radio broadcaster – including the BBC – has commentary, puts the station at the very heart of Premier League football in the UK."

The Saturday evening fixture gave the station a massively strong line-up with the live football coming straight off the back of the hugely popular *Matchday Live* and followed by *Call Collymore*, which was always a lively phone-in show.

Matchday Live is one of the staples of the station and has played a huge part in establishing talkSPORT as the go-to destination for football fans up and down the country. As host Adrian Durham says, the audience knows there is going to be something for everyone: "It's all about the football: whether you support a National League team or a Premier League team, your side's goal will get a mention. It's fast-moving, it's live at the grounds, it covers everything. It's absolutely why I got into radio. I get to host a solid football show for five-plus hours on a Saturday from a Premier League game. It wipes me out – I have no on-site producer, I gather together all the goalscorers myself, as well as half-times and full-times, often without adequate WiFi and sometimes with my feet turning into blocks of ice. I don't get home until late Saturday night, but the show is a joy to host.

"I know there was a moment some years back when to cut costs the idea of not bothering with anything outside of the Premier League was discussed among management at talkSPORT, but thankfully it was dismissed. Something like that would mean the end of me on that Saturday show."

In the summer of 2010 talkSPORT would be an official broadcast partner at its second World Cup finals, in South Africa, following the success of their coverage of the tournament in Germany four years earlier.

As well as the football rights, talkSPORT also signed a deal for the exclusive broadcast rights for the 2011 Rugby World Cup in New Zealand – another bloody nose for the BBC – and a further indication they were now becoming a major player, not some cocky, wide-boy upstart.

talkSPORT was growing up, and it was growing up fast. But anyone who imagined that over the course of its second decade it would leave behind the madness and mayhem of its first ten years could not have been more wrong.

If anything, the fun and games were only just beginning …

'Clips of the Week': The Top 20 All-Time Greats

'Clips of the Week' is one of the most established features on the station, broadcast every Friday at 3.30pm within Paul Hawksbee and Andy Jacobs' long-running afternoon show. It celebrates the on-air gaffes and foul-ups from that week. But it could have been killed off almost before it started. In the early days, Alan Brazil was frequently the butt of the joke, leading to then Programme Director Mike Parry instructing Hawksbee and Jacobs that they should refrain from taking the mickey out of Brazil as he was the star of the schedule and so deserved more respect, suggesting some of the banter was going a bit far. But no sooner had that message been taken on board, then owner Kelvin MacKenzie, insisted he loved it and the pair should continue in exactly the same vein.

In between chapters, we celebrate 20 years of talkSPORT with our 'Clips of the Week: The Top 20 All-Time Greats'. Here's No. 20 to kick us off.

'CLIPS OF THE WEEK'

The Top 20 All-Time Greats

#20

Newsreader Liz Saul, proving she's not quite the football expert that you might imagine:

"David Beckham will be officially presented as an LA Galaxy player tomorrow night. He and Posh leave Britain for America this afternoon. Becks is following in the footsteps of some of the sport's biggest names such as ... Joanne Croff, Franz Berkinboirger and ... Gyorgy Best."

Chapter 2 ⚽

Collymore in Bedroom Farce at 2010 World Cup, South Africa

Long considered the preserve of 'white van man' and the bolshie upstart of British radio, the station was to prove itself to be much more than that. It did so again with its exemplary coverage of the 2010 World Cup finals in South Africa. This was the second successive tournament at which the station had been an official rights holder following its inaugural campaign in Germany, 2006.

But even before that tournament started there was drama for talkSPORT at the draw in December 2009, amid fears that a member of the production team had been killed.

A four-man party – Programme Director Moz Dee, presenter Mark Saggers, Outside Broadcast Manager Matt Smith and producer Dennie Morris – had been dispatched to Cape Town for the draw and to do a recce ahead of the event in the summer of the following year.

All was going swimmingly until one evening after a few beers. Dee befriended some locals and was drinking with them in a bar on trendy Long Street in the city centre. He was joined by Morris. The pair continued into the night, before leaving the pub together, by which time Dee was less than steady on his feet.

With Dee using Morris as a makeshift crutch, the pair began to wobble their way towards their respective hotels. But as that rather comedic scene was playing out, a young lad ran towards them, dipped his hand in Morris's jacket pocket and raced off with his mobile phone.

It seems likely some of the locals in the bar had spotted their fancy phones and viewed them as easy targets. That may have been the case, but Morris wasn't prepared to give up his mobile without something of a fight. He set off in pursuit of the opportunistic phone pincher.

This wasn't the best news for Dee, however. With Morris sprinting off into the distance, and Dee no longer having anyone to hold on to, he was left to fend for himself.

By now Morris, still in hot pursuit of the pacy pickpocket, was about to fall foul of Cape Town's clean-up routine. Anyone who has spent time on Long Street in the evening will know that the streets are cleaned each night with a mixture of water and detergent. And that put paid to the chase. As Morris rounded a corner, he lost his footing, slid along the pavement and could only watch helplessly as his attacker, and his phone, disappeared into the night.

With nothing more he could do, Morris returned to his hotel room, blissfully unaware that he was at the centre of a ridiculous murder mystery.

Dee, against all odds, had made it back safely to his own hotel, but there was clearly some alcohol-befuddled thinking on his part. For some reason, even though he had been with Morris just a short while before, he had decided to phone the studios in London to find out if anyone had heard from the producer. Unlikely of course, given that he had just witnessed him being robbed of his phone.

But Dee was not thinking about that when he was informed no one had heard from Morris. Instead, he broke down in tears and could be heard sobbing down the phone: "Dennie's dead ... Dennie's dead ..." Fortunately, of course, Dennie wasn't, although he had scuffed his knees slightly sliding along Long Street.

It was yet another talking point on a trip that had started on a bizarre note when Dee arrived in South Africa without any clothes – well, apart from the ones he was wearing. For some reason known only to himself, he had decided not to take a suitcase.

That meant he had to quickly buy a whole new wardrobe on arrival, which he did, and clearly from some lesser-known South African fashion emporiums. More Daktari than Ralph Lauren! He also managed to deck himself out in a pair of shoes that were too small for him, meaning they caused his heels to bleed. Suffice to say, no one from Paris or Milan was likely to be signing him up to model their next collection.

The trip, however, proved worthwhile in terms of planning for the finals the following year. It was Matt Smith's job to organise the trip, as he had done in Germany in 2006. Essentially what happens is the station buys the rights and then hands it over to someone, in this case Smith, to plan all the logistics.

It is quite a task, particularly as the goalposts often move with frequent changes to presenter line-up, travel and accommodation along the way. But while the demands may change, the budget doesn't, so it's very much a juggling act.

It's also very difficult when you're up against a better-resourced broadcaster, who has much bigger budgets and plane-loads of people going out to tournaments. talkSPORT would typically have around just 20 people for a World Cup even though they were producing double the amount of programming.

This led to Smith having to carefully manage the numbers and think 'outside the box' to balance the books. One thing had become abundantly clear to him during the recce. Given the tight talkSPORT budget, staying in hotels was out of the question as the costs would be prohibitive.

The better option therefore was to find a lodge big enough for the whole team to live in throughout the duration of the tournament, flying in and out of venues to cover games. An added bonus of that approach was that it meant talkSPORT could build its own studio on site.

Smith decided a lodge in Johannesburg would make for the best base, and the team were delighted with what they found when they arrived at their World Cup 'home'. And a formidable team it was, including Stan Collymore, Mark Saggers, Ray Parlour, Micky Quinn, Darren Gough, Adrian Durham, Matt Holland, Ian Danter, Jim Proudfoot and Andy Townsend.

The lodge exceeded expectations, complete with its own tennis court and swimming pool (although June in Jo'burg is not necessarily the best time for a dip given it's their winter!), but the huge security gate and barbed-wire fences took a little getting used to for people more accustomed to leafy suburbia. It certainly looked a bit fearsome compared to a two-up, two-down in middle England, but it soon began to feel perfectly normal.

Ray Parlour, for whom this would be his first trip with the talkSPORT team, comments: "It was a great World Cup, probably the best one I've been to. South Africa was really good and well organised in the end because we thought it was going to be a bit of a nightmare."

With a regularly stocked drinks cabinet and five-star food being prepared by on-site chefs, the team wanted for nothing.

But all being under one roof naturally made for a unique environment. "It was lively," says Liam Fisher, who was a producer at the time but would go on to become talkSPORT's Programme Director and later national controller of Wireless Group's stable of national stations. "It felt like the set of *Big Brother*. That is probably the best way of describing it, trying to avoid the weekly eviction."

It was fortunate no one was trying to tune in to *Big Brother* the night the talkSPORT team turned up at their new home, because Stan Collymore managed to break the brand new plasma TV within hours of their arrival. Stan had decided it would be a good idea to watch a DVD through his laptop on the giant screen in the living room. Having disabled the TV's cable connections, a process that took a considerable amount of time, he hooked up his laptop instead. He turned the TV back on only to be confronted by a completely blank screen. He tried, in vain as it eventually turned out, to restore the TV to its original settings before it was finally agreed by those gathered in the lounge that, yes, the television was indeed broken. And so a call went out to the lodge owners to try to remedy the problem. Not the best of starts.

Technology also played a part in a brilliant wind-up that saw sports reporter Ian "The Moose" Abrahams display previously unimagined athletic prowess. He had been annoying people with his habit of leaving the audio equipment in the studio on, meaning someone else always had to be responsible for turning it off. Eventually, his colleagues grew increasingly tired of this sloppy attitude and so, having one evening discovered the kit had once again not been switched off, Adrian Durham sent The Moose a text asking him if he was the guilty party. The Moose apologetically replied that he was, whereupon Durham told him he'd better get back to the lodge straight away because something had happened with the equipment and there had been a fire.

Dashing out of the local bar where he was winding down at the end of the day, The Moose probably shattered a couple of long-standing athletics records as he raced back in double-quick time, only to be met by the sounds of increasingly loud and raucous laughter among his colleagues as they took in the sight of the by now extremely concerned and extremely sweaty reporter, wondering why there was no smoke.

Humour is key on big tournament trips where people are thrust into the strange environment of living with work colleagues for maybe six to seven weeks at a time. It's a bizarre situation and means individuals often need to display levels of patience alien to them. That was certainly the case for Matt Smith who, having discovered there were not enough single rooms in the lodge to go around, was forced to share with a snoring Moose. And no one wants that.

Mind you, at least if he was snoring, he was safely tucked up, unlike one night when there were fears an intruder had got inside the property and was trying to get into the bedrooms. Adrian Durham described it as like "hearing this elephant charging down the corridors". But with all the pre-tournament scare stories about crime in South Africa, it was no laughing matter.

Durham nervously sent a text to Ian Danter, who was in the room next door, asking if he realised someone had been trying to get into his room. Danter, who as well as being a huge Birmingham City fan, was also a member of a Kiss tribute band and the man the breakfast producers had on speed dial to cover for one of Alan Brazil's not infrequent no-shows, laughed it off by joking it was probably Mike Parry getting back after a night out. But Durham was still not convinced, asking his colleague: "How do you know it's not some axe murderer?" And it was then that the tension was eased when Danter replied, quite brilliantly, "Because I think he would have got in."

Whoever the mystery pachyderm was, he must have eventually found his way back to his own quarters, unlike one evening when Morris recalls waking up to find a disorientated Stan Collymore had come into the wrong room, trying to get into what he thought was his bed.

Collymore is about 6ft 3in. It's fair to say Morris is more like an English Jimmy Krankie and he had to literally stand on his bed and was physically hitting Collymore in the chest to force him out of the room. What a sight that must have been. You don't even get that on *Big Brother*.

If a mistake was made, it was probably the fact that talk-SPORT didn't effectively convey the atmosphere of South Africa in the build-up to the tournament. Lessons learned were put into practice at later tournaments in countries like Brazil and Russia where the flavour of the host countries was really captured.

Not to say that the team didn't get out and about at times. And of course when you're on trips of this kind it's important to be culturally aware of your surroundings. Just ask former Newcastle and Coventry centre-forward Micky Quinn.

He and Liam Fisher along with ex-Ipswich, Charlton and Irish international Matt Holland and a number of other presenters and producers hired a minibus to take them on a tour of Johannesburg and Soweto. As part of the tour they went to Winnie Mandela's house, where the prime exhibit is the chair that Nelson Mandela, a relatively slight man, used to sit in.

The chair is in the corner of a room and people respectfully file past it and take photos. Not Micky Quinn. Instead he promptly sat his fairly ample posterior firmly in the centre of it and asked Fisher to take his picture. It was a tight squeeze and it took considerable effort to unwedge his behind from Mandela's favourite recliner. So here is this piece of history, meant to be preserved for generations to come, and Quinny had probably taken a quarter inch of leather off it in one go.

Jon Norman is a time-served talkSPORT producer who divides his sporting passions between football (Fulham FC) and cricket. He and drive-time presenter Darren Gough also ran into some problems of their own in Cape Town. Fortunately, unlike Morris and Dee a few months previously, neither of them had their phones stolen nor did they fall over in the middle of the street, though they both feared for their safety.

This time it was to do with growling mutts. Matt Smith had arranged for them to use the studios at the home of cricket writer Neil Manthorp, who was out of the country at the time. But when the pair arrived at the front gate they were met with the sight of Manthorp's dogs, big Rhodesian Ridgebacks, roaming the grounds. Neither was too keen on entering and after calling Smith to tell him the situation, they were advised to call the gardener who would grant them safe passage past the guard dogs. This was definitely one occasion when the dogs' bite would be much worse than their bark.

"Yeah I know, I s**t myself," says Goughie. "We went to his house and I didn't like the look of his dogs. Killer dogs basically. Ridgebacks. I love dogs but in Cape Town security is strong and two middle-aged white guys turning up? I wasn't so sure the dogs were going to be that friendly. I wasn't going anywhere near them, they just looked angry. There are certain dogs you look at and you think, 'I'm not going to pat that' and Neil's dogs were like that. There was no way I was going to chance just walking in."

Stories like that give everyone a laugh and are remembered, embellished and retold for years. And the team spirit created proves vital on tours when things don't always go as planned.

One such incident occurred on day one at the opening ceremony [followed by the opening match, South Africa-Mexico] in Johannesburg, with Fisher admitting the station wasn't quite as fully prepared as it thought it was for such a showpiece occasion with the eyes and ears of the world watching and listening.

talkSPORT suffered production issues which is not uncommon on the first day but in this case the issues were of the most basic level. First, there was only one road in and out of the stadium and it was heaving by the time the team joined it in their cars.

It became clear that they hadn't left enough time to get there for the ceremony as they were now stuck in a long tailback that wasn't for moving. An executive decision was made to jump out and haul the kit for the last half mile on the basis it would be quicker. With all hands to the pump, the queuing motorists were treated to the sight of talkSPORT's crack national broadcasting team sprinting up the highway with assorted cables, microphones and other paraphernalia over their shoulders.

Despite somehow getting to the stadium before the start, all the 'apparently' meticulous planning and the well-lubricated 'recce' in December failed to uncover that British-style plugs would not fit into the stadium sockets in the media booths – or, more likely, someone just forgot. Additionally they found that no one had brought the batteries nor enough cables required to get half the kit functioning. This was the cue for Fisher and the team to go humbly to their big rivals at the BBC and beg, steal and grovel. And to be fair to them, they were extremely helpful, probably on the basis that it can happen to any of us at some stage. But for a period, the station's broadcast from the opening ceremony was actually not being transmitted back to the UK. Perhaps the ultimate irony was that back in the studios in London the technical operator was still pumping out the station's promotional trails for the event, loudly proclaiming, "Live and uninterrupted coverage of the World Cup." Well, not exactly.

It's virtually a criminal offence in broadcasting to be off air. The commentary team was on their knees and humiliated at having to go cap in hand to their arch rivals for help. The issues led to a frosty atmosphere back at the Johannesburg lodge that night and cross words were exchanged. Frustration stemmed from the passion to get things right. Grievances were aired and the team moved on.

Liam Fisher explains: "That's what you have to do at a tournament, because you've got three games the following day, and again the day after that. There's no time for lengthy inquests, you just have to get on with things very quickly.

"Mark Saggers was very bullish about what had gone on, and made it clear it wasn't good enough. No one was disagreeing with him, but suffice to say he was angry that evening when we sat down for dinner, but I'll always remember – and it still makes me shiver slightly to this day – that he ended the evening by kissing me on the cheek. So it can't have been that bad."

In another universe, Programme Director Moz Dee was unaware of the day's shenanigans as he'd been entertaining the sponsors, Barclays. He wandered into the lodge in the midst of the very heated inquisition, opened the door without a care in the world and with a big smile said, "Everything alright fellas?" If looks could kill.

Mark Saggers had arrived at the station a year or so earlier after leaving the BBC. His last job for Radio 5 Live had been at the 2009 Champions League final where Barcelona beat Manchester United, and so it was that he awoke the following morning in Rome, on the day of his 50th birthday, out of work. "That's part of life as a gob on a stick and you have to get on with it," he reflected.

He met with Dee, who had worked with him at the BBC, and, although at that stage he wasn't sure where to place him in the schedule, Dee was keen to get him on board. Saggers says: "I'd always listened to talkSPORT, as the competition, and I'd heard so many people at the BBC be very disparaging about it but I thought even in those days it had plenty to offer. *The Alan Brazil Sports Breakfast* was different to anything else out there, and Mike Parry and Andy Townsend were laugh-out-loud funny. I knew Adrian Durham did *Drive* and Paul Hawksbee and Andy Jacobs were a fixture in the afternoons so I was under no illusions. I was going to be doing what I'd done all my career really and basically fill in and hopefully prove myself."

His first show was a baptism of fire and highlighted just how different life was going to be at talkSPORT compared to the BBC. He had interrupted a family holiday in Majorca to fly home on his own to present a Saturday afternoon show between 12 noon and 6pm. On arrival at the studio he was told his guest would be former England international rugby prop Jeff Probyn and that, with the British and Irish Lions playing in South Africa that same afternoon, the pair would "do some rugby". So far, so good until he asked, "Who do we have at the rugby?" He was told,

"No one. Jeff will do it from the studio." "OK, and what other guests are lined up?" "Er, no one, Mark. Just you, Jeff and the rugby for six hours."

Saggers figured there would be no one left listening after about 25 minutes, but that was pretty much a good indication of what talkSPORT's summer schedule in non-football tournament years looked like back then.

As he drove back to Gatwick to re-join his family, Saggers admitted he wasn't feeling too sure about his talkSPORT prospects, but he was determined to make it happen. And following further discussions with Dee, he was paired with Micky Quinn to host *Weekend Sports Breakfast*. And that's when he really began to feel at home. The show was a lively mix of news, interviews and fun, and the audience lapped it up, as was shown by a sharp increase in listeners.

Saggers was also able to utilise the excellent contacts he had built up over the years to deliver a couple of brilliant exclusives in his early years at the station. In January 2011, he broke the news on the night of the transfer deadline that Fernando Torres would be joining Liverpool in a record £50 million deal. Then he captured the interview the whole of the UK media wanted as Chelsea chairman Bruce Buck and Chief Executive Ron Gourlay joined him and Quinn in the studio to reflect for the first time on the news that Blues captain John Terry had been found guilty by the Football Association of racially abusing QPR defender Anton Ferdinand.

The Stamford Bridge club had held their usual pre-match manager's press conference on the Friday following that verdict but Buck, who was in attendance, refused to answer any questions on the subject. Instead he told the assembled media they would get the full story by listening to Saggers and Quinny on talkSPORT on Sunday morning, and that was when Buck issued a formal apology on behalf of Chelsea FC to the Ferdinand family, while also confirming Terry would remain as Chelsea captain. Naturally with these stories being picked up by the national press and accredited to talkSPORT, it was great publicity for the station.

The relationship between Saggers and Buck also led to a memorable afternoon at Stamford Bridge when he and Quinn were invited into the directors' box to watch Chelsea play Liverpool. Lifelong Red Quinny figured it would be entirely reasonable to turn up in a red shirt, red tie and a suit with a red lining! He probably would have got away with it had he not jumped up to celebrate Liverpool's winning goal, while of course sitting in the Chelsea side of the directors' box. Buck was gracious in defeat but, on bidding the pair farewell, he did inform Quinn he would never be allowed in there again.

Saggers and Quinn enjoyed a largely good relationship, but towards the end of their time co-hosting *Weekend Sports Breakfast* there were occasions when tempers would flare. Notably early one morning the pair almost came to blows in an argument about players' wages, with Quinn sticking up for the pros and complaining that Saggers was sucking the life out of him. So ferocious was the argument that producer Ian Morris felt he needed to try to separate the pair, much like a boxing referee, despite the fact he is considerably smaller than either man. Morris, who had only recently arrived at talkSPORT, says: "I was thinking to myself, what am I doing in this toilet of an office at 6.30am in between two grown men hell bent on having a full-on row?"

Saggers' angry outbursts are the stuff of talkSPORT legend and every producer he's worked with has been on the receiving end of his ire at some time or another. But that passion is what makes him such a brilliant broadcaster. When he gets going, he lets rip with both barrels. He has produced some memorable rants on air over the years, but one of his most famous outbursts, among his talkSPORT colleagues at least, never made it to the airwaves.

In the immediate aftermath of Frank Lampard's 'goal' for England against Germany at the World Cup in 2010 being ruled out – the officials decided the ball had not crossed the line – Saggers really lost his cool. That would have been 2-2 as half-time approached, and Saggers could not contain his anger. The ball was at least a yard over the line. Credit at this point must go to talkSPORT audio guru Owain Jones back in London, who had the good sense to record Saggers off air, resulting in some of the best unbroadcastable content talkSPORT has ever created as the furious presenter tore in to FIFA.

An elated Saggers was shouting delightedly: "Come on. Come on. Yeeeeeeeessssss. It's a goal. It's a goal. It's a goal. It's a goal. It's a goal ..."

Gradually, as Saggers started realising the goal was not going to be given, his voice began to take on an air of incredulity and sheer disbelief.

"It's a goal ... It's a goal ... It's a goal ... It's a goal ... Boo ... Boo ... It's a goal. It's a goal. Ooooohhh, [sees TV replay], miles over the line. You cheating bastards. Ah, f*****g hell, it's this far over. Ah, come on. You bastards. Boo."

Germany went on to win that last-16 match 4-1, and eventually finished third after beating Uruguay in the play-off. But who knows how history might have changed had Lampard's effort been correctly awarded. In fact, history probably did change as a result of that incident. To many people watching, given what they know now, it certainly felt like the beginning of the movement to use technology smarter and introduce VAR (Video Assistant Referee).

"The two FIFA officials were sitting in front of us, and at that stage I was a fan because I had handed over to the commentary team," says Saggers. "And I started, 'It's a goal, it's a goal'. They [the FIFA officials] looked around, and I was like 'FIFA ...' It was passionate, from the heart, and the station decided to play it (minus the swearing of course). I didn't know it had been recorded but that clip went around the world. And I still maintain that was part of goal-line technology coming in to the game, I really do believe that. It was a big moment for me, but I didn't do it deliberately, I didn't know I was going to say that."

Whether Saggers and talkSPORT can take all the credit for the game's recent VAR evolution is unclear but the FIFA executives who heard his furious remarks must have recognised something had to be done – if only to ensure this radio presenter didn't one day self-combust in the commentary box!

And he nearly did, six years later in Nice at Euro 2016. But more of that later.

'CLIPS OF THE WEEK'

The Top 20 All-Time Greats
#19

Alan Brazil's broadcasting skills are not in question, but just occasionally his 'quick questions', in this case to former Villa keeper Nigel Spink as Aston Villa under Alex McLeish faced a relegation dogfight in season 2011/12, become slightly longer than intended.

Alan: Nigel, in a strange way, you know I've looked at the remaining games for the Villa and, yes, they are in trouble. There's no doubt. And how they're going to get out of it is simply togetherness because they haven't got the players to come back in, you know if there's major problems. He's got kids ... but the remaining games, West Brom vs Villa, Villa at home to Spurs ... er ... Tottenham by the way are struggling, Norwich against Villa and, of course, Norwich's Paul Lambert gets a mention which I think's a bit unfair on Norwich and the season they've had but you know I think Alex has got to and, knowing him as I do, I think if he can, you know, he's got to stay for the last three games. I can't see what good it will do bringing someone in now if they can get someone at this late stage, someone that's going to make a difference, and I think ... listen, at the end of the season Alex might look at it and say, "OK, we kept them up by the skin of our teeth or we didn't, I'll go," that may well happen, but the story for me is West Brom in great form go to Anfield, Roy Hodgson beats his old club, West Brom big, big favourites here, you can't see the Villa getting anything but, maybe a point ... but it just might lift them ... I don't know, it's a local derby, form goes out the window, the atmosphere will be red hot, the Albion fans will be wanting four or five, and it might just lift Villa, it might get them something that could keep them up?

Spink: Yeah, maybe.

Chapter 3

Noisy Boys Get Rowdy at Radio Oscars and Brazil Goes AWOL

"**A**nd the winner is ... talkSPORT ..."

Cue pandemonium as all 23 (that's right, all 23) people on the two talkSPORT tables invaded the stage to accept the award for UK Station of the Year at the prestigious Sony Awards in London's swanky Grosvenor House Hotel in May 2011.

Now the eagle-eyed among you may have spotted that 23 is an odd number. You might expect two tables to yield an even number of guests. And you would be right. There was indeed one high-profile absentee from the celebrations who shall be revealed shortly.

Picture the scene as talkSPORT's merry (in some cases, very merry) band of brothers and sisters took to the stage to receive their accolade, having beaten the other nominees, BBC Radio 3 and BBC Radio 4, to the top prize.

The Sonys (now known as the Radio Academy Awards) are the radio equivalent of the Oscars, minus the eye-wateringly expensive designer dresses and the $100,000 goodie bags. While the event may lack some of the glitz and glamour of Hollywood's celebration of the great and the good of the silver screen, it is an extremely well-regarded ceremony held in the highest esteem possible by those working in the industry in the UK. The fact that talkSPORT had forked out for two expensive tables at the event – unheard of for a single commercial radio station – suggested that management may have been quietly confident that something was afoot.

Winners of such awards are, for the most part, largely humble in victory, while the losers are suitably gallant in defeat. talkSPORT, of course, raised (or should that be lowered?) the bar. And then proceeded to drink it dry.

Once all 23 of the gleeful recipients exited the stage, the celebrations got truly raucous. Jenni Murray, Radio 4's *Woman's Hour* presenter, was later on stage receiving the Gold Award, the final presentation of the evening for 'a career of exemplary broadcasting'. She was being praised for her incisive yet sensitive interviewing skills, her championing of the women's perspective and the inspiration she gave to others. At this point, it was the recipient herself who was forced to turn to the audience and shout, 'Will you please be quiet?' It was aimed at the talkSPORT posse who by now were serenading the room with a boisterous rendition of 'Championes, Championes' as though they had, in fact, been crowned Premier League champions. Which in some ways, they had.

talkSPORT's Laurie Palacio, a stalwart of the backroom team who at the time was producing *The Late Show* with Ian Collins, was there that night. He says: "I just remember being really, really proud because we had been to these occasions before – and since – and we were always at the back of the room, maybe a table because the bosses didn't want to pay for 15 tables like the BBC can. But there was just something in the air, the mix of people around the tables felt right, we were on the crest of a wave off the back of the World Cup [in South Africa in 2010], and to get the recognition from your peers, especially in radio where you have this domination by the BBC, it's a bit like Leicester winning the Premier League.

"That's how I remember it. We shouldn't have had a prayer of winning, but we did because our World Cup coverage was the best we had done up to that point and our audience figures were flying. Programme Director Moz Dee was a Claudio Ranieri-style Tinkerman, Keys and Gray were like our Jamie Vardy and the whole year had been headline after headline. I'd never known anything like it.

"I'd been so used to us cutting our cloth accordingly, so much so that in some years we hadn't even entered the Sonys because we just thought: 'What's the point, we're just making up the numbers?'

"The looks around the room when we were announced as Station of the Year I'm sure were, 'Who are these people? Where have they come from? Why are they making so much noise? And why are there so many of them on stage?'

"I'm not sure who started the chants of 'Championes' ... Moz, probably. But it felt right. We were a football station and we were ultimately being slightly laddish, admittedly perhaps more Millwall than Leicester City at that stage."

That award sparked a never to be forgotten 48 hours of revelry that will forever be the stuff of legend among those who took part in it. But we must pause briefly at this juncture to re-visit the case of the 'missing guest'. Who was the mystery man or woman who had gone AWOL just at the point of talkSPORT's greatest triumph?

Of course, it could be none other than Alan Bernard Brazil, a man with 'previous' for going missing. Although now known to most as the longest-standing breakfast show presenter on UK radio, he was also a very talented and highly successful foot-baller. He had signed for Ipswich as a youngster and played with them in the hugely successful Bobby Robson era when the team was challenging in the early 80s for the top flight league title. It may be hard to imagine now with The Tractor Boys having recently been relegated down the divisions, but under Sir Bobby, Ipswich had been formidable. With Brazil scoring goals for fun alongside Paul Mariner and fellow Scot John Wark, Ipswich were runners-up in the old First Division twice in successive seasons and also won the UEFA Cup in season 1980/81. Robson would later leave Ipswich in 1982 to manage England while Brazil joined Spurs and then Manchester United, eventually retiring prematurely at the age of 27 due to a persistent back injury.

But back to the awards ceremony and Alan Brazil.

This is a man who had tickets for two World Cup finals, and didn't attend.

This is a man who had tickets for a Champions League final, and didn't attend.

This is a man who had tickets for Ricky Hatton vs Floyd Mayweather, and didn't attend.

These are all fine examples of when he has been near major sporting occasions but found the bar a more attractive prospect.

And while it may be an apocryphal tale, there is also the story of Rod Stewart inviting Alan as one of his special guests to his concert in London. Halfway through the show Rod stopped singing to introduce some of the celebrities in the crowd. As he introduced 10,000 people to Alan Brazil, the spotlight landed on the chair where Alan should have been. But he wasn't.

Alan and Rod may seem unlikely friends but it's a relationship that stretches back well over 30 years. Alan explains: "My relationship with Rod Stewart developed during the 1982 World Cup in Spain. The Scotland bus, which included me, Alex McLeish, Asa Hartford, John Robertson and Alan Rough, stopped at his villa. I had a picture taken with him which I still have in my house. I just met him now and again and now we're good buddies. He is a massive football fan. Some people think it's all show. It's not. I stayed at his house in Essex one Friday night before a Celtic vs Rangers game. We played snooker and his games room is like a shrine to Celtic – pictures, scarves, rosettes, cuttings everywhere. He really is a massive Celtic fan with two big Celtic flags in his grounds. We flew up by private jet the next day, also with Gordon Strachan. They were on the water. I was on the bubbly."

All those events were during Alan's free time, but he's also been known for going missing when he should be working.

It's the stuff of talkSPORT folklore that when the intro music to *The Alan Brazil Sports Breakfast* goes on beyond the usual 30 seconds or so, it's because the big man has only just arrived, or is asleep on the sofa. He's had so many close shaves down the years his show really should be sponsored by a well-known brand of razor.

On one memorable occasion, Brazil was dispatched to Amsterdam to cover an England international with his co-host, and incidentally at the time the station's Programme Director, Mike Parry. All was going well on the night before the game as the pair enjoyed a couple of quiet drinks in the hotel bar before retiring for an early night prior to the following day's breakfast show. At least that was the plan until a pack of British journalists arrived.

They were there to cover the match the following evening, and also to mark the retirement of legendary *Sun* journalist John Sadler. With Parry knowing most of them from his days on Fleet Street, and Brazil familiar with many from his playing days, the party was soon in full swing.

When the journalists moved on to their next destination, Brazil and Parry also decided they should prolong the night for a while longer, so they headed to a local casino. Good sense got the better of Parry, however, who returned to the hotel in plenty of time to get some sleep ahead of their morning's work. Brazil, though, had met up with some friends of his former Ipswich team-mate Frans Thijssen, and continued into the wee small hours before heading back to the hotel for a couple of hours' sleep prior to going on air.

As he was undressing, however, there was a knock at his door and he opened it to find Parry standing there. Parry was amazed to find Brazil was up and awake. Alan announced he was just going to have a shower and then he would be along to the studio in a hotel room just down the corridor. As soon as the door closed, however, he collapsed on the bed.

He was awoken by the sound of one of the show's assistant producers thumping on the door but, having convinced himself it was Sunday, he told the persistent knocker exactly where he could go and what he could do for waking him up on his day off.

Moments later, after more furious banging on the door, this time by Parry himself, Brazil checked his watch and was horrified to see it was seven minutes to six. He scrambled out of bed and headed to the studio where he found Parry manning the show on his own. So he lay down on the sofa where he spotted a dish of M&Ms on an adjacent coffee table. The temptation proved too great to resist. So, as Parry was broadcasting to the nation back in the UK, Brazil started throwing the sweets at his head, popping one into his mouth before launching the second at his old mate, muttering repeatedly: "One for me, one for him ..."

Parry was apoplectic at this stage and, at the next ad break, threw Brazil out of the studio, calling a team meeting for noon to discuss the Scot's unprofessional behaviour. By then of course Brazil had had a few hours' kip and had sobered up considerably.

So by the time he joined Parry in the hotel lobby he was his usual charming self. Whenever Parry attempted to lay into the miscreant, an FA bigwig would walk by. Parry would cut off mid-sentence and instead play the part of dutiful corporate colleague exchanging pleasantries with the official.

Sensing an opportunity, Brazil reckoned it would be impossible for the pair to achieve any closure in a busy public place, so suggested it would be better for the pair to iron out their differences in an Italian restaurant over the road. After copious amounts of Pinot Grigio, they were once again best buddies, on their way to the match. And Brazil was off the hook.

Long before former Crystal Palace manager Iain Dowie coined the phrase 'bouncebackability' as his team climbed out of the Championship relegation places in December 2003 to win promotion to the Premier League via the play-offs in May 2004, Brazil was proving he had more lives than the proverbial cat. But his luck very nearly ran out in March 2004.

The Cheltenham Festival is one of the highlights of Brazil's sporting year. He usually presents his show from there and is finished by 10am. He is then free to enjoy the delights of the racing … and the Guinness tent. What could possibly go wrong?

Brazil was already in a mood during this particular festival because he had been told he would be broadcasting from the course for only three days – Tuesday to Thursday – before heading back to London and presenting Friday's show from the studio where the special guest was to be Chelsea chairman Ken Bates. Brazil was having none of it. Particularly as Thursday was Gold Cup day. And he wasn't missing that.

With Thursday morning's show wrapped up, he headed straight for the Guinness tent. Parry was still the station's Programme Director and was once again cast in the role of good cop, trying desperately to persuade his old mate that they needed to get back to the capital.

Once Brazil had got himself settled in the Guinness tent, however, there was no moving him. Eventually Parry decided to get the train back to London leaving Brazil to make his own way back. Parry's parting shot was to warn his colleague it was now up to him to be back in time for Friday's show at 6am or there would be hell to pay.

In fairness to Brazil, he was determined to do the right thing but it's always difficult at Cheltenham. Old friends turn up and Rod Stewart was in one of the boxes that day. He did start off in the direction of London but decided to stop at a local village hotel with the intention of rising at 3am and heading back to London for work. All good in theory. In practice, however, it was a recipe for disaster. He checked in and sat by a crackling fire enjoying the warmth and a large glass of red. And then just as he had one foot on the stairs heading up for an early night, the porter told him that Brazil's old mate Jim Steel, a fellow Glaswegian and a former Southampton player Brazil knew through Mick Channon and Alan Ball, owned the best pub in the village. He decided it would be rude not to go over and say hello. Brazil had just got a new phone which was also his alarm but he wasn't entirely confident that the batteries were working properly so as he left the hotel he asked the porter to give him a wake-up call at three in the morning. The porter said "No problem" and assured Brazil that he'd be woken. Brazil got to Steel's pub. It was St Patrick's Day and Brazil re-acquainted himself with the owner. The Guinness and the Irish songs were flowing in the packed bar. The next thing Brazil remembers is waking up in his room sensing something wasn't quite right. He looked at his watched, grabbed his stuff and leapt downstairs to see the porter there. "Why did you not wake me at three o'clock," shouted Brazil. "Because you didn't get in until twenty past four, sir," was the reply.

He immediately realised he had no chance of making it to London in time for his show. His new phone was now flat, so he was forced to call his producer from a pay phone to explain the situation, only to be cut off mid-conversation.

Parry was furious at having to present the show and conduct the interview with Bates alone, but there was nothing he could do. To further complicate matters Brazil had booked the coming week off to go skiing with his family so opted to go straight home and deal with the inevitable consequences on his return from Méribel. The station's owner at the time, Kelvin MacKenzie, was none too impressed but he knew there was little choice with Brazil. Indulge him or fire him and, as the station's main man, the latter had never been viewed as a serious option … up until now.

The following evening Parry received an angry phone call from MacKenzie.

"Mike, I haven't heard a word from Brazil."

"Well, he is going skiing actually, Kelvin."

"Skiing?"

"He had already booked the week off after Cheltenham, Kelvin."

"I haven't heard a f*****g word."

"Well, to be honest Kelvin, neither have I."

"I'm not putting up with it. You ring him and tell him that unless I get a fulsome apology then he is out."

Parry knew that spelled the end for Brazil at talkSPORT, knowing full well the Scot would never apologise. As Brazil himself said: "I don't tend to think too much about tomorrow – my body will take me where it wants to. If I am feeling tired, I might have a few early nights. If I don't feel tired, I will have late nights. I do believe what my body tells me. Bodies are brilliant things, it is remarkable how they can recover. You put it under pressure and it responds. I rarely listen to what my boss tells me, but if my body tells me … Woah! Woah!"

With the chances of Brazil saying sorry being slim to none, Parry began the thankless task of searching for a replacement. Brazil simply shrugged his shoulders and assumed something else would turn up. And it did. His old job.

Parry had moved to fill the Scot's sizeable shoes with regular station contributor Paul Breen-Turner, a Spanish-based DJ and radio presenter. Ironically PBT, as he was known by all at talk-SPORT, had been introduced to the station by Brazil after Breen-Turner had arranged for the breakfast show host to use a studio at his radio station for an overseas broadcast. The pair struck up a friendship over a few post-broadcast *cervezas*.

But before Breen-Turner could utter a single '*Hola*' on the airwaves, a torrent of emails, texts and phone calls demanding Brazil's reinstatement flooded in, eventually leading to MacKenzie being persuaded by Parry to bring Brazil back. 'Brazilbackability', you might say.

Brazil recalls: "Parry had phoned me up and said, 'It's over. Kelvin's decided that's it.' So I said, 'OK, no problem,' and they brought [Paul] Breen-Turner in. I got back to London from skiing and Parry called me to say, 'It's dire. We got emails galore. You've got to come back.' I asked him what Kelvin had said and he said, 'I've not spoken to Kelvin yet but I think I could talk him round'. So I put the phone down. Two days later he called again saying, 'Kelvin's warming to it,' and when I asked Parry if he'd spoken to him he said 'No'. So I put the phone down again. By the end of the week he phoned a third time and said, 'I've got four thousand emails here. You've got to come back.' I said, 'Well maybe, maybe ...' And eventually got my job back."

But back to the night of the Sonys and there was no persuading Brazil to stay put. Many of the other talkSPORT employees at the awards were astonished Brazil had turned up in the first place, so they weren't entirely surprised that, having lost out to BBC Radio 5 Live for the title of Breakfast Show of the Year, Brazil decided he'd had more than enough of the evening. The Breakfast Show Award was the first to be announced, and the big man was not in the mood for an evening of glad-handing among his broadcasting peers. Miffed at being beaten by his rivals at the Beeb, Brazil stormed towards what he thought was the exit from the packed room, only to take a wrong turn and end up in the kitchens at the Grosvenor House Hotel with no way out. Undeterred, he could be seen, and heard, gesticulating wildly at kitchen staff demanding to know how he could exit the building before rather sheepishly having to re-enter the main ballroom where the awards were taking place and walk back past the tables, and amused looks, before making his escape. As shows of petulance go, it was as effective as attempting to slam a revolving door!

Brazil recalls: "We had two tables and Moz Dee was on a table right next to the stage, and I'm on a table right next to the kitchens! You couldn't get a worse table. Everyone is telling me I've won it but I said, 'Don't believe it'. I said to Ronnie Irani [breakfast show co-host at the time], 'Stuff this, we might as well go. We haven't won an award.' But he wanted to stay. Danny Baker won the award so I got up and left. I ended up walking into the kitchens thinking that was the way out. I couldn't get out of there. The chef was there, knife in hand, and they were all shouting at me to get out, and I'm shouting at them, 'I'm trying to get out'. All the guests were looking in and thinking what's all that noise in the kitchen."

The remaining members of talkSPORT's celebrating crew were not going to let the absence of Brazil get in the way of a good time, however, and they soon decamped to the station's usual haunt, Little Italy in London's Soho, where the party went on long into the night ... and into the next day.

At around 11am the following morning, bleary-eyed Programme Director Moz Dee (at least people assumed he was bleary-eyed but you couldn't really tell as he was wearing dark glasses) marched triumphantly into the office, clutching a Sony Award having been up all night, beaming from ear to ear, chanting 'Championes' at the top of his voice. It was quite the 'rock star' entrance.

And that set the tone for the remainder of the day (and night) as the entire talkSPORT office – editorial, sales, engineering, presenters, management, cleaners, security, work experience and related spouses – decamped back to Little Italy to continue the party.

Producer Laurie Palacio remembers: "At Little Italy on the night of the awards, the Champagne was flowing, we were all singing and dancing to the old classics like '500 Miles' and whatever. Chris Evans, radio royalty, turned up to join the party. I remember going outside, and somehow we'd got hold of these huge cigars. Me, Moz and some of the guys were there and we were chuffing on these cigars, high on success, booze and emotion. Everyone was there including Chief Executive Scott Taunton who announced to the team: 'It's never going to get any better, lads.' It was said in a very sort of contemplative way, but we loved it.

"It was effectively a two-day festival, and the following day was great because it meant the guys who weren't there on the award night got to share in the overwhelming sense of achievement. There was no talk of being serious and business as usual. It was, 'These moments don't come along very often, let's go for it'."

Inevitably, as is so often the case on such occasions, the free booze swilling around the Frith Street bar led to one or two, shall we say, 'confrontations'.

During workplace social gatherings such as these, people who don't usually cross paths in the course of their day-to-day activities regularly find themselves engaged in conversation. And so it was that one member of the radio sales team, when asked by a couple of writers from *Sport* magazine (talkSPORT's then sister publication) what he did, promptly replied: "Don't you know who I am? I'm the guy who pays your wages." Fortunately, the boys from *Sport* had not been drinking for anywhere near the same length of time as the self-confessed King of Sales and they let that frankly ludicrous boast slide. That same chap was not so fortunate later on in proceedings when he decided it would be a good idea to get a member of the station's senior management in a headlock. Suffice to say, it wasn't ... either for his evening, or his career at talkSPORT.

The over-exuberant celebrations should not, however, detract from what was a significant achievement in talkSPORT being recognised by the radio industry in this way.

Mike Bovill, who had joined the station straight out of university as a newsreader and at this point was Head of Content, says: "None of our programmes had ever won a Gold Award, that's the context of it. The creative team had won awards, but none of our editorial had ever won a top Sony Award, which was the industry standard. Moz has to take an enormous amount of credit. We hadn't had anyone in the building like him before. He recognised that you had to play the game, and he did it brilliantly. He scattered the stardust, he made headlines, and he transformed the perception of talkSPORT far more than the output itself. The programmes didn't change enormously, but it's what people thought of us as a radio station that was the context behind us winning that award.

"We had the rights for the 2006 World Cup in Germany and we did a great job, but in 2010 it was the idea that it [the World Cup] was in safe hands with talkSPORT. We had the big names, the big games, we had coverage of every match, and we had an advertising campaign, which was rare at that time. And all of that almost allowed the industry to take us seriously."

'CLIPS OF THE WEEK'

The Top 20 All-Time Greats

#18

Commentators are there to create pictures in the mind for the radio listener and Graham 'Beeky' Beecroft excels at it. Sometimes when the unexpected happens, as it did during this 2010 World Cup group match, simplicity is key.

'He could have played for four countries altogether. Here's Krasić from the right-hand side ... clips it back ... Žigić with a header down ... It's there! It's been belted home by Milan Jovanović and Serbia, after Germany have been reduced to ten men, have taken the lead here. Sensational ... He's fallen down the moat!

'CLIPS OF THE WEEK'

The Top 20 All-Time Greats

#17

talkSPORT presenters are paid to talk about sport but when they drift into other disciplines, such as arithmetic, it's not always their strong point. Here's Ray Parlour:

"Moose, you speak to a lot of the fans – is it split? You know, 50% want him to leave and 50% want to keep him? Or is it the other way round?"

Chapter 4

Keys and Gray Fall Out of Sky and Land on talkSPORT

"It was just banter ..."

Those words have haunted Richard Keys in a million and one virals and memes on the internet. At the time, in January 2011, they were being used to excuse his remarks about Sian Massey, a female linesman. He landed in the hottest of hot water with his paymasters at Sky TV, following an off-air exchange with his long-time broadcast partner, Sky's senior co-commentator Andy Gray. The remarks were never meant to be seen or heard but were subsequently leaked to the media.

This is how the conversation between the pair went, ahead of a Wolves–Liverpool match at Molineux:

Keys: Somebody better get down there and explain offside to her [the female linesman].

Gray: Can you believe that? A female linesman. Women don't know the offside rule.

Keys: Course they don't. I can guarantee you there will be a big one [offside call] today. Kenny [Dalglish, Liverpool's manager] will go potty. This isn't the first time, is it? Didn't we have one before?

Keys: [Referring to Karren Brady's newspaper column] The game's gone mad. Did you hear charming Karren Brady this morning complaining about sexism? Do me a favour, love.

And that was the start of a media furore and firestorm that would eventually bring about the departure of the men who had fronted Sky's football coverage since the inception of the Premier League in August 1992. There were more headlines and column inches devoted to the fall-out than anything that took place in an actual sporting arena in the days that followed.

The reaction to the comments was nothing short of astonishing. It was the lead story on the TV news that day, made front-page headlines in the national press and social media was going off the scale in its condemnation of Keys. His charge sheet prior to that consisted of nothing more serious than crimes against fashion for some of those frankly hideous garish blazers he wore in the early days as football began its takeover of living rooms across the globe. But that was to be just the beginning.

Within days, more footage had been leaked online, this time with Keys goading former Liverpool star and now Sky pundit Jamie Redknapp about a former girlfriend.

That left Keys clinging to his job by his fingertips, with colleague Gray having already been sacked for "unacceptable behaviour" following the leak of more footage. An archived video had emerged of him asking Sky colleague Charlotte Jackson if she'd mind "tucking that down there", referring to his microphone while gesturing towards the front of his trousers.

That tape was leaked following further damning evidence from Molineux that had also been released into the public domain, where Gray was caught in another off-air exchange with reporter Andy Burton about Massey.

Burton said, "Apparently, a female lino today, bit of a looker," with Gray responding, "A female linesman?"

"He [a Sky Sports crew member] says she [Massey] is alright," Burton continued. "Now, I don't know if I should trust his judgement on that?"

Gray then said: "No, I wouldn't. I definitely wouldn't … I can see her from here."

Gray had already been suspended by Sky for his part in the original Sian Massey controversy, and it was the storm surrounding the Charlotte Jackson video that ultimately sealed his fate.

Clearly, it appeared to be an orchestrated campaign from within to bring about the downfall of two of the most high-profile sports broadcasters in the country.

All of this, however, would lead to Keys and Gray joining talk-SPORT. But prior to that was a day that would go down in the annals as one of the craziest in the station's history. And when it comes to talkSPORT, that is really saying something.

The duo's questionable behaviour had dominated the news for days. And social media was in meltdown. It is doubtful they could have been treated any worse had they been accused of crimes against humanity. They were hung, drawn and quartered by the keyboard warriors. It was an extraordinary time.

The pair were being hounded constantly by news reporters and photographers, with the media camped outside each of their houses. They were prisoners in their own homes as their professional and personal lives were picked apart by all and sundry.

They were under immense scrutiny and pressure with their careers hanging in the balance. Gray later admitted the ugly scenario left him feeling suicidal. The media and the public were demanding their pound of flesh, in answers and apologies. And it was talkSPORT that provided the platform for Keys, still employed by Sky at this stage, to have his say.

Keys' relationship and friendship with talkSPORT's Programme Director Moz Dee – both Coventry City fans – was strong. They had known each other for many years and it meant Keys chose the station to air his side of the story for the first time. Sky was supposedly keen for him to apologise and put the whole sorry affair behind him. Even before his public declaration of remorse, it seemed his fate was sealed.

On that Wednesday, talkSPORT became the epicentre of the country's main news story. Only a handful of senior staff at the station were trusted with the identity of the mystery interviewee who would be arriving later in the day. They were sworn to secrecy.

But such is the way in modern media that rumours began to spread and, before too long, the usually quiet Hatfields, the street where the studios were then based, was a scrum of activity.

Paparazzi and TV news trucks were fighting for space. Traffic was gridlocked in the surrounding streets as cameras and vans were rammed into any available space on the now crowded street. And the cameras weren't there to film the rather bemused bunch of lads who suddenly discovered their lunchtime game of five-a-side on the pitches across the road from the studios was going to be a bit more interesting than usual.

There were rumours Keys had to be smuggled out of his house in the boot of his car in order to initially throw off the paparazzi. The scene could not have been more frenzied if it had been heralding the arrival of the Queen, rather than a chat with a bloke whose job was to 'do' the bit of the football that took place either side of the on-field action. The only thing missing was snipers on the roofs poised with telescopic rifles.

Instead of its usual place in the natural order of things (i.e. reporting the news), talkSPORT was thrust into the limelight and cast in the role of actually 'being' the news.

The size of the crowd gathering outside the front doors was leading to some anxiety amid concerns that, should events escalate, receptionist and effervescent Essex girl Zoe was perhaps not the strongest last line of defence.

This resulted in one of those 'you couldn't make it up' talkSPORT scenarios where CEO Scott Taunton was racing around the building looking for the biggest blokes that worked there.

And so it was that John Mahood, an amiable, but admittedly burly Irishman, swapped his day job as Art Director at *Sport* magazine – talkSPORT's free sister publication that was distributed outside Tube stations in London – for the newly created (albeit short-lived) position of Head of Security.

While all this was going on, Keys was spirited in via the rear of the building in scenes that would not have looked out of place were Her Majesty's Prison Service transporting a maximum security high-risk prisoner to court.

At the same time as all this commotion and carry-on was unfolding, Paul Hawksbee and Andy Jacobs, the hosts of the much-loved 1pm–4pm show, were being briefed as to the identity of their mystery guest.

Jacobs says: "We knew they had chosen us because they thought we would be like *Hello!* magazine. We're not known for our tough interviewing style, but we both also knew that if we gave Richard an easy time we would be the ones who would be slaughtered. So we had to be much harder than we would normally be. It's not our style to put people on the spot, but he had transgressed, he had made mistakes and we had to hold him to account, which I think we did."

They certainly did, and it was to be a remarkable hour of radio. Although the pair were not afraid to ask the tough questions, for long periods they were able to simply sit back and listen as Keys unburdened himself. Clearly he had a lot to get off his chest. He repeatedly apologised to Massey, at the same time alluding to "dark forces" at work – a barely concealed reference to the person or persons he believed were responsible for leaking the footage that had already brought down Gray and was about to do the same to him. All this as he faced up to the possibility of a 20-year career at Sky Sports coming to an unedifying end.

Keys says: "I was told [by Sky] go in, and to keep saying sorry. But you're in such a state of confusion. To begin with they [Sky] wanted me to go on BBC Radio 5 Live with Victoria Derbyshire but I said no and I rang Moz [Dee] and asked for the favour of some airtime. I did all the things they [Sky] wanted but as I left [the talkSPORT studios], I thought, 'I'm done'.

"I used that phrase 'dark forces' because I knew, whichever way we turned, we were getting blocked. I was getting manipulated enormously over what was happening and I knew where all this was coming from. I know the individuals, I know all those things.

"As I left [the talkSPORT studios], I thought to myself, they've sacked Andy and I would be working now with one or two people I didn't really like and I wasn't sure I wanted to continue doing that. I left talkSPORT, drove to Sky and told them, 'Make me an offer, I'm leaving'. My security pass was taken off me and I was escorted off the premises. I got home and felt nothing but relief. The following morning, panic. And then of course an enormous wave of damaging content came out, all of which was edited as you would expect."

Keys' remarkable interview with Hawksbee and Jacobs dominated the news that day, so big a story that it was the lead item on TV news bulletins that night. Even at this stage there was no suggestion that the pair would end up working at talkSPORT although that is exactly what would happen.

Jacobs added: "It was funny being on the news! Over the years we've been known for one thing but we can turn our hands to other things. We actually got nominated for an award for that interview. Maybe we should just be like Paxman every day."

It's certainly true that H&J, as they are commonly known, have a much-deserved reputation for their excellent on-air bonhomie that translates through the speakers and helps put both guests and listeners at ease.

But that relaxed style has, on occasions, caused them to be separated when it's been felt the station needed to adopt a more serious tone. The most famous incident became known as 'Ridley's Puddle'.

It was soon after the huge tsunami had hit Asia in December 2004 and there were fears it might happen again. Paul and Andy were due to be on as usual at 1pm, but Bill Ridley, a vastly experienced journalist who was Programme Director at the time, decided he would bring in experienced journalist Mike Parry alongside Paul just in case this awful disaster struck. So while Andy sat outside in the office twiddling his thumbs, Paul was interviewing Parry, who basically knew no more than he did, but he was claiming this huge wave was going to strike. He expressed concern and he hoped it wouldn't result in a terrible loss of life. In reality, this 'wave' simply lapped up on to the beach, not even enough to disturb a young lad with his bucket and spade.

Parry, of course, was a Fleet Street stalwart and, like Ridley, a widely respected news journalist. But he was also the man who advocated wing mirrors for racehorses!

The first time Parry saw a picture of Osama bin Laden following the 9/11 attacks in New York, he announced on air: "He looks a bit like Mick Fleetwood, of Fleetwood Mac. Not that I'm suggesting that Mick Fleetwood had anything to do with this atrocity." He was the man to bring gravitas to any situation.

Not that Parry or anyone else was needed to bring gravitas to the situation surrounding Keys and Gray. It was the end of an era for the duo at Sky TV's studios in Isleworth, but would soon herald the start of a new one for them in Hatfields, SE1.

talkSPORT has never been afraid to make controversial appointments when it comes to on-air talent, deeming that past indiscretions should not forever be held against the perpetrators.

And so, just a couple of weeks after their acrimonious departure from Sky, Keys and Gray were announced as the new hosts of the 10am–1pm slot on talkSPORT. The duo's arrival was to cause controversy not only because of who they were and their so-called 'crimes', but also because of the identity of the man they were replacing on the airwaves.

The previous incumbents of the 10am–1pm slot were Mike Parry and Mike Graham (aka 'The Two Mikes'), and listeners were outraged that Parry had been axed to make way for the former Sky Sports duo. Of course, what those listeners were not privy to were some of the extraordinary shenanigans that had been going on behind the scenes.

Parry is, unquestionably, one of the most exuberant characters in talkSPORT's colourful history. A former Programme Director, and a former co-host of *The Alan Brazil Sports Breakfast*, 'Porky' is a larger than life force of nature. His love of the good life had got him into many a scrape, even after he was supposed to be slowing down following life-saving heart surgery.

His madcap on-air antics made him a beloved figure among the listeners, but it was widely rumoured that Moz Dee was not a fan of 'The Two Mikes', believing they lacked 'stardust'. What they certainly didn't lack was work ethic, as their producer Dennie Morris knew only too well.

He was playing football one Saturday afternoon and answered the phone at half-time to hear Parry complaining that he'd been trying to get hold of him for the past 45 minutes! Morris told him he was playing football but Parry's response was, "We've got a show to do on Monday". Clearly to expect his producer to be running around with his phone in his hand while trying to score a goal was nonsensical. But that's the sort of person he is.

Morris believes Dee's lack of enthusiasm for the show and his regular criticism eventually pushed Parry over the edge. That build-up of pressure probably led to the creation of Parry's bizarre alter ego, Padre Parry.

At some point someone thought it would be a good idea to kit the presenter out in a sort of bishop's outfit and he would then preach his sermons of wisdom to the nation. These sermons would find their way on to YouTube. On one memorable occasion, whilst dressed in the bishop's outfit, he was looking through *The Sun* newspaper and stopped on page three and was wrestling with this internal conflict because of the guilt he felt looking at a picture of a topless girl. He then actually started frothing at the mouth (courtesy of stuffing it full of Refreshers) before passing out on the floor. Quite bizarre, but very amusing for Parry's legion of fans.

Even Morris, Parry's most ardent advocate, admitted that was probably the moment at which he realised things were not going in the right direction.

But with Parry and Graham already with a less than supportive boss, Parry chose the worst possible time to incur Dee's wrath with a drunken escapade at the NEC Bike Show in Birmingham.

Things had begun to unravel the night before. Parry and Graham had met at Euston to get the train. Graham tells the story:

"Parry had nipped off to get a couple of libations for the journey but came back with three carrier bags full of wine and other bits. It was only a journey of one hour and twenty minutes! That set the tone. We were staying at the NEC Hilton in Birmingham where we made good use of the bar facilities and where coincidentally there was a wedding party going on. Of course we joined them and were singing songs and joining in and having a jolly good time. It all got a bit lively and the last thing I remember was Parry on all fours pretending to be a motorbike with producer Dennie Morris running alongside him. The security weren't impressed and told us if we persisted we'd be thrown out."

Suffice to say this didn't go down too well with the other drinkers in the bar and nor did it go down too well the following morning as they got ready for the live broadcast. It was perhaps not the wisest decision to stick Parry and Graham on mini motor-bikes and let them have a little ride around the exhibition as part of the Bike Road Safety Seminar. They were seen to be speeding around the exhibition with attendees diving out the way, an esca-pade that reportedly didn't impress the sponsors, although Morris is adamant that by the end of the show the pair were being treated like conquering heroes. They were also clad in leather biker's kit to present the show which made it incredibly hot and compounded the pain and sweats of the previous night's excesses.

What is certain is that Dee was not impressed when news of the prank reached him, and by this stage the writing was very much on the wall for Parry. It was clear he was drinking in the last-chance saloon.

Hazy recollection means it is unclear if he had spent a large chunk of the day in said last-chance saloon on the evening he ill-advisedly sent Dee a text essentially telling his boss where to go. But he inadvertently chose the very time the two most high-profile broadcasters in the country had unexpectedly become available for work to fire off that particular broadside. It could certainly be described as accidental timing of quite epic proportions.

Also unknown to Parry, after angrily compiling his missive and hitting the 'send' button on his mobile, was that he effec-tively delivered one of the most spectacular letters of resignation of all time. Dee received it in a private room at the Dean Street Townhouse in Soho, with the entire executive board of UTV in attendance. More unfortunate timing for Porky.

His fate was sealed. He was out and Keys and Gray were in. That proved no great surprise to the staff at talkSPORT Towers, all of whom had been wondering, ever since that Keys interview with H&J, when the former Sky duo would be added to the talent roster.

Programme Director Moz Dee said at the time: "The events of the last couple of weeks have been a lesson and have changed them.

"One thing that hasn't changed, however, is that they are two iconic broadcasters who have a wealth of experience in the world of sport and that's what we have to do now – move forward with them as sports broadcasters.

"I think it's a sensational coup for talkSPORT and great for radio. These men have carved out amazing careers in television and were at the forefront of the Sky revolution. I think they are going to have a massive impact on the radio scene."

But the boisterous, bubbly duo of old was not evident in those early days. Keys looked ashen and shell-shocked as he adapted to the somewhat less salubrious surroundings than those he had been used to. Gray sheepishly introduced himself to the production and digital teams on the programming floor, showing no hint of the misogynistic bully that had been portrayed in the media in the preceding weeks. Both had lost weight and looked shadows of their former selves.

Indeed, they were so subdued throughout that first week of broadcasting that there were genuine fears they would not reappear the following Monday for the start of week two. Both executive producer Steve Morgan and producer Jon Norman look back now and wonder if the pair should have actually been on air in that first week. Both felt it was perhaps too much, too soon given the very public ordeal they had just endured.

Keys admitted: "Those first few days were impossible. I'd never been through anything like it. I'd worked in the press for years and thought I knew how things worked, but that was a revelation how somebody could almost crush the life out of us. Andy has gone public and said he considered suicide at different times. I would be lying if I said I got so low that I would seriously contemplate that, but we weren't on the floor, we were beneath the floor. We were statue-like [in the studio]."

Gray admitted to having the same feelings: "On the Sunday night before I walked in on the Monday, I wasn't going [to talkSPORT]. I said to my wife, Rachel, 'I can't do this, I'm empty, it's too early'. And she told me it wasn't and that it was exactly the right time. She told me, 'You're going to get up and come with me to London and stay in the hotel that has been booked for us and you're going to get up in the morning and walk into that studio with your head held high'. Had it not been for Rachel and Richard, who was very proactive, then I don't know where I would have been, I really don't, because I was as low as I've ever been in my life. When you don't fancy being here any more, that's pretty low, and that's where I was."

The story had transcended sports radio, even sports media, due to the amount of publicity surrounding their arrival at talk-SPORT. In the midst of all this were two guys who had been publicly shamed, rightly or wrongly, and had lost their liveli-hoods in a very public manner. Fleet Street had gone to town on them. But at the end of the day they were two human beings who were now having to get on with life, and their life now was this show.

Steve Morgan and Jon Norman had very deliberately set the first show up to be jam-packed with guests. What really gave that first show a shot in the arm was a guest appearance in the studio by former Chelsea, Manchester United and England mid-fielder Ray Wilkins. At that stage, all their old buddies at Sky had been told to keep away from the show, but Wilkins agreed to appear for the final hour and that was just what the pair needed, a friend and an ally in the studio.

Wilkins would go on to become a regular co-host and pundit on talkSPORT, always with a friendly smile and a word for everyone he met there, whether one of the reception staff, an assistant producer, the CEO or the latest work-experience kid. Everyone got the same kind treatment.

Ray was loved by all the staff at talkSPORT and also many others outside. His death at the age of just 61 in April 2018 shocked and saddened everyone. Tributes to Ray flooded into the station and perhaps the most telling and most poignant, which revealed the type of bloke Ray was, came from an ex-soldier who phoned into the Jim White show (with Bob Mills) to tell his story:

"I'd just like to say Bob mentioned just then that he [Wilkins] was a football man. I disagree. He was a real man. I'm an ex-soldier and I had some time when I was homeless and I was outside of Brompton station.

"What happened was, Ray came over to me and I recognised him straight away and he just took some time to sit and chat and we were both sat on my bit of cardboard together. And we were chatting about the army. I was a gambler at the time. I'm still a gambler but I'm recovering. But he took the time and he even took a phone call during that and he said [to the caller], 'Look, I'll call you back, I'm busy at the moment,' and we were sat chatting and he gave me £20 and told me to get myself a hot meal and then took me across the road to buy me a coffee.

"As the bill came I said to him, 'Can I please buy this? I want to feel like a man.' And he said that he totally understood all of that. That night I took that £20 and I got some shelter and a hot meal. During that time when I was in the shelter I met a guy who was helping ex-soldiers who put me in touch with decent people who would help me. I'm now fully recovered, not gambling. I have my own place. A beautiful girlfriend who I am about to marry. And I put it down to the time that that man took, to give to a man that was nothing to him. A stranger … and … I'm sorry if I'm getting emotional, but he was a real hero to me and to millions of others across the world. Thank you for giving me the time to say thank you to a man that I never got to say thank you to, not really. Anyone who phones in today with a memory is basically saying to his family, thank you for giving us Ray Wilkins."

It was typical of Wilkins to help out two old mates by appearing in their first broadcast. Such was the focus on Keys and Gray's talkSPORT debut that other national media outlets were actually blogging the show live, so while the production team had their heads down in the control room trying to get through that first morning, producers of other shows were coming in to tell them what the bloggers were saying. This information was met with a firm, "Get out the studio, this is not what we need right now".

By the time they got to the end of Friday's show in that first week, there was a collective sense of relief from Keys, Gray and all the production team that they had pulled it off. But Morgan's unease about the future was such that, for the first and only time in his radio career, he walked down to the car park with the presenters to say goodbye. Usually, presenters and producers have a quick catch-up outside the studio, maybe a brief chat about the next show and then go their separate ways. But on this occasion, Morgan wanted to say a more private goodbye because he was still uncertain if they'd return on Monday such was the pressure and intensity clearly weighing them both down.

All weekend, Morgan was expecting a call from Keys to tell him the pair had decided this was not right for them and that they wouldn't be returning on Monday. In fact, so convinced was he, that when the call had not come through on Sunday afternoon he was getting people to ring him to make sure his phone was still working.

As it was, he did get a call, but not until 7.30am on that Monday morning, by which time he was already in the office. Seeing Richard Keys' name flash up on his mobile, his first thought was that Keys had left it a bit late to bail out, but when he answered the call he discovered the problem was a simpler one to fix. Keys had lost his security pass and was outside the building unable to get in. Morgan went down to the car park where he was met by both Keys and Gray, rejuvenated, refreshed and looking as though they meant business, with Keys reeling off a whole litany of ideas, guests, things they needed to do.

"Once we'd settled, it helped me laugh again and it became the best two years of my career," says Keys. "It was fantastic. We were surrounded by good people who helped us laugh again. It was just good fun. It came at a time in my life when I needed the change; it was the right time but in the wrong way. It was really enjoyable."

Gray echoes those sentiments: "I'd never done radio to that extent and I remember saying on the day of the first show, 'We've got to talk for how long? Three hours?' And then after the first hour I couldn't believe we still had another two hours to go. And then we had to do it four more times that week. And then another five days the following week.

"But after a week, I thought, 'I can do this'. Keysie definitely wanted to do it. He was determined to do it. He was the driving force for the show with the help of Jon [Norman] and Kathryn [Anastasi]. It took me a while, probably longer than people realised, to settle in and feel accepted, but once we had, we felt very much part of the talkSPORT family. No one pre-judged us and they all gave us a chance, and it was brilliant. I loved it."

They were back and once they got their feet under the desk, it soon became apparent Keys and Gray were anything but wall-flowers. Revelling in the dressing-room-style atmosphere that pervades the programming floor at talkSPORT, the pair soon introduced their own brand of humour into the building.

A favourite prank was to pretend someone was waiting outside the programming floor and making unsuspecting producers get up out of their seats and open the door. Keys would give a loud knock on the wooden table in the centre of the green room, while Gray would bellow: "Come in. Give it a pull." In the beginning, this led to those members of staff seated nearest to the door to the office – which could only be accessed with a security pass – regularly getting up to open it, to be greeted not by a grateful visitor but by the sound of Keys and Gray sniggering hysterically. And on it went, day after day: "Knock, knock. Come in", until the only people listening to them were themselves.

Another regular cry was that of 'legend in the building' with Keys marching out of the studio to greet one of his many football chums who had agreed to come in to be interviewed. He'd be closely followed by Gray echoing the same sentiment. By the time they had walked the 25 yards or so from the studio door to the green room, the call of 'legend in the building' would have rever-berated around the floor no fewer than five or six times, with Keys immediately being parroted by Gray. They were relentless.

"It was a great atmosphere," says Keys. "That daft trick with the door, we just had fun, it was like being back at play-school." And they were part of the team very quickly. Andy Gray famously was asked to leave the local watering hole, The Windmill, while leading the programming team in a mega-mix of Christmas carols. It had just got too raucous for the staff and the other customers. As they left they pleaded, "Have a heart, it's Christmas," but immediately decamped to the next bar and carried on.

The great thing about them is they were prepared to take as much stick as they gave out. As they returned to normality, they began to tease people more at which point one day Morgan turned around to Keys and said, "Oh, is this the culture of bullying at Sky I'd read about?" Keys just laughed it off. They were more than happy to laugh at themselves as well.

"Keysie has a far more wicked sense of humour than I do," says Gray. "He's very sharp. But if you're going to give it out you have to take it back. I was brought up in a football environment, in a dressing room from the age of 17 where you had to stand up [for yourself] and you lived by the sword and died by the sword. If you were a shrinking violet it was very difficult to succeed in those days. I'm happy for people to take the mickey out of me and, as a Scot living in London, that's happened many times."

And from those difficult early days, the show blossomed into one of the most popular on the station, attracting a previously unthinkable audience of more than one million listeners to that 10am–1pm time slot.

They produced some absolutely electrifying, unmissable radio. Keys had a contacts book unrivalled in the world of sports media. He knew everybody and he used those contacts to attract guests talkSPORT had never previously been able to secure. They had the likes of Wayne Rooney, Frank Lampard, Manchester City boss Roberto Mancini, England rugby World Cup winning hero Jonny Wilkinson and Liverpool legend Graeme Souness. Producer Jon Norman recalls the Souness interview as being one of the most memorable of all time at talkSPORT Towers.

"Richard Keys could do something I'd never seen anyone do and that was to get something out of a guest I hadn't heard before. I'd been watching Souness on air for years and suddenly time stood still as he recounted how, on the night he had a triple heart bypass, he stayed awake all night watching the clock because in his head he thought if he went to sleep he'd never wake up again. That was spellbinding.

"Similarly with Jonny Wilkinson. Keysie had a way of disarming a guest with only five or six words. 'What are you doing here?' was his first question to Wilkinson. 'You hate this? Why are you here?' And you could see it in Wilkinson's face, the reaction of a man who had done a million interviews, but suddenly wondering where this guy was coming from. But he was then put at ease and what followed was an amazing interview.

"Such was their standing in football that we had Wayne Rooney ringing the studio the day after getting in trouble for swearing on camera while celebrating a goal. That sort of thing had become the norm. It was incredible."

Keys and Gray also managed to convince the station's bosses to let them travel regularly to European games, meaning they would leave London on Monday afternoon after their show, and then present Tuesday's show from whichever European city was hosting that week's biggest Champions League clash. Keys would then introduce coverage of the night's live football with commentary from Sam Matterface and Gray, before presenting Wednesday's show from the same city, making the most of local contacts and journalists. They were right at the heart of the action and the stories.

On one occasion, however, the 'local flavour' brought on to the show nearly came back to bite producer Jon Norman. Keys, Gray, Norman and the team were in Barcelona for the Champions League semi-final, second leg against Chelsea. On the morning of the match, their guest in the studio was former Nou Camp striker and Scotland World Cup team-mate of Alan Brazil, Steve Archibald.

With time to kill before heading to the stadium for that evening's match, they decided to go for lunch at a restaurant recommended by Archibald. Having had a look at the menu and seeing that main dishes were around €27, and with no one drinking because they were working at the match that night, Norman figured it would be safe to offer to pick up the tab and claim it back on expenses. And that's when he found out about blue lobsters.

The alarm bells probably started ringing when he noticed Archibald tuck his serviette in and roll up his sleeves like a man about to tackle a giant T-bone steak. At this point the waiter pushed through with a trolley on which was a de-shelled blue lobster. Norman was thinking it was a lot of food for two people, assuming Archibald and Keys were sharing, but then the food

Keys had ordered arrived. So it was one lobster for just the one man – Archibald.

It was too late to retract the offer of hospitality. Norman had to leave slightly earlier than the others to get to the ground to make sure everything was in order. He bid the guys farewell and went to the counter to pay, where he discovered that a single lobster had cost €400. The entire bill came to €650. Fortunately, his boss felt sorry for him, saw the funny side and agreed he could put it through on expenses. But you can be pretty sure he no longer lets anyone order blue lobster if it's his credit card in the firing line.

The eye-watering cost of an unusually coloured crustacean was, in truth, a small price to pay for the on-air brilliance of the duo, with Gray's superb analysis and Keys' bulging contacts book and sensational interview skills. It made the show one of the most popular on the station.

That was recognised in April 2012 when, just 14 months after their acrimonious departure from Sky and their controversial appointment at talkSPORT, the show won a Sony Gold Award as Best Sports Programme at the UK radio industry's annual awards. It was the first time an individual talkSPORT show had won gold.

"I was hugely proud," says Gray. "When Moz [Dee] told us he thought we had a chance of winning that award I was chuckling to myself because I thought there was no chance, and that someone would say, 'No, we can't give it to those two'. I thought it would be impossible for us to win it."

Keys added: "Winning that Sony Gold was unbelievable, not least for the people who trusted us. Our producers didn't really know us, [at the start] our technical operators certainly didn't know who we were, so I felt really good about that award for the support they gave us. Their trust was so important. It was incredible.

"We were given freedom to do the show we wanted. I went to Moz and asked if he'd ever rung a radio show, or knew anyone who had, and he said no. So I asked why are we broadcasting to the small number of people who make calls to radio stations rather than to the enormous amount of people who just want to listen to what someone has got to say. And in fairness to him he said, 'Let's do that'. It changed the whole dynamic of the show from a phone-in-led one, to a show littered with interviews with some of the biggest guests in UK and world sport.

"No one had ever put sport out in the mid-morning slot. Go all the way back and Moz tried to get me to Radio 5 Live. It was at a time at Sky when I was really unhappy and we nearly did it. But that was the time of the day we were talking about – mid-morning. That was the time slot I wanted. I didn't know at the time that Mike Parry had fallen out with Moz. I think that show fitted neatly at that time of the day and to win that Sony Gold award 12 months later was a compliment to talkSPORT's production team. It was different. It was brilliant.

"I hope others thought it was worth listening to, the figures eventually said that was the case. I think everyone's figures at that time were going in the right direction."

Perhaps inevitably, the success of the show led to them being lured back into the world of television and so, after two and a half years, they left their five-day-a-week role at talkSPORT Towers in the summer of 2013 to take up the new challenge of presenting live football for Al Jazeera in Doha.

Keys says: "I think it was agreed by everybody that maybe for a number of reasons it was the right time to call a halt, but I would have loved to have carried on and I'd like to think at some point there is a reunion to be had.

"talkSPORT is unique, there is nothing else like it. Those that are part of it, have been part of it or who might be part of it in the future should cherish it because it is something very, very special.

"If I said I owe my life [to talkSPORT], that sounds dramatic. But to a large degree that is true. I certainly owe my professional life to those two years at talkSPORT and I will never, ever forget them. Ever."

'CLIPS OF THE WEEK'

The Top 20 All-Time Greats
#16

Alan Brazil has always had a way with names. And here he is demonstrating that with the old Boy Scout motto of 'Be Prepared':

Brazil: Once a Scout, always a Scout. Do you know who the head of the Scouts is at the moment?
Irani: Go on ...
Brazil: Er, what's his name? Bear Grease.

'CLIPS OF THE WEEK'

The Top 20 All-Time Greats
#15

When a call comes into the studio and the details are logged on to the presenter's screen, it's not always foolproof. Here's Stan Collymore getting a little mixed up:

Stan: James is a Liverpool fan in Hitchin. [Starts singing] How far to Hitchin, it's Hitchin I'm missin' ... it's an old song, that is. James, good evening.
Caller: Er, it's Jamie.
Stan: Sorry, Jamie. How are you pal?
Caller: And I'm in Letchworth, by the way.

Chapter 5 ⚽

An Englishman, a Scotsman and a Northern Irishman Walk into a Station ...

The departure of Keys and Gray left a hole in talkSPORT's weekday schedule. And Colin Murray was identified as the man to fill it.

Northern Irishman Murray was a well-known face and voice having worked on high-profile TV and radio shows for the BBC, including *Match of the Day 2* on BBC 2 and *Fighting Talk* on BBC Radio 5 Live. He had also presented Channel 5's live UEFA Cup coverage.

It was another exciting signing for talkSPORT, although one that then Programme Director Liam Fisher thought had slipped through the net following his early exchanges with Murray.

"What impressed me most from the moment I met him was that he was full of energy, full of ideas, full of creativity. But he didn't want to come to us to begin with," says Fisher.

"After he joined he said to me that after our first meeting he walked away with only 1% of him thinking he would make the move to us, 99% of him was thinking he would stick with the BBC. And they can give a broadcaster like Colin a lot of opportunities. They've got the news stations, the music stations, and one of his greatest gifts is he's able to do a lot of different types of programming.

"But then, on a long drive up to Manchester he thought about the show he could do for talkSPORT, the ideas he could come up with, and the freedom he would have to develop his ideas and just deliver them. Freedom he didn't have at the BBC. By the time he got to Manchester he told me he was 70% sure he was coming because he knew there was loads he could do and he wanted to get involved."

On announcing his decision in the press to move to talkSPORT, Murray said: "I'm truly excited about creating this programme, and I hope it will become the morning 'go-to' for UK sports fans. I will be joined by fascinating and knowledgeable guests every day, offering up different opinions on issues and topics that you want to hear about throughout the week."

He certainly did bring plenty of energy, and plenty of guests, as *Colin Murray and Friends* continued the success of the mid-morning slot vacated by Keys and Gray. 'Friends' would include, among others, Mike Tindall, Steve Bunce, Danny Murphy, Didi Hamann, Stuart Pearce, Des Kelly, Daley Thompson and Kelly Sotherton.

Occasionally Murray's energy and creativity was a bit much for some of his colleagues on the programming floor who would have to listen to him repeatedly cutting and tweaking musical beds for his show. He was apparently unaware that a pair of headphones would relieve the rest of the office of the sound of his drum 'n' bass soundtrack, or whatever his musical choice of the day was. It used to particularly annoy news reader Robyn Schönhofer who sat on the desk opposite. Schönhofer took it upon herself one day to hand Murray a set of headphones to put on, thinking he'd take the hint. However, Murray, blissfully unaware, didn't. He looked at her with a vacant stare and said: "No it's alright, I'm fine thanks." Cue a stroppy march back to her seat by Schönhofer.

But he definitely delivered some fresh radio that had never been heard on talkSPORT before. One such innovation was 'Trust Darts', where some of the game's leading players would face off against one another live on air. The premise was they would throw the darts at their own board, and then announce their score. Their opponent would take the score on trust, before having their shot.

Murray was the man responsible for the 'Ponty Party'. A group of around 200 fans and talkSPORT listeners, including himself, former Arsenal favourite Perry Groves, and boxing broadcaster and walking encyclopaedia Steve Bunce travelled with the Welsh part-timers from Pontypridd in July 2014 for a pre-season clash with La Liga giants Valencia.

The game came about because of connections Ponty boss Dominic Broad had in Spain, but the Welsh minnows were struggling to finance the fixture. When Murray heard about it he persuaded his show's sponsors, Wickes, to get on board and sponsor the trip.

A year later Pontypridd returned to Spain to take on Deportivo La Coruna before, in May 2016, facing up to perhaps their toughest challenge – a visit from the talkSPORT All-Stars. This team included ex-Liverpool stars Danny Murphy and Didi Hamman, former Ipswich captain Matt Holland, ex-Sunderland star Micky Gray, 2003 Rugby World Cup winner Mike Tindall and two-time Olympic decathlon champion Daley Thompson.

Despite the stellar names in their line-up, the visitors were beaten 3-1 on a rain-soaked pitch in a match that was broadcast live on talkSPORT. It captured the locals' imagination, with the attendance of 1,600 smashing the previous record of ... 64.

Murray, who hosted the coverage before bringing himself on for the second half, said: "It was great to get an away goal, so when we take them back to ours we'll be all-out attack. It was great that we've come here, had a wonderful reception and broken the attendance record by 2,000%. We've had such fun."

Former Liverpool and England ace Murphy told the local media: "It was hard work. It's the first time I've played since I retired [in 2013]. I felt fine to start with but gave too much in the opening 20 minutes, and we struggled to cope with their fitness.

"We knew they'd be fit and strong, but I was surprised by the quality we came up against. They are a good team and we couldn't match that. It wasn't much effort for us to come here and play, and it means so much to them and all the people watching. I think people enjoyed it.

"I played a lot in the lower leagues but it's been a long time. It's quite nice to play in that atmosphere, and with the ball not running properly through the puddles. But I wouldn't like to do it every week."

In other firsts for the station, Murray's show hosted the FA Trophy draw live on air, and broadcast coverage of a 2014 charity cycle ride as some of talkSPORT's presenters and staff rode 150 miles from London to Amsterdam in aid of the station's charity partner at the time, Prostate Cancer UK. It was an eclectic mix of fun and games, big-name interviews and raw passion. It was a format that was well loved, with audiences around the one million mark and new listeners being attracted to the station.

Another man bringing a new audience also joined the station around the same time as Murray. Johnny Vaughan was brought in to host a new Saturday morning show, *The Warm Up*. Both Vaughan and the show were truly unique in talkSPORT history, in terms of both content and personality. But amazingly, only a few days before its debut in August 2014, no one at the station was sure it would even happen.

Deputy Programme Director Steve Morgan, who had previously worked in light entertainment TV, had been handed the task of running the show but, the Wednesday before it was supposed to air for the first time, Vaughan had still not signed on the dotted line. Frantic bosses were putting enormous pressure on Morgan. All he really had was the name of a show, but no host and only a couple of days to go before it was meant to start. That night, however, thankfully Vaughan called Morgan to casually ask what was happening with the show on Saturday. Morgan said: "I was like, 'Are you doing it?' And he replied, 'Of course I am, I'll come in and see you tomorrow'. He came into the office on the Thursday and was like a whirlwind. He was just fantastic. But it was squeaky bum time for me."

By his own admission, Vaughan, the former host of the breakfast show on Capital Radio, was initially unsure of making the move to talkSPORT, describing it as: "The backstreet bookie of broadcasting." But he threw himself wholeheartedly into the challenge.

There were some great ideas brought to air, including 'The River Niall', where ex-Sunderland chairman Niall Quinn was the first interviewee, and then he would nominate someone to be the next one the following week and so on. There was also 'Slaughterhouse', a rugby league segment hosted by three men who worked in an abattoir. Yes, really.

Morgan says: "It was incredible. It was brilliant. I could never have suggested that as an idea, it would have seemed ridiculous. It just happened spontaneously on air. We rolled in a piece of music from *Wild at Heart*, the David Lynch movie, and it was this heavy piece of guitar music, really fast and frenetic, and then Johnny just naturally, over the top of it, said in this deep, menacing voice: 'You're listening to Slaughterhouse' and he went into it.

"Vaughan on air was like conducting lightning. You can't box someone like that in. He's like a freeform jazz trumpeter. You can show them the notes, but it doesn't necessarily mean that's what they're going to play. You just have to try to keep in time if you can. The trick was to do the programme meeting as the show went on."

One of the abiding memories of Johnny in the studios was that he always turned up with his bulldog Geoff who was given free rein in the production offices and studios. Geoff also travelled with Johnny into the studios by the car laid on, which cost talk-SPORT substantial additional cleaning charges, due to Johnny feeding the canine companion on the back seat.

Vaughan's time at talkSPORT was sweet, but sadly short. In the autumn of 2015, after just two years, he returned to music radio. Morgan admits he felt a great loss at the time. "I genuinely felt bereft because I felt it had a far longer lifespan," he says. "At the end of the show each week I remember feeling like you do at the end of a good meal and you've had a bit of cake and you're going round the plate for a few more crumbs thinking: 'I could have done with more of that.' That was what it was like. He was phenomenal."

Another man whose departure came as something of a shock to everyone was Murray's when, in the summer of 2016, he announced he was quitting his mid-morning show in light of the takeover of talkSPORT by News UK. As an avid Liverpool fan, he felt he was unable to continue in his new role due to the association with *The Sun* newspaper.

So for the fourth time in only six years, following Parry and Graham, Keys and Gray, and Colin Murray, talkSPORT was on the look-out for a fresh host for their midweek morning slot.

It's remarkable to think that since 2000 Alan Brazil has hosted breakfast and Hawksbee and Jacobs have been on in the afternoons, while Adrian Durham has been hosting the drive-time show since 2006. But while those shows have enjoyed reigns of longevity similar to Sir Alex Ferguson at Manchester United, the 10am–1pm slot has, in recent years, been more like the Crystal Palace job.

Finding the right person to fill the vacancy was not an easy task, but talkSPORT has never been afraid to think outside the box. And so it was that they turned to the hugely respected journalist and broadcaster Jim White, a man who has enjoyed a 40-year career in sports broadcasting, most notably for Sky Sports, but who had never previously presented a radio show in his life.

He says: "I knew it would be different to TV and it is, but it's brilliant. It's tough; tougher than I ever imagined it would be. Every single day is a test and a challenge because you start with a blank canvas at 7.30am each morning, but I'm so glad I did it. I'm thankful to Sky for letting me do it, but I'm really grateful to talkSPORT for giving me the opportunity."

The big thing in White's favour, as had been the case five years earlier with Richard Keys, is that he brought with him a huge contacts book. "If I didn't have the contacts I've built up over the years, this would have failed spectacularly," he admits.

And on no occasion do those contacts come in handier than on transfer deadline day. White has become synonymous with the last-minute spending frenzy that takes place on the final day of January and August each year, with his trademark yellow tie on display on television sets in pubs, offices and living rooms all across the country.

And his insider knowledge proved invaluable in August 2017 when he got the jump on one of the biggest Premier League moves of the day that saw Alex Oxlade-Chamberlain join Liverpool from Arsenal for £35 million.

It was being widely reported, including by White's colleagues at Sky Sports News, that the England midfielder was all set to join Chelsea and that the London rivals had agreed terms on the deal. White, however, received a text message from someone close to the player who told him he would be going to Liverpool. White was able to break that news live on talkSPORT. In the next commercial break he phoned his mates at Sky to tell them what was going on. As a result, White was able to deliver the scoop of the week on talkSPORT in the morning and then follow it through on Sky in the afternoon.

There have been times when White's confidence in his sources has been tested. None more so than when he received the tip-off that England captain Wayne Rooney was to be left out of Gareth Southgate's team for the World Cup qualifier in October 2016. White went 'balls out' with the information on talkSPORT. But he discovered later in the day as he made his way to the Sky studios that two people were going to feature in the pre-match press conference – Southgate and Rooney. Would Rooney really be facing the media if he was about to be dropped for the first time in his international career?

"I don't mind telling you, I thought: Oh God, was my information right?" But it turned out White's inside track had been accurate. Southgate and Rooney had simply agreed to appear together to banish any speculation about ill-feeling between the pair.

The exclusives White's contacts provide are just one aspect of the show, however, with a format similar to that adopted by Colin Murray, of having one host joined in the studio by two regular co-hosts. White's usual partner in crime being comedian Bob Mills.

"I can always rely on Bob," says White. "If there's a comment the man on the street wants to make about his football club, Bob is that man. He's a Leyton Orient fan and knows exactly what a good owner can mean to a club and what a bad owner can mean to a club. He's been through it. He knows how fans think, and he's got great humour. He's wonderful." Bob was once asked by Jim what the biggest game in the UK was that day, alluding to the fact that Liverpool were playing Manchester United and in Glasgow the Old Firm match was on. But Bob, quite simply and emphatically, said: "There's only one match in town. The Orient are going to Barrow." And he meant it.

The mix of White's nose for a story, Mills' man-of-the-people attitude and humour, the expert opinions of former players like Danny Murphy, Micky Gray and Perry Groves, plus the outspoken former Crystal Palace owner Simon Jordan, makes for a heady mid-morning cocktail that has proved to be a winner. But there's no question of White taking that for granted.

"I've got a lot more creative licence at talkSPORT compared to Sky. You can develop ideas; you can go off in a different direction. They give you that freedom and that's one of the magical things about talkSPORT. They allow you to breathe. They let you go in a direction that maybe my bosses at Sky would be a bit reluctant for me to go in. It's not as structured as Sky, and that gives you great scope to operate."

And, of course, there's always the possibility of an unexpected exclusive as he discovered one day on his way to Waterloo Station when he spotted American actor and star of *Breaking Bad* Bryan Cranston. White approached him and told him he was a fan, and the pair got chatting. Cranston said Donald Trump is the worst thing that's ever happened to the USA and he talked about the protests by NFL players – 'taking a knee' during the national anthem – and how his sympathies lay with the players.

That was a talkSPORT exclusive that also made major headlines across the pond, much more a case of 'breaking news' than *Breaking Bad*.

But that was now the established way at talkSPORT. The bad old days of fighting for scraps had been consigned to history, and the good times were rolling. And they would go on rolling in ways that few would have dared to imagine.

'CLIPS OF THE WEEK'

The Top 20 All-Time Greats
#14

Time checks are an essential part of any radio station's output but occasionally presenters can go a wee bit overboard. Like Alan Brazil one morning reporting live from The Open:

'It's gone 9.32. Don't forget, Andy Gray coming up at 10 o'clock here on the *Sports Breakfast*. 9.32. Tiger after his ball on the left side. 9.32 here on talkSPORT.

OK, Alan, we get the picture, it's thirty-two minutes past nine.

Goughie Goes All Kate Adie
at Euro 2012

The sporting year of 2012 was always destined to be a momentous one for British sport, and so it proved.

There was the success of the London Olympics, and 'Super Saturday' when Great Britain won three athletics gold medals in the space of 44 minutes, courtesy of Jessica Ennis, Greg Rutherford and Mo Farah. There was more to celebrate. Andy Murray won the US Open, his first major, and followed that up with gold at the Olympics. Chelsea won the Champions League, Bradley Wiggins took the yellow jersey in the Tour de France and Rory McIlroy claimed the PGA Championship. It was quite the haul.

But 2012 was also to prove a momentous one for talkSPORT.

With the BBC holding all the rights to the Olympics, it was the European Championship finals in Poland and Ukraine that were the real focus of talkSPORT's efforts that year. The station was determined to pull out all the stops to make the tournament as memorable as possible for its listeners. And it certainly was memorable, although not necessarily for all the right reasons.

By now talkSPORT was a veteran of several major tournaments, a world away from those dim and distant days of Euro 2000 when the best they could do was broadcast games from a TV in a hotel room in Amsterdam. And, as such, the scale of their ambitions had risen considerably.

And those ambitions were clearly stated even before a ball had been kicked. Poland and Ukraine were joint hosts of the tournament and that added a significant layer of logistical complications for the man whose job it was to plan coverage of the event. At that stage, however, no one had any inkling of the challenges they were about to face.

The team was about to unwittingly walk headlong into a maelstrom of issues, which first became apparent in the penultimate week before the start of the tournament.

As part of the build-up, and in order to truly bolster the excitement back home, it had been decided that the drive-time show would go on a road trip across Europe. Broadcasting each day from a different city en route to Poland, the show would arrive at its destination on the day of the opening game.

Darren Gough recalls: "[It was] my favourite trip when we did the drive-time road trip. It was just unbelievable. Amazing. It was one of the best trips I'd ever been on. We went Lille, Eindhoven, Wolfsburg, Berlin. It was tiring, but [we were] doing the show, having a night out, then travelling to the next spot. It was hilarious in our own little wagon with pictures on the side of the van of me and Adrian."

The trip was being sponsored by Vauxhall. It was with a sense of excitement that the five-man team, presenters Adrian Durham and Goughie, producers Laurie Palacio and James Dodd, and video editor James Bragg, left the UK as it would be the first time that the station was planning to produce substantial digital content from a major event – a lot of it coming from the road trip.

The Vivaro van was indeed complete with cartoon caricatures of Durham's face on one side and Gough's on the other. They set off on Sunday, 3 June, stocking up on sweets and enjoying a McDonald's on the A2 en route to their ferry to France. As Palacio says: "We were all really looking forward to the trip. What could possibly go wrong?"

At this stage, Palacio and the team were confident everything was in place for a smooth journey from London to Warsaw, via France, Holland and Germany – a distance of approximately 1,000 miles.

It soon became apparent, however, that the meticulous plans Palacio believed were in place were sadly lacking. The true scale of the problems facing the whole talkSPORT team would only emerge once the whole party arrived in Poland and Ukraine, but more of that later. Right now things were beginning to unravel. They discovered there were no hotels booked and no studios booked to broadcast from. Nothing. Palacio and company were on their own.

In those days 3G wireless mobile was in its infancy and 4G was unheard of. Connectivity was patchy at best as the team arrived in France. They needed somewhere to sleep and a venue from where they could broadcast. But as is the talkSPORT way, rabbits were pulled out of hats at the eleventh hour and the trip was somehow stitched together thanks to some frantic phone calls and several favours being called in.

In the end, the team managed to broadcast from a radio station in Lille, a recording studio in Eindhoven, a shopping centre in Wolfsburg (to this day no one really has any idea quite why they came live from a shopping centre) and a radio station in Berlin, all of which were arranged on the fly as they navigated their way across Europe.

Generally, wherever they went, people were happy to help and they created some great 'colour' pieces from Eindhoven in Holland and Lille in France. So they arrived in Wolfsburg in Germany with a similar level of optimism. However, that was soon to be dashed. First, not only was there no accommodation booked, there were no rooms to be had anywhere. Sensing mutiny, Palacio took the executive decision to book the whole party into the only remaining rooms in the town, at the ultra-plush and ultra-expensive Ritz Hotel. Palacio had blown a week's expenses in one night. But the next day more problems were to come.

As the technical guys made ready their space in the shopping centre for the afternoon's drive-time show, Palacio, Dodd, Durham and Gough made their way to Wolfsburg's Volkswagen Arena, where they were met with a less than friendly welcome.

The plan was to secure a tour of the stadium and conduct an interview with the press officer and one or two members of the behind-the-scenes staff. However, on arrival in the reception they were greeted with a hostile, "Who are you, and what are you doing here?"

The press officer appeared. Usually clubs are very accommodating when it comes to visiting foreign media, but not this chap. He was absolutely furious that a band of upstarts had simply turned up at the stadium without emailing in advance to seek permission. It was all quite surreal and things escalated when he threatened to call the police unless the talkSPORT crew vacated the premises immediately.

That prompted a hasty retreat and resulted in a madcap scenario of Durham, Goughie and producers dashing across the car park to make a swift getaway in a huge Vauxhall van complete with the faces of Adrian Durham and Darren Gough on the side. Not exactly inconspicuous if the police did arrive.

But obviously it did all add up to a great tale for the show that afternoon. Whether the accountants had such a good laugh when they got the expenses bill from Wolfsburg is very much open to debate.

It was to the credit of all concerned that the listeners were none the wiser about the problems the team overcame every day just to get on air. Due to the talkSPORT team's resilience, they delivered four days of superb radio, with entertaining guests, before arriving on schedule in Warsaw on Friday, 7 June, the day before the tournament kicked off with Poland taking on Greece at the Stadion Narodowy.

Goughie says: "I think we did some of our best stuff, then, me and Adrian. When we do an outside broadcast I excel in that sort of environment."

Their arrival, however, was not without incident. They had driven from Berlin to Warsaw without stopping as they were running slightly behind schedule. This was mainly because it had taken a while to rouse a couple of members of the team that morning following a lively night out. On arrival in Berlin the team were so excited they'd made it this far that they skipped dinner and went out to sample Berlin's nightlife. It was a very, very late night and ended up with Palacio having to physically drag people out of bed the next morning to start the last leg of the tour (Berlin to Warsaw) in order to make it in time for Durham and Gough to host an evening show live from Warsaw.

When they arrived in Warsaw it turned out that the apartment where the studio had been set up was very close to the stadium that was playing host to the opening game. That meant that by the time of their arrival the exclusion zone for vehicles was well and truly in place. There followed a frantic drive around Warsaw, a city none of them had been to before, without a satnav, desperately trying to persuade police officers to let them through the barricades to reach the studio. But, of course, at this point none of them had their tournament accreditation.

Eventually, they had to abandon the van, leaving Durham & co. to run to the studio arriving just in time to begin broadcasting. They couldn't have cut it any finer if they had tried. But if they thought that was the end of their problems, they were sadly mistaken. Instead they walked into a full-blown crisis.

By now several other members of talkSPORT's production and commentary teams had arrived at their respective bases in Warsaw and Kiev and a picture was emerging of what a mess they were in.

Outside Broadcast Manager Matt Smith, the man who was supposed to have fully organised the trip (including hotels, travel arrangements, accreditation, commentary positions, match tickets – the whole shooting match), had left much of it uncompleted. And he was nowhere to be seen.

Smith, affectionately known among his colleagues as 'Villa' because of his allegiance to his local club, was a hugely popular member of the talkSPORT team. He was liked by all, great company on a night out and someone who had shown himself eminently capable of organising coverage of major events such as the World Cup in South Africa in 2010, the Rugby World Cup in 2011 and talkSPORT's live Premier League and Champions League football.

There had been hints maybe all was not well ahead of Euro 2012 when Smith's PowerPoint presentation of the plans made little or no mention of where the games were being played or who was due to be where, when and how. But, at that stage, there was no real inkling of how ill-prepared the whole venture was. Smith had delivered before and people were confident he would do so again.

Alarm bells began to ring as the teams arrived in Warsaw and Kiev to find no one waiting with keys for their apartments, as expected. Several phone calls and much kicking of heels later, keys were delivered. Suffice to say the apartments did not bear any resemblance to the Wolfsburg Ritz.

That first night in Warsaw will also be remembered as the starting point for Ian 'The Moose' Abrahams' culinary tour of Poland's capital, once known as the 'Paris of the North' and reckoned to be one of the most beautiful cities in the world until the Second World War. It remains an enchanting city and one that every member of the talkSPORT team who spent time there grew extremely fond of. But The Moose is a man who likes his home comforts and was known for eating tuna fish at his desk at ten in the morning much to the disgust of his colleagues. As the team was waiting for the keepers of the keys to arrive, they retreated to a local restaurant. The Moose has pretty simple tastes, and is not one to experiment with local delicacies, so opted for burger and chips. Now there's nothing wrong with that, of course, but it was the beginning of 30 consecutive days where he had burger and chips for dinner and the same for lunch. There's little doubt he would probably have had the same for breakfast if it had not been for the delightful little patisserie across the road to which he took a particular liking.

His diet caused widespread amusement among his colleagues, but laughter was in short supply when the team arrived at the stadium in Warsaw to collect their tournament accreditations to discover there was no evidence of an accreditation application for Richard Keys, the man who was due to utter the opening words of talkSPORT's match coverage in that very stadium, just hours later.

That resulted in what would be the first in a series of slightly frantic phone calls and email exchanges between talkSPORT and UEFA as the station's senior staff attempted to rescue their tournament, and piece together the missing pieces of their itineraries and planned coverage. Eventually, after some begging and pleading, UEFA agreed to the request to expedite Keys' accreditation and he was able to take his place in the stadium to present the station's live match coverage as their Polish hosts drew the opening match 1-1 with Greece.

It wasn't the start the Poles were hoping for and the mood around the city that night was relatively sombre, despite the locals' obvious pride at hosting such a prestigious event.

But their mood was positively euphoric compared to that of the talkSPORT team as a war council was assembled – Moz Dee, Steve Morgan, Mike Bovill, Kay Townsend and Lauren Webster in London, and Liam Fisher and Laurie Palacio in Warsaw – to attempt to fill the gaps in the itinerary as the hunt for Smith, and some answers, continued.

At one point someone contacted Palacio to tell him he thought he'd spotted a strangely vacant looking Smith crossing his hotel lobby but, by the time he got outside to attempt to confront his AWOL colleague, Smith, if indeed it had been him, had vanished once more. It was like the hunt for Keyser Söze!

Smith had completely vanished off the grid. No one knew where he was and no one could contact him as he had turned his phone off. In fact, he was in Warsaw at this point but, for reasons that would emerge, he was in no position to do his job. So much so that he actually arrived at the stadium for the opening game, collected his match ticket and then turned around and walked away again.

Liam Fisher, who was the senior producer on the tour and later became Programme Director, remembers spotting Smith in the outer confines of the stadium, but that was the last time he saw him.

Fisher said: "The next time I really thought 'Where's Matt?' was about halfway through the first half when I looked around and realised he still wasn't there. But then it's about getting the game done. Keys and Gray hadn't done that sort of broadcast for talkSPORT before at a major tournament, so that was my main concern. And within all that you're thinking about how you're getting people back to hotels and apartments after the broadcast.

"It was only really when we were packing up after the game that I began wondering where Matt was and started to think something really didn't feel right about all this. And then further into the evening it really hit home that he'd gone missing. There were stories he was spotted getting into a cab to the Ukraine to take some kit there. It was rumoured that someone had seen him throw his phone into the Vistula river. It went from, 'Where's Matt, he should be here, he's letting us down,' to more of a safety issue where you're thinking, 'Is he OK, what's happened here?' We were trying to get hold of him to make sure he was alright, but it's difficult because you really are spinning plates. At that point the tournament had started, there were games going on and the *Drive* team had arrived from their road trip. You're trying to manage all of this as well as what is becoming a big issue with one of the guys who was key to the whole tournament."

What has since emerged is the harrowing tale of a man battling drinking and gambling addictions, who by this point was so far in denial about his illness that by his own admission he didn't even realise there was a problem.

On leaving the stadium in Warsaw, Smith went to a bar and began drinking. And he stayed there until he borrowed someone's phone to call a driver to take him, through the night, the 250 miles to Lviv in Ukraine, where Germany were taking on Portugal that day.

That reflects where he was mentally and emotionally. He says: "When I look back now I don't even know why I was thinking of going to the next game, I hadn't even turned up to do my job at the first one. I was completely down the rabbit hole. My mind was just black, a complete fog.

"My addictions had really taken a grip on me. My thinking was not straight. I was completely and utterly delusional."

On arrival in Lviv, he met up with Sam Matterface and Stan Collymore, and was told people in London were trying to get hold of him, but he refused to speak to anyone. It was collectively agreed that the only sensible course of action was to get him home as quickly as possible.

Flights were arranged, but on receiving the details via email, Smith was not happy. The reason? The flight coincided with England's first game against France and he wanted to stay out there to watch that. "That was my state of mind at the time," he says. "How absolutely pathetic and ridiculous."

On arrival back in London, Smith went straight to Ronnie Irani's house where he took refuge and from there the full story emerged. Irani at the time was the co-presenter on *The Alan Brazil Sports Breakfast* so knew Smith well.

Smith says: "The reason I didn't communicate what was going on, or what the plans were, was simply that I couldn't. I'd lost all ability to do anything. Within the space of a week my entire world had come crashing down, a result totally of my own behaviour. But I was so far in denial about my illness I didn't even know I was ill.

"I never once thought, or intended, that I was going to hurt people, and my colleagues in particular. That wasn't what I wanted to achieve. I was in a dark place in my mind.

"Admitting responsibility for those things doesn't absolve me from what I did, it doesn't do that. All it does is say I was responsible. It doesn't remove the facts of what I did, and I have deep regret and shame around those things.

"My state of mind ... at that point I didn't even think I was going to lose my job, even though it was obviously gross misconduct on my part. I was so in denial and delusional."

Following meetings with CEO Scott Taunton, Smith was given a leave of absence and entered counselling but admits he didn't engage with the process. He didn't want to stop. All he wanted to do was drink and gamble.

"I couldn't have asked for more support from Scott," said Smith. "There was an investigation and everyone involved managed it in a magnificent way. They protected me as much as they could, but I couldn't stop. And I didn't stop until two years later when I hit rock bottom and went into rehab.

"Ronnie [Irani] had introduced me to a man called Paul Spanjar, who runs the Providence Projects in Bournemouth. Because of that introduction, two years later I contacted Paul and said I was ready [to enter rehab] and they gave me a charitable place. I turned up there with one bag, that's all I had. I was basically homeless, I hadn't spoken to my mum for a year and a half, I hadn't spoken to anybody. I had just gone completely off the rails.

"Scott [Taunton] did the right thing by letting me go [from talkSPORT], and I'm really grateful he did because if I had been able to carry on I probably wouldn't be alive now."

And thankfully Smith is now a full five years into recovery and back to the very capable person that he was prior to his illness.

By now UEFA had been made fully aware of the impossible situation the station found itself in. Smith was the only person who had the access details and passwords to the UEFA 'FAME' system which is used by media companies to arrange coverage of international tournaments such as the European Championship finals. It meant Palacio had to go to a UEFA office and present his passport and explain the situation once more in order to convince them he was legitimate and should be allowed access to the system.

Once he had the keys to the kingdom, so to speak, he and Fisher were confronted with the full horror of the bleak picture. As Palacio remembered: "We discovered odd things, like we had 'observer seats' for an England match, but no commentary positions booked. There may have been a good reason for this, but we couldn't get hold of Matt to ask him. So we had to effectively start from scratch double-checking everything and it was an intensive couple of days to-ing and fro-ing with UEFA officials. They were actually very helpful once they realised how precarious our situation was given our lack of access to things we urgently needed including commentary positions."

For Production Manager Kay Townsend and Office Manager Lauren Webster, it meant one of the longest weekends of their lives. The two of them spent the best part of two days and two nights in the talkSPORT office as a barrage of phone calls and emails bounced around between London, Warsaw and Kiev as they tried to stitch together the plans for the tournament. At one point, ex-Wimbledon FA Cup-winning manager and now evening presenter Bobby Gould popped out of the office and returned with a pair of ear protectors from Argos for each of them just so they could block out the noise and concentrate. At times of adversity heroes emerge and without the sterling efforts of those two, who knows how things would have turned out? Not well, it's probably safe to say.

Of course, it wasn't only in Poland where problems were aris-
ing. The team in Kiev had their own issues to deal with. The
'living' apartment which had been allocated to Mark Saggers
and Dennie Morris had no actual furniture to speak of. There
was a big TV on the wall that didn't work and couldn't actually
be plugged in anywhere. The beds weren't really beds and
Saggers' en-suite shower was a rubber hose you fixed to the taps
"like your parents had when we were kids".

Those issues paled into insignificance once they arrived at the
second apartment that was to be used as the studio. Saggers
described it by saying: "It looked like a condemned building. It
looked like the sort of thing you see in a horror film. There were
hard nuts walking up and down the corridors in vests. I don't
know what else it was used for but it did not look right." Morris,
his producer, was equally unimpressed. "We walked up to this
tower block. It was like something out of *Hostel*. But worse. It
was the most intimidating place you've ever seen, like something
you would get on a really rough estate."

While footballers at tournaments are cosseted and feted in
the best hotels surrounded by security and with every need
catered for, the talkSPORT commentary team had to fend for
themselves for five weeks. So you do experience some rather
unusual situations and predicaments. As was the case here for
Saggers and Morris.

The building was truly awful. One fire escape had been bricked
over, and there was a metal door that didn't open across another.
The pair figured there was no way they could invite guests there
in case something happened. Calls were made to London to
express their concern but, at this stage of proceedings, with
everything else that was unfolding, there was little anyone could
do to alter the situation. There was no choice but to roll with it.
At one stage in an amusing tale Saggers and Morris feared they
were about to meet their maker and in a not so amusing tale they
were genuinely in fear for their lives.

They were in the lift one day. "The lift was one of those long
ones, like you could fit a coffin in," says Morris. A woman got in
with them. The pair described her as a cross between a classic

Eastern European femme fatale and a Bond villain. When she put her hand slowly into her bag they both looked at one another convinced this was the end, that she was going to pull out a gun and they were going to be killed. Luckily, her hand emerged clutching nothing more threatening than her keys!

But a more sinister and serious predicament would emerge. Somewhere along the line, someone had, perhaps in casual conversations, unwisely promised various people in Kiev all sorts of things including match tickets. But there were no tickets acquired. One of those people happened to be a rather menacing expat who now lived in the Ukraine. And he was now stalking the station's personnel. So he and a few accomplices had found out where talkSPORT was broadcasting from and ended up loitering with intent in the dark shadows outside the building. Presumably in the hope of menacing the team and disrupting broadcasts.

This went on for a few days and then things took an even more sinister turn. Calls started coming into the control room back in London. The caller sounded very threatening and said he was owed money or tickets, and made it clear he wasn't messing around. During the calls he also went on to say that he knew exactly where Mark Saggers was broadcasting from and was outside that building now. This was relayed back to Kiev, and Saggers and Morris were put on alert. As they were making their way from the studio apartment back to their living accommodation, it was like a scene from *Scooby-Doo* with the two of them creeping stealthily on tip toes down the streets and peering round every corner before venturing on. Every rustle in the bushes made them jump. Worse was to come as another call came in to the station with the message that there would be broken legs if no tickets were forthcoming.

By this time the production team had worked out who the guy was. True enough he didn't appear to be a pleasant individual and although none of the threats was carried out it made for a worrying time for the presentation team.

He wasn't the only gangster figure that they would come across in Kiev. Saggers and Morris used to frequent a particular restaurant around the corner from their apartment, and it was often full of gangster types. On occasions there would be armed guards stationed outside and people would come in and hand over wads of cash to the local godfather. The talkSPORT duo sensibly just kept their heads down, and ate their borscht, just in case 'Bond Lady' made another appearance.

So there was some levity despite the difficult situation. And one duo you can always rely on to find the silver lining are Keys and Gray, who were on their first and, as it turned out, last talk-SPORT tour.

For the first week in Poland they were accompanied by Liam Fisher as their regular producer. The pair were delighted to have come up with the nickname L.i.am, as in Will.i.am, even though someone had already claimed that accolade. And from that day on, that's how they would refer to Fisher and they still do to this day. For the intrepid duo, if it's a good joke, it's still a good joke hours later. In fact, it doesn't even have to be a good joke.

In fairness to Keys and Gray, this trip was probably a culture shock to them. More used to the relative comforts of life on the road with Sky, they were unfamiliar with the concept of just a five-minute walk to the train station. According to Fisher, even though he would be managing all the kit, and all they had was a small holdall each, the pair regularly lagged behind moaning about how long the walk was. Well, it would have been a lot shorter if they had just walked a bit quicker.

Once on the trains, however, they seemed perfectly content with the surroundings, particularly Keys. Fisher remembers being on one particular journey with them as they rushed through the Polish countryside, past disused train stations that had a real old communist feel to them. And there was Keys, a man Fisher had watched fronting Premier League coverage on Sky for the past 20 years, poking his head out of the window and seemingly fascinated by the trains.

Jon Norman recalls a similar train journey with Keys and Gray on what he describes as the "Miss Marple Express". The three sat together in one small cubicle, with the two broadcasters basically taking it in turns to try to fart … and keeping score. "It was something of a low," admitted the producer. Keys offered an alternative view, however. "The farting was to try to get the damn thing to move a bit more quickly. You could have walked quicker. It was transport from the land that time forgot."

That wasn't the only issue Norman had with transport. By his own admission, he does not have the best sense of direction. On the way back from Spain's victory over the Republic of Ireland in the group stages in Gdansk, he inexplicably chose to jump off the tram one stop too soon. Norman found himself amongst a heaving mass of Ireland fans as the doors closed behind him. He had to navigate the crowded cobbled streets, complete with 30kg of broadcasting kit, as Keys and Gray – still on the tram, of course – collapsed into a fit of giggles at his predicament.

But after all the initial teething problems the tournament was now in full swing and it was business as usual for talkSPORT. Watertight plans were now in place. The matches were coming thick and fast, and there was plenty to talk about.

One major talking point was the security issue surrounding the biggest game of the group stages. Poland took on Russia in Warsaw. The tournament organisers' worst nightmare became a violent reality as rival supporters were involved in a series of sickening clashes before and after their Group A match at the newly built Warsaw National Stadium. The clash always had the potential for trouble given the years of conflict between the two countries and the Soviet Union's domination of Poland after the Second World War. It was like a red rag to the Polish people given that they had suffered enormously under the Soviet regime.

UEFA had been criticised at the time for scheduling the match on 'Russia Day' which commemorates the establishment of Russia as an independent country after the dissolution of the Soviet Union in 1991. The criticism was well founded as Warsaw turned into a battle zone. Pre-match, armoured vehicles, water cannon and Robocop-style police officers were swarming around the stadium and the city centre. Tension had been heightened when it became known that Russian fans were intending to march from the centre of Warsaw to the stadium to commemorate the day.

There were over 180 arrests with 15 fans badly injured. Fights, some premeditated, were breaking out everywhere before kick-off, with the police fully stretched using tear gas and rubber bullets alongside their water cannon to try to quell the growing violence. Post-match the violence continued with running battles in the streets back into town.

The tension in the city all day was acute, and the talkSPORT team was able to watch it all unfold from the balcony of their studio apartment that overlooked the Stadium Narodowy. And so it was that during the build-up to kick-off, with violent clashes taking place just a few hundred metres away, Darren Gough decided to turn all Kate Adie and wade into the war zone.

Despite Palacio trying to persuade the former England fast bowler that heading down into the melee was perhaps not the best idea, Goughie was not to be deterred and so he and video editor James Bragg, who probably weighs about ten stone wringing wet, marched into the madness.

Goughie admits that he's always liked a 'danger element' in everything he does and even once took part in a sting on the Donal MacIntyre *Undercover* programme. And he saw plenty of danger that day in Warsaw.

"On that day, we could see them all coming across the bridge, all fighting. That was intimidating. Everybody charged into the other side and I'm right in the middle of it. It was an amazing experience but I've always liked that. I'm a sportsman but I've always had that journalistic side so I didn't want to miss it. It all kicked off on that bridge [Poniatowski]. It was horrible. It was the worst organised game ever. For Russia to play Poland on that day. It was crazy."

From a health and safety perspective it was certainly not the wisest move, but from a content perspective it was dynamite, with Gough broadcasting live on air from right in the centre of the disturbances. At one stage he could be heard saying: "I'm in the middle of it, I've just seen Darth Vader." There was indeed a bloke wandering around dressed as the *Star Wars* villain. It was a tourist attraction, but only he knows why he thought it was a good idea to be encouraging locals to have pictures taken with him at the same time as missiles were raining through the air.

To put the atmosphere that night into context, Gray, who had been covering top-level football for 20 years, described it as "the most intimidating I've ever been in as a commentator".

He and Keys were enjoying the camaraderie that comes from working at tournaments for talkSPORT, but there was one rumour doing the rounds in Eastern Europe that reportedly was really winding up Mark Saggers.

He had apparently received word that Keys and Gray had a penthouse suite in Warsaw. Over time the story was suitably embellished until they were staying in seven-star accommodation with panoramic views across the entire city. So while Saggers was broadcasting from what he believed to be a condemned drug den complete with murderous women in lifts, Keys and Gray were having cocktails and Jacuzzis in their luxury abode.

In fact, the studio in which Keys and Gray were working was as far from palatial as the one Saggers was dealing with in Ukraine, although they didn't have to share bunk beds as Saggs and Morris once did in Donetsk. But on the plus side, Saggers never had to suffer the trauma of walking in on The Moose sitting on the toilet as Keys did one morning. So it was very much swings and roundabouts.

"The studio [in Warsaw] was like somebody's front room," says Gray. "And it overlooked the ground. We couldn't work out why we overlooked the ground when we were a radio station. It's not like anyone else could see it." He was right about "somebody's front room". The studio doubled as The Moose's accommodation for the tournament so broadcasting would take place while The Moose's underpants were drying on radiators.

Gordon Strachan, who was a guest one day on the *Keys and Gray* show, perhaps best summed up the facility. He says: "I thought I'd got in a taxi to come here today, not a time machine!" And when David Moyes, in a cab on his way to guest on one of the shows, was told that the studio was less than 'salubrious', he replied, "Well that might make a difference to me if I knew what it meant".

One man who probably wished he could have had a time machine, or even a taxi for that matter, was Palacio, for whom there was to be one final twist in the tale of his tournament.

He had initially been assured he would be able to fly back to London from Warsaw. But with just a couple of days of the tournament left, he found out that he was, in fact, expected to drive an additional car that the team had rented for the trip all the way back to the UK. A journey of a mere thousand miles.

At one stage it looked as though the road-trip van would also have to make the return trip, but the sponsors were persuaded to allow that to be dropped at a local Opel garage. There was no such compromise with the car, so Palacio and video editor Bragg had to put the pedal to the metal and drive back to Blighty.

This time, however, there was no leisurely meander through Germany, Holland and France. Instead, between them they drove virtually non-stop to get home in near record time. To add insult to injury for Spanish-born Palacio, they were on the ferry from the Hook of Holland to Harwich while the final was being played, and unable to get a signal on the radio. As they drove off the boat, they tuned in just in time to hear Juan Mata net the fourth goal for the Spaniards in their victorious romp over Italy.

It was an inglorious end to the tournament for Palacio, to go with his ignominious beginning. But, despite all the early problems, it had been a success for talkSPORT, as the end-of-year listening figures would demonstrate.

Somewhat bizarrely perhaps, those figures were also boosted by talkSPORT's coverage of the main event of 2012 – an event at which they were very much outsiders.

The Olympics of London 2012 was the hottest ticket in town, but talkSPORT was not invited to the party. With the BBC owning the rights lock, stock and barrel, every other broadcaster, be they TV or radio, was cast in the role of envious bystander.

But that was not going to stop talkSPORT. Of course it wasn't. If they couldn't actually be in the Olympic Stadium, they would pull out all the stops to be as close to it as they could.

They rented studio space above a car park in Stratford and also hosted the *Hawksbee and Jacobs* show from a boat at Fish Island, which backs on to the Olympic Park. It was basically as close as you could get to the Olympics without actually being on Olympic property.

With medal alerts from a dedicated Olympic news desk at the studios in Hatfields and interviews with all of Team GB's major competitors, it amounted to a thoroughly decent package that brought listeners a nice all-round flavour of the Games.

Crucially, however, it also freed up plenty of airtime to discuss the forthcoming Premier League season which, with Euro 2012 now virtually a dim and distant memory, for salivating football fans it was a real plus.

So while BBC Radio 5 Live was concentrating on archery and the finer points of dressage, talkSPORT was debating Arsenal's attempts to close the gap on Manchester City and Manchester United, and how long Roberto Di Matteo would stay as manager of Chelsea.

And it worked. People in the UK loved the London Olympics, but they didn't want it 24 hours a day, seven days a week. They wanted their football fix. And talkSPORT was happy to provide it.

The station was flying, audiences were growing and the numbers firmly validated the decision that had been made in April that year to axe all non-sports content.

Up until that point, although sport dominated the schedule, there were still around 40 hours a week of non-sports related content, including George Galloway's current affairs programme, *The Mother of All Talk Shows*, which aired on Friday nights, and *The Late Show* with Ian Collins, which was on weeknights between 10pm and 1am.

It was a bold decision, making talkSPORT the first sports broadcaster in Britain to offer nothing but sports-related programming, but it was a decision Programme Director Moz Dee backed fully.

He called it an "exciting yet natural step," adding: "We want to change expectations of overnight radio, focusing on up-to-the-minute sport news and information from around the globe.

In an official announcement he said: "It gives us a great opportunity to work with an international network of sports reporters covering everything from American sports to British teams and athletes competing on the other side of the world, and makes us the only UK station focused on sport all of the time."

While Dee was driving the station forward he was quietly contemplating his own future. There was widespread shock when, just days before Christmas, it was announced that he and Sales Director Adam Bullock were leaving talkSPORT to set up their own business. And that was pretty much that. The pair ceased to be part of the business, effective immediately.

So talkSPORT welcomed in the New Year with huge uncertainty surrounding two key areas of the business – programming and sales. Calum Macaulay, who had been talkSPORT's Marketing Director at launch in January 2000 and was currently the Managing Director of the independent local radio stations that were part of the UTV group, took up the reins as Managing Director of talkSPORT. Following a recruitment process involving internal and external candidates, Liam Fisher, who had been Dee's number two, was named as Programme Director.

When you read player pen pics in matchday programmes, you often read the phrase 'progressed through the junior ranks' and that statement could certainly be used to sum up Fisher's rise to the top, having joined the station 12 years previously when his job was to answer the phones and make the tea on the Tom Watt show – and that was a man who was very particular about his tea.

Like Macaulay, Fisher had witnessed first-hand the evolution of the station from its early days under Kelvin MacKenzie. And now, he was the man tasked with making the big decisions. And it's fair to say the first decision he made was certainly a big one as he proposed a huge change to the much-loved *Alan Brazil Sports Breakfast* show.

For the previous six years or so, Brazil had been joined in the studio by his regular partner, former Essex and England cricketer Ronnie Irani, the man he referred to as 'Chicken' – Ronnie Irani/ Chicken Biryani/Chicken. But Fisher decided the format needing spicing up, and that meant 'Chicken' was off the menu.

Fisher says: "The show had worked really well for a number of years, and Ronnie had been Alan's longest-serving 'radio wife', but it needed freshening up. It wasn't necessarily a reflection on Ronnie himself, but Alan benefits from having a different person alongside him every few years, and it felt like it was that time."

Instead of placing another regular co-host alongside Brazil, however, it was decided to build a roster of former sports stars that could slot in alongside him. Whilst this may not sound dramatic, it was pretty revolutionary in radio where the norm is to have the same two presenters on the breakfast show every day or a set 'posse' so listeners breed on familiarity. But the new breakfast show's format started working.

The rotating guest format not only has the effect of keeping the show fresh, it also keeps Brazil fresh (well, fresh-ish depending on how he's spent the previous day!). He feels he's getting something, and someone, new and exciting to work with every day.

Brazil says: "I worked with Parry. He's an acquired taste. Marmite – you either love it or you don't. Beeky [Graham Beecroft] is just Beeky, a great foil, good fun and a nice guy, and knows his north-west football inside out. I spent six years with Ronnie. Ronnie was different. Knew cricket and I class Ronnie as a good friend. He was devastated when he left. I think he was going in for a rise if I remember or pushing for another contract, then got the bad news that he was out. He phoned me and he was heartbroken.

"But I thought, OK let's change it. Maybe it's the time. Some people said the rotating schedule wouldn't work, but I knew in my heart it would and I think I've proven that now. I'm delighted with the format with people like Ally [McCoist], Sam [Allardyce], Dean Saunders, and Ray Parlour. Brilliant."

The rotating schedule at inception included David Ginola, Brian Moore, Neil Warnock and also Dominic Cork, the ex-England, Derbyshire, Lancashire and Hampshire cricketer.

Brazil recalls: "Corky was great. 'Half pint' as he's known. He made the fatal admission, as we were going to Cheltenham, that his wife had told him, if he was going with me, that he had to drink half pints of Guinness, not pints. 'Otherwise I'll get so pissed that I can't talk.' It was the worst thing he's ever done! So I brought it up on the show and called him 'half pint'! When we got to Cheltenham on the Wednesday, everyone is like, 'Hey, Al, how's it going? Hey, half pint!' Corky was gutted, saying, 'I should never have told you'. The whole of Cheltenham was calling him half pint."

It also makes it easier to persuade people to do the show, leading to a higher profile of co-host. For instance, sports stars like Lawrence Dallaglio and Sir Bradley Wiggins are unlikely to commit to doing five days a week, but they'll happily do one. And that means when someone like Joey Barton becomes available, it gives the station the flexibility to slot him in. The format certainly seems to work, as the listener figures demonstrate, with the show currently attracting a weekly audience of 1.4 million.

The rolling roster has, however, caused one issue over the years, although for talkSPORT, not the co-hosts. In fact, it could be said to have worked extremely well for the co-hosts. At one stage it seemed no sooner had they taken their place in the studio than they were swapping it for a place in the dug-out.

Sam Allardyce (Everton), Neil Warnock (Cardiff), Joey Barton (Fleetwood) and Stuart Pearce (West Ham, assistant) all went back into football within months, and in some cases weeks, of starting a regular gig at talkSPORT.

So if anyone fancies a career in football management, maybe the best bet is to forget about the coaching badges and just send talkSPORT a demo tape instead!

'CLIPS OF THE WEEK'

The Top 20 All-Time Greats

#13

Never let common sense get in the way of a good question. Here's Darren Gough talking to a guest:

Goughie: Alexandra, where are you from?
Alexandra: I'm from Finland.
Goughie: Finland, eh? Do you speak Finnish?

Er ... possibly, Darren.

Chapter 7

Stuart Pearce Misses a Penalty and Moose-Baiting at 2014 World Cup, Brazil

A World Cup finals in Brazil is probably one of the most evoc-ative sporting images you could summon ... the Copacabana Beach, Christ the Redeemer, the sounds of samba, the sight of the yellow and green tops everywhere.

While England is rightly recognised as the founding father of the modern game of football, and the place where the first rules were drawn up, there can be no question that Brazil is the spiritual home of the sport.

And so it was with eager anticipation that talkSPORT was looking forward to covering its third finals, following Germany in 2006 and South Africa in 2010. And this was to be the biggest and best yet, with talkSPORT bringing listeners live commentary of every game, while also being dedicated to producing 18 hours of radio a day live from the host nation. Effectively the station was decamping to South America for seven weeks, including an initial detour via Miami to cover a couple of warm-up friendlies.

The amount of broadcasting talkSPORT was planning from Brazil meant that, as well as organising all the travel and accom-modation to get the presentation and commentary teams around such a vast country, they also needed a base in Rio from where they could co-ordinate proceedings and broadcast the bulk of their non-match coverage.

That planning on the ground began seven or eight months prior to the big kick-off, with the station using the draw for the finals as an opportunity for a recce and for Head of Live Sport Mike Bovill to make contact with someone offering apartments at the Copacabana Beach.

Bovill admitted they weren't perfect, but they fitted enough of the requirements of the station to make them a very good option, offering a fantastic location right on the beachfront and big enough to just about accommodate the whole team. So he agreed to take all three for the duration of the tournament. So far, so good.

But then came the issue of payment. The talkSPORT accounts team, like many of their counterparts in the world of UK media, were never all that keen on prising apart the old corporate wallet, and the issue was further complicated by the fact the landlord wanted the deposits paid in US dollars.

The upshot of the impasse was Bovill having to cough up the cash out of his own pocket. This not only meant it had been a very, very expensive trip for him, but it was now his money on the line when the time came to collect the deposits at the end of the tournament.

At that point, there was nothing more Bovill could do but keep his fingers crossed he would never have to explain to Mrs Bovill where all that cash had gone and to get on with the serious business of planning the tour.

With England the only home nation to have qualified for the finals, that simplified things slightly, particularly compared to the situation the station would face two years later at Euro 2016 when England, Wales, Northern Ireland and the Republic of Ireland all reached the main event.

For now, though, the focus was on the Three Lions with Roy Hodgson's men set to play their group games in Manaus, São Paulo and Belo Horizonte. Manaus, however, provided the biggest challenge given that it was the furthest north of the 12 venues being used to stage matches, a distance of almost 2,700 miles from Rio, and deep in the middle of the Amazonian jungle. Old Trafford or the Emirates it is not. This was by far the most remote fixture that talkSPORT had ever had to cover and was the equivalent travel miles of getting a crew from London to Syria for just one match. The problems of covering matches in 2012 in the Ukraine seemed almost trivial compared to Manaus. Everything was problematic. From ensuring everyone had the correct injections to cope with potential jungle diseases, to broken transmission lines and lack of normal stadium technical support. Let alone getting the kit halfway up the jungle.

Bovill always knew that fixture would potentially present real problems. "The industry standard up to that point was using ISDN lines in stadiums, which are essentially dedicated communication lines for broadcast, and Brazilian telecoms did not offer that service. Although FIFA were insisting those lines had to be in place by the time of the finals, there were always concerns, particularly regarding Manaus."

But as he got set to leave London for Rio in early June as part of talkSPORT's advance party, Bovill had far more pressing concerns than whether the jungle telegraph would be operational. Top of his priority list at that point was to find out why, as he sat on the plane looking out of the window at Heathrow, he was staring straight at several boxes of talkSPORT kit sitting there on the tarmac.

He made polite enquiries to the British Airways stewardess, but she swore blind they were not the talkSPORT cases and that they were for a different flight. At this point, Bovill gently reinforced the point that, in fact, said cases lying on the tarmac were plastered with talkSPORT logos. As means of identification are concerned, it was fairly unambiguous.

Eventually the stewardess returned and confirmed that, yes, that was talkSPORT's luggage and that the plane would be taking off without it. Good start. British Airways 1, talkSPORT 0. And perhaps an omen as to how England were to fare in the forthcoming tournament.

So Bovill had to fly across the Atlantic knowing that on arrival he would have no means of broadcasting back to the UK. Oh, and he would have no clothes either.

It took several days for the kit, and Bovill's underpants, to arrive in South America but, in the meantime, as is the talk-SPORT way, they had made done to ensure they could get on air as they waited for the second wave of staff to arrive with more kit.

The kit on this occasion did make it on board the flight, as did seven or eight more of the production and digital teams, as well as presenters Alan Brazil and Adrian Durham, and lead commentator Jim Proudfoot.

While most of the team was housed in Premium Economy, a class that for most of them was a significant step up, Mr Brazil gratefully took his place in first class. He would occasionally pop back through the curtain to see how his colleagues were getting on 'back here' but, for the most part, he was happily glugging away up front.

Not that the boys behind him were too far behind him in the glugging stakes. After a bite to eat, maybe a movie and a couple of G&Ts, some of the lads gathered towards the front of the section for a chat about the plans for the next few days, and the sort of content they were hoping to produce in the five or six days before the first game. As many people will attest, all the best ideas are written on the backs of fag packets in pubs so the lads were lubricating to get the creative juices flowing.

It was all very good-natured, with other passengers occasionally dropping by for a chat and a drink, with Alan Brazil wandering back through from time to time, and the BA staff were happy to keep the booze coming. Around 90 minutes or so before the plane was due to land, one stewardess came back through the curtain with her tunic laden with the mini bottles of wine you get on flights, and she placed them down gently on one of the empty seats. "This is the lot lads," she said. "Between you and Alan Brazil, we're out of wine." British Airways 1, talk-SPORT 1.

So it was a happy band that arrived in Rio at around 8pm on that Saturday evening. It was a somewhat less happy band that emerged from the airport around three hours later having taken what seemed an eternity to get through customs.

Many international airports operate carnet systems for clearing customs (basically you just fill out a big form stating everything you've got with you), a method used by media organisations to allow their kit into countries without undergoing rigorous search processes. Galeão International Airport in Rio, however, does not, meaning all the kit had to be searched. And with each member of the team having their own bag, plus carry-on luggage, plus at least one box of kit each, it was a truly laborious process.

So by the time everyone arrived at their Copacabana apartments it was almost midnight. But there was still one more shock in store for Dennie Morris and Jon Norman, who were due to share an apartment with Mark Saggers. Saggers, who had arrived earlier in the week with Bovill, had all the keys to the apartment *inside* the apartment in which he was sound asleep! Morris recalls that, "After a fair bit of pounding and hollering, the door was eventually opened by a very sleepy presenter clad only in his electric blue underpants. I think they were the tightest pair of pants I'd ever seen and left nothing to the imagination." That's a sight that will quickly sober you up.

Also having had something of a surprise on arrival was Adrian Durham. Having reached his Copacabana accommodation he was approached by a member of the management who enquired whether he had any Brazilian currency on him. And indeed he did because his wife works at a bank so she had exchanged plenty of cash for him, enough to probably get him through the whole tour. Or so he thought. In fact, it barely got him through the first night because he was told the owners of his apartment hadn't been paid yet and wouldn't hand over the keys until they had been reimbursed in full, in cash. So that was that: Durham had to hand over every last Brazilian Real he had. On the plus side, he did get it back at a later date.

Despite the late hour, however, and the burning retinas of a couple of team members and the burning hole in the wallet of another, it was decided that, as it was the first night, it was only right that everyone should gather on the Copacabana for a couple of nightcaps and to really get the tour started. Little did they know then that, for at least one unsuspecting drinker that night, this was about as good as the tour would get and it would be downhill from there on in.

As the team in that first week set about creating the content for the radio station and its website that would bring a flavour of the build-up back to those in the UK, Bovill was dealing with an issue not of his making but one that he now found himself very much at the pointy end of.

As part of the build-up to the finals, talkSPORT had collaborated with a band named The Strikers to release their official World Cup record, 'Welcome to Brazil'. The station had previous when it came to cracking the charts, with 'Come On England' reaching No2 during the 2004 European Championship finals and leading to a never-to-be-forgotten appearance on *Top of the Pops*. Sadly, 'Welcome to Brazil' did not scale such dizzy heights.

All good, clean knockabout fun, of course, but the issue for Bovill was the record featured recordings of some of the station's presenters, including Stan Collymore and Mark Saggers, while the likes of Adrian Durham, Darren Gough, Andy Goldstein and Jason Cundy appeared in the video. And that spelled problems.

The station's management naturally wanted their talent to participate in the song, and they now wanted them to sign legal waivers granting permission for their contributions and their images to be used, but they weren't willing to pay them.

Now at this point it's worth pointing out that the bean counters at talkSPORT know the value of a tenner. But it's also worth pointing out that, by and large, so do the presenters.

Mark Saggers certainly took exception to the idea of non-payment, and made it absolutely clear to Bovill that under no circumstances would he be signing the legal document. By now the team had been in Rio for a few days, and they were getting ready to fly to São Paulo for the opening game of the tournament. Despite Bovill's best efforts on behalf of his bosses in London, Saggers remained unmoved.

And so it was that, at virtually the crack of dawn, as Bovill assembled a crew of grumpy presenters, grumpy pundits and grumpy producers, and tried to get them aboard their minivan for the trip to the airport to catch their early morning flight, he was still being berated by an angry man over a piece of paper that Bovill quite frankly had long since stopped caring about. Understandably he had much bigger issues to deal with than a middle-aged radio presenter moaning about signing away his musical rights. In truth, however, that pretty much set the tone for the entire tournament.

While Bovill was engaged in contract wrangling with talk-SPORT's great and good, the remaining guys on the ground were having a brilliant time producing audio and video content from Rio in the lead-up to the weekend's opening set of fixtures.

Among the highlights was a trip to the top of Sugarloaf Mountain, where not only did the team enjoy a panoramic view of the city, but they also had a bird's eye view of England's (not so) secret training camp. Long before Leeds United manager Marcelo Bielsa became embroiled in the 'Spygate' controversy in early 2019, anyone with a cable car ticket and a pair of binoculars could have had a sneak peek at Roy Hodgson's plans for the Three Lions. Not that any of their opponents needed too much inside info to get the better of them in Brazil, of course, so abject were their performances.

On the subject of World Cup mismatches, talkSPORT also found themselves on the end of a hiding when they rather foolishly challenged Flamengo's professional beach football team to a game of five-a-side on Copacabana Beach. It's fair to say the locals took it easy on their visitors, coasting to a 5-1 victory, with talkSPORT's consolation goal swept home gloriously by Darren Gough ... from about four yards out. Mind you, the Brazilian lads probably hadn't been out drinking Caipirinhas until 2am like some of their somewhat dishevelled opponents.

The Copacabana Beach was also the scene of another memorable moment involving talkSPORT's tournament debutant, Stuart Pearce. The former Nottingham Forest full-back, known as 'Psycho' in his playing days, did have prior experience of World Cups, but his previous involvement saw him marauding down the left flank terrorising opposition right wingers. Sadly, the lasting memory of his time at Italia 90 was his penalty being saved in the semi-final shoot-out against West Germany. But proving what a good bloke he is, he was happy to recreate the moment on the beach for a talkSPORT video – where he once again missed from the (sandy) spot. To this day, the people who were there with him are unsure if he missed deliberately just for the cameras, but they suspect he probably did.

Even though few of the talkSPORT team knew Pearce very well at this stage it quickly became clear he is a thoroughly good fella, and The Moose had good reason to be thankful for that one day on the metro en route to the Maracanã Stadium. As they were approaching the station, producer Andrew McKenna generously bought the travelling party an acai drink each (acai berries are a lot like grapes and they are turned into a superfood drink that is sold all over Rio). The berries, and consequently the drinks, are purple. Very purple. You definitely don't want one spilled down your shirt on the way to a football stadium to cover a World Cup match. Especially not if you're a very recognisable former England captain. But that's exactly what The Moose did as he somehow tipped about a third of his thick, gloopy drink all down Pearce's pale yellow top. He certainly got the Psycho stare and a couple of choice words, but if he'd been a nippy little winger he'd have probably got a lot worse.

In fact, the only time Pearce's face really betrayed his emotions and gave anyone a sense of the menace he oozed during his play-ing days was after he had worked on his final game at the tournament, in Fortaleza, before leaving Brazil to take up his new role as manager at his former club Nottingham Forest. From Fortaleza, he was facing an arduous journey back to London via Rio and São Paulo, so he was not best pleased when a local waiter informed him he could have flown direct from Fortaleza to Lisbon and then on to London, a journey time of around ten hours, rather than the multi-stop, multi-layover monster awaiting him. Still, this was talkSPORT after all and that travelling maybe explains why he was so keen to stop the journeys with The Moose, in favour of an arduous 46-game season in the Championship.

Amid the fun and games on the beach, however, the serious business was just around the corner and the tournament got the start it deserved in São Paulo as the hosts recovered from the shock of Marcelo's 11th-minute own goal to run out 3-1 winners against Croatia, with national hero Neymar netting twice.

All went seamlessly for talkSPORT during that opening game, and indeed the first few games, despite the fears about ISDN lines, internet access and such like, fears that were so genuine that when the production teams had initially touched down in Rio the week before they were still far from 100% certain they would be in a position to broadcast from their Copacabana apartments.

Those concerns proved to be largely groundless, but the fears as highlighted earlier about what they might discover in Manaus were not.

On the day before the game, the man in charge of all of talk-SPORT's operations in Brazil, Mike Bovill, flew from São Paulo to Manaus and, after ensuring Stan Collymore and Mark Saggers were safely checked into their hotel, headed for the Arena da Amazônia to make sure everything was in place for live commentary of England vs Italy the following evening. He was pleasantly surprised that, indeed, ISDN lines were in place, the commentary position was excellent and everything was working as planned, allowing him to return to the hotel a fairly contented man. His contentment would not last.

On arrival at the ground the following day, they were met by some possibly slightly overly officious officials. Even though talkSPORT had the correct pass to get them into the media car park, the local police were refusing them access because their minivan was not actually a car. So they were stopped around a mile from the stadium and instructed they would have to walk the rest of the way. Stan Collymore, however, was having absolutely none of that.

Now, against this backdrop, it's worth remembering that in the build-up to the tournament there had been numerous scaremongering stories in the UK media about the dangers of working and travelling in Brazil, and everyone was warned they should be on alert at all times.

Despite its often laddish reputation, talkSPORT takes the health and safety of its staff on trips such as these extremely

seriously. So, before they left London, a couple of training ses-
sions had been arranged where a former SAS soldier and personal
safety expert gave them simple hints and tips on how to behave
and how to avoid any potential flashpoints.

The one thing he made clear was that the biggest danger any
team like this faces on tour is the behaviour of one of their own
members. And so it was to prove.

Touring with Collymore was never completely straightforward, not for the people around him, and probably not for Stan
himself. He was a brilliant broadcaster and a great addition to
the radio station, but for all the magic he produced on air, he
could occasionally cause mayhem off it.

On this occasion in Manaus, Collymore reacted to being told
he would be making his way to the ground on foot by marching
aggressively up to a heavily armed military policeman, waving
his accreditation in the officer's face and shouting "FIFA" at the
top of his voice. It was certainly an interesting tactic in his bid
to be allowed access to the car park.

Remarkably there were no serious repercussions and Collymore
even commandeered a police car to drive him to the stadium
entrance, leaving Bovill and the other members of the production
team to carry the heavy kit to the ground in the beating sunshine.

Incredibly, Collymore had pulled a similar stunt in America
during England's pre-World Cup tour to Miami shortly before
they arrived in Brazil, a trip that perfectly highlighted the light
and shade of life on the road with the former Liverpool and
Aston Villa striker.

Collymore was accompanied by fellow presenter Ian Danter,
commentator Jim Proudfoot and producer Laurie Palacio, and
everything went gloriously for the first two or three days.
Collymore loves Miami, and is familiar with the city having spent
some time there. He took it upon himself to be the trip's unofficial tour guide, organising cycling tours of South Beach, seeing
the sights and dining out in some very nice restaurants.

On the night after the first England game, a 2-2 draw with
Ecuador that took place at Miami's Dolphin Stadium, Collymore
took the rest of the talkSPORT team to a late-night bar called

The Back Door. There were some doubts among the others as they were led through this dark residential area, finally emerging from a little alley at what appeared to be a fire door. But Collymore opened the door, had a quiet word with the doorman and the group was welcomed into what is known as The Fox Hole, which is where all the Miami bar workers congregate at the end of their shifts, complete with Miami Dolphins cheerleaders behind the bar serving the drinks. It is one cool place to be, and everyone had a fine time, all thanks to Collymore.

So far, so good. Cycling, beaches, eating, drinking, cheerleaders – what's not to like? But then came the day of the second game of the tour against Honduras, once more being staged at the Dolphins Stadium.

For some reason, the stadium management had decided to change the location of the media entrance for this match. But, despite the fact the Americans take security at venues extremely seriously, Collymore figured he knew best and, even though the entrance had been moved, he marched up to the location of the previous one, where he was politely, but firmly, told there was no admittance.

But after some shouting about "British media", the security guard eventually relented and allowed them through, with Palacio apologising profusely and offering platitudes about "stupid British tourists getting lost". And he was still apologising after they set up their equipment in the stands when he received a visit from stadium security who started asking him questions, checking accreditations and letting them know in no uncertain terms they were in the wrong in forcing their way into the arena through the wrong entrance. Palacio managed to talk the stadium officials out of giving talkSPORT anything more than a slap on the wrist, but that was classic Collymore – wining and dining with cheerleaders one night, then having to apologise to security guards for his behaviour just a couple of days later.

But back to Manaus, and the problems for Bovill were far from over because, on entering the stadium, he discovered those ISDN lines that were working perfectly the day before were no longer working at all.

It was *the* nightmare scenario … middle of the Amazon rain-forest, no one at the stadium seemingly able to offer any assistance, no one knowing what the problem was, and FIFA and the host broadcasting team having difficulties communicating with Brazilian telecoms, who had put the lines in. However, it wasn't just a problem for talkSPORT: none of the ISDNs in the stadium were working.

Poor Bovill now found himself running around the stadium in the searing heat and stifling humidity trying to find someone who knew what the hell was going on and who could answer the one question that mattered: would the lines be fixed in time for kick-off?

Of course this situation was not unexpected, so talkSPORT had wisely put in place plans B and C. Plan B involved having a commentary team on stand-by in London who could, if the worst came to the worst, broadcast the game 'off tube' from there. And as part of this plan, Adrian Durham, who had only recently come off air and was now hastily heading back to the apartment/studio in Rio, would host the show if required.

Plan C would be to revert to a good old-fashioned solution of transmitting a live commentary down the phone.

Plan B inadvertently caused another problem: Durham and the Rio-based crew, who had all supposedly finished work for the day, had retreated to a local bar to watch the England game. But when that plan was kyboshed by events in Manaus with Durham and the team now back at the studio, it left a very unhappy Darren Gough bemoaning the fact that he now had no one to watch the game with, no one to have a beer with and that he now wanted to go home. Back to Blighty. Right then. That night.

What a start for the boy Bovill. He had annoyed Saggers by being forced to ask him to sign his musical life away; he had annoyed Collymore because the talkSPORT vehicle was a mini-bus and not a car; and now he'd annoyed Gough by making him leave the pub in Rio – even though he himself was around 3,000 miles away trying to sort out the Manaus carnage. As World Cup hat-tricks go, that was an effort to rival Geoff Hurst in 1966. And this was only day three, remember.

So while Bovill was sweating and fretting in the jungle, producer Jon Norman and a couple of others were in Rio trying to dissuade Goughie from doing the off. Eventually, a very simple scenario was presented to him: he could go home that night at a cost of several thousand pounds (which he would have to pay himself), or he could go to the World Cup opening weekend's most exclusive party at the Budweiser Hotel (the American brewing company had taken over the Pestana Hotel on the Copacabana for the duration of the tournament) for which someone had somehow managed to wangle him a VIP ticket at the 11th hour. It would have been easier to get the ISDN lines in Manaus working than to get access to that particular shindig but once again talkSPORT had pulled off the seemingly impossible! Funnily enough, by the following morning, Goughie seemed to have forgotten all thoughts of Heathrow.

"I'd got invited to the party which was unbelievable. I went on my own! Everyone else had gone. There was loads of people there, lots of ex-footballers, all the old Dutch players. So I found something to do in the end."

Back in Manaus, however, as talkSPORT's favourite Yorkshireman was probably quaffing his first ice-cold Bud, Bovill was still working on the connection issues. The problem had at least been discovered: someone outside the ground had put a spade through all the lines. As you do. And then, of course, having done that, the entirely appropriate course of action is to not tell anyone and hope no one will notice.

At this stage in proceedings, reassurances were being made, lines were being tested, but still nothing worked and, in the end, it was clear nothing was going to work. But cometh the hour, cometh the man.

"At that point," says Bovill, "we basically railroaded FIFA into giving us a TV commentary position and, via Switzerland, we managed to connect back with talkSPORT Towers in the UK. It meant we were a bit late on air, but we did manage to bring listeners live commentary from the stadium."

Sadly, England couldn't follow Bovill's lead as, despite a promising and positive performance, they were unable to overcome adversity and slumped to defeat, a loss that eventually led to the Three Lions crashing out in the group stages. So while Bovill bested FIFA in his own 'Rumble in the Jungle', Hodgson was left to rue his side's 'Crumble in the Jungle'. Meanwhile, Collymore was probably continuing to 'Grumble in the ...' – oh, you get the picture.

Moaning presenters are not uncommon on tour and it's often a delicate balancing act for their respective producers to keep them sweet. One key issue always remains the same: food.

Where they are eating takes up a huge amount of energy each day, with producers under a great deal of pressure to ensure the talent are suitably fed and watered. And that pressure is ramped up when you're somewhere like Rio where, quite frankly, the food is terrible. In many places they serve you both chips and rice, just in case you're not getting enough carbs, and then scatter something akin to semolina dust on top of it. It is not good.

Some presenters are more fussy than others, with Andy Jacobs being a particular food snob. Whereas his presenting partner Paul Hawksbee is usually happy with a pie and a pint, Andy prefers a little more refinement. He also loves a guidebook, which resulted in one of their more memorable culinary experiences in Brazil.

Having done some research, Jacobs had read about something called a Uruguayan sandwich in a guidebook that recommended what looked like the perfect spot for a bite to eat one day. So he, Paul, producer Tom Hughes and several others set off in search of this magnificent sarnie.

As previously mentioned, the team was staying in apartments right in the middle of Copacabana Beach. The home of this must-have sandwich, however, was Leblon, a three-mile walk around the bay past Ipanema.

It took the hungry party about an hour to get there, fuelled by buckets of Caipirinhas that were being sold on the beach for a pound, with one or two fearing the potent contents of their buckets were going to render them blind.

Eventually they arrived in Leblon, the home of the much vaunted and eagerly anticipated Uruguayan sandwich restaurant. Which, in truth, turned out to be a burger van on the beach! Cue disappointment all round and some hastily issued apologies from Jacobs.

So that turned out to be not Andy's best idea ever, much like his idea of getting the metro out to the Maracanã Stadium one afternoon.

They were heading to the stadium to watch Spain train and, in theory, taking the metro was an inspired suggestion, particularly as they had begun the journey in the talkSPORT minivan only to find themselves stuck in horrendous traffic on Atlantic Avenue, an occupational hazard in Rio.

So they abandoned the van and headed for the closest metro station. The trains are air-conditioned, they go straight to the stadium, it's quicker than driving ... what could go wrong?

Well, what could go wrong was the fact Brazil were playing Mexico in Fortaleza in that afternoon's 4pm kick-off, meaning half of Rio was trying to make their way home to watch the match. There were thousands of people using the same route, and absolutely no room to move. People were taking run-ups to try to get on to the train.

On such occasions it's useful to have something weighty to use as leverage to push your way on and off the train. Fortunately, Hawksbee and Jacobs had just the thing, accompanied as they were on this particular trip by The Moose.

He made the perfect human battering ram as they were forced to barge their way through the crowd at the Maracanã. People knew that was where they were getting off because some of them spoke English, but it was clear no one was going to smooth the passage for them. In Rio, it's every man, woman and child for themselves, so the only way they could get off was by using The Moose as a sort of American football-style blocker.

But that was just the start of the fun with The Moose on an afternoon that would see him get a stern rebuke from a well-known comedian. After watching Spain's light training session, the group had retired to a small bar around the corner from the Maracanã where they decided they would watch the Brazil game.

They had all had a beer, but The Moose is not much of a drinker, and so ordered a Diet Coke. But the barman didn't hear him properly. Brazil were playing so it was quite lively in there. So the barman figured his customer requested another beer, and duly placed one in front of him.

Now The Moose is not known for his patience, or indeed his manners, when it comes to dealing with staff in bars and restaurants and he made it very clear, in his own inimitable way, that he wanted what he had asked for, not a beer.

TV and radio comedian Andy Smart had gone along for the ride with the boys and, not really knowing The Moose, couldn't believe what he was witnessing and, incredulous, he turned around to him and said: "How dare you talk to them like that?" Not that a couple of sharp words was likely to be enough to silence an angry Moose.

Having said that, not everybody is always so happy to see Andy Smart, either. Or at least not to see him in all his unclothed glory. That occurred one night following a day's racing at Cheltenham where Smart had been a guest on the *Hawksbee and Jacobs* show and had stayed around post-show for a night out. But with nowhere to stay, the production team had kindly offered him the use of the sofa in their flat. But as Hawksbee and Jacobs' producer David Walker was getting ready for the final day's show on the Friday, happily minding his own business and ironing his shirt in the kitchen, a fully naked Smart who, up until this time had been hiding his modesty under a thin sheet, decided to get up for a stretch. Fortunately, he had his back to Walker.

But recognising the correct etiquette of staying on a stranger's sofa notwithstanding, no one could doubt Smart was in the right when it came to his reaction to The Moose and restaurant personnel. Safe to say he's probably not the first person who's asked him why he was behaving like that, and he wouldn't be the last on this particular trip.

But it wouldn't be the only time The Moose lost his rag. Ray Parlour was with The Moose for an evening out with some of the production guys, and they had gone to a relatively upmarket burger joint at Ipanema. As already stated, The Moose is not a boozer, so he asked for a strawberry milkshake while the other lads all went for a nice cold lager.

Parlour recalls: "He wanted strawberry milkshake but they'd run out and he was fuming, shouting 'I want to see your manager, I want to see your manager'. And the guy, the waiter had a smirk on his face and was laughing with us, but The Moose went mad saying, 'You're an absolute disgrace'. And we were all taking the mickey out of him. And he was getting really upset just for not having strawberry milkshake."

The Moose finally reached boiling point when he banged his fist down on the table and screamed at the top of his voice: "My strawberry milkshake. NOW. Or the manager."

Parlour is an arch mickey taker who loves those situations and for whom there is nothing better than winding The Moose up. He was loving the increased rage on the big man's face as he egged him on to complain ever more vociferously about the continued absence of his milkshake.

Parlour was, by now, in hysterics and he absolutely collapsed in laughter just seconds later when the manager appeared from inside the restaurant to inform The Moose that, sorry, but they were definitely out of strawberry milkshakes. It was genius comic timing.

Parlour had also been at the centre of 'Moose-baiting' at the previous World Cup in South Africa in 2010. He did so brilliantly when the pair acquired one of the new Jabulani tournament footballs. They had started knocking the ball around the garden of the lodge where they were resident. Parlour was full of praise for The Moose, telling him he was a natural, asking him if he had ever played professionally and talking about how, despite all the brilliant players he'd played with, he'd never seen anyone strike a ball as cleanly as The Moose. The Moose was loving it, explaining that one of his old teachers had told him back in the day he could have been a pro and Parlour was agreeing, really bigging him up. Parlour takes up the story:

"We were in the back garden. I'd just turned up, it was my first World Cup and the first time I'd been away with the team and The Moose. It was the first morning. So were in the back garden and I'm kicking balls at him and he's useless really. But I went,

'Moose, I'll tell you what, has anyone seen you play football yet? You're not bad you know?' I kept a serious face and we kept on playing. So that night he's told the whole of the house that 'Ray thinks I'm a good player'. Anyway, at eight o'clock in the morning, the next morning he's knocking on my door with this football kit on asking if I want another kickabout in the garden.

"I said, 'Oh go on, then,' so I got up and go into the garden again and now as I'm booting balls at him I said, 'Moose, have you ever thought of going into coaching?' And again I kept a serious face. He says, 'Yeah, Ray, I'm looking into it. To a bit of serious coaching.' That night he told the whole house again that, 'I might be doing my coaching badges as Ray thinks I'll be a good coach'. In the end, he was useless, absolutely hopeless but we kept it going and I was just winding him up every day. It got to a stage where everyone was saying, 'Please don't say anything again to him today'. As it had got to the stage where he'd always tell the house how good he is and all that I'd said."

Whether or not The Moose really was a budding professional footballer in his younger days remains unconfirmed, but to one member of the talkSPORT team there's no doubting he never would have made it as a cricketer.

Andy Jacobs says: "I played cricket with The Moose once when I invited him to play with our team. He turned up and we were fielding first and the whole time he was saying to me, 'Can I have a bowl, can I have a bowl, can I have a bowl?' Not realising you're guesting in a team where there's a certain order. In the end we let him have a bowl and of course he wasn't very good, at which point he claimed he was more of a batsman really. So he went in at No4, got out first ball and went home."

In Rio, The Moose was making his presence felt too. Given the four-hour time difference between London and Rio, he was up and about in the apartment he shared with several of his colleagues at 2am every morning delivering his news bulletins back to the UK on *The Alan Brazil Sports Breakfast*. It wasn't the noise that was the problem, it was the fact that more often than not he was clad in little more than a towel, much to the chagrin of his housemates who would get up for breakfast to discover a virtually naked Moose in the centre of the apartment. That is not the way anyone wants to start the day.

Also having to make an early start each morning was producer Ian Morris whose task each day for the first week of the tournament was to go and collect Alan Brazil from his luxury hotel at the other end of Copacabana Beach and deliver him to the main apartment where the studio was based. This was a job he shared with Jon Norman, meaning one or the other had to walk along the beach at around 1.30am every morning to get the big man there for the start of the breakfast show at 2am each day. It's all glamour on tour with talkSPORT.

Morris probably also still wakes up in a cold sweat following a night out with Hawksbee and Jacobs in Rio. They were all watching a game in the fan park on the Copacabana when he asked them what they were all doing for dinner, and they said they were going for sushi, which he admitted he'd never had before. As has already been ascertained, Jacobs is a food snob so they warned Morris they had heard this place was very good albeit not very cheap. But he really wanted to go, so he did, only to discover that, first, there was not a lot of it and, second, it was not simply 'not cheap' but rather really expensive. As Hawksbee says: "I felt sorry for him. He's probably never had sushi since because he thinks every time he has a mouthful of salmon it costs him about five quid."

That World Cup in Brazil was the first tournament Hawksbee and Jacobs had broadcast from as part of the talkSPORT team, and they loved every minute of it. Or most of them at least.

It's fair to say Andy probably wasn't too happy one day at the beach, when he'd gone down there to recreate the well-known advert for Southern Comfort that features a guy strolling along the sand in just a pair of swimming trunks and shoes. Having finished filming he went to collect his glasses from cameraman James Bragg, only to discover the young video genius had somehow dropped them while walking along the beach. And with it being the Copacabana, they would have disappeared within about ten seconds.

Bragg was mortified at what he'd accidentally done, but fortunately Andy had a spare pair of specs in the apartment and was quite prepared to forgive the innocent mistake. But it did lead to the very funny sight of him having to be led by the arm from the beach and back to the apartment block. As anyone who has ever crossed the roads in Rio will agree, it's not something you want to attempt when lack of glasses render you effectively blind.

His eyesight wasn't the problem when Jacobs discovered something equally vital was missing as they set off on their Rio adventure. As they were checking in at Heathrow, with Hawksbee and producer Hughes all sorted out and clutching their boarding passes, Jacobs, who had been feverishly searching through his bag, was forced to admit he had his wife's passport with him instead of his own.

Now Andy has something of a reputation for being hard on people, but what they don't realise is that he is much harder on himself. If he makes a mistake, no one can slag him off as much as he does himself, and by all accounts – well, by Tom Hughes' account anyway – the self-loathing on display that day at Heathrow had to be seen to be believed. Fortunately Jacobs doesn't live too far from the airport and potential disaster was relatively easily overcome.

For the most part, however, despite the doomsday scenarios that had been painted in certain parts of the media, the finals went off without a hitch. And the locals all seemed happy to mingle with the talkSPORT team.

Several of them went to watch Brazil's round of 16 match with Chile in Lapa, a vibrant, bohemian suburb of Rio, kind of like a Brazilian version of Shoreditch. A big TV screen was erected at one end of the main street, and hundreds gathered to watch it, enjoying drinks and food in the street. There were two rows of seats set up at the very front, right before the TV, but right up until kick-off no one was sat in them. Brilliantly, it turned out they were reserved for the local OAPs. Actually, you wouldn't get that in Shoreditch.

There was also the incredible experience of watching a World Cup quarter-final in Brazil's largest favela, Rocinha. Built on a steep hillside overlooking Rio, it's home to around 70,000 people and provided the venue for one of the most memorable nights on tour as several members of the talkSPORT team watched Brazil's 2-1 victory over Colombia and then partied into the night with the locals. There were a few quizzical looks, however, as to whether the almost non-stop loud bangs that could be heard for miles around were all fireworks or if some were actually gun shots.

While the on-field battle for supremacy was raging in Brazil, however, talkSPORT was at the centre of more controversy much closer to home. In fact, so close it was happening right outside their front door.

Ahead of the World Cup, Collymore had posted a comment on Twitter about Britain 'thieving' the Falklands, a comment that sparked outrage among veterans of the conflict with Argentina, particularly as it came on the anniversary of the sinking of *HMS Coventry*, leading to 19 deaths.

Collymore had tweeted: "Falklands? Wasn't anyone's. Just thieved it, as we do. What glory, what triumph. A f*****g island with sheep. Rule Britannia."

That post was subsequently deleted, but still there were calls for the former striker to be sacked by talkSPORT, with the station receiving more than 500 complaints, although he insisted his comments had been taken out of context and stressed he did not mean to demean the soldiers who served in the 1982 conflict.

But with no apology forthcoming, a group of around 40 veterans staged a silent protest outside the talkSPORT offices on Saturday, 21 June, fixing 258 poppies to fences surrounding the football pitches opposite the studios to represent the UK service personnel and civilians killed in the Falklands War.

Campaign spokesman and Falklands veteran Dougie Brimson, who organised the protest, said: "On 25 May Stan Collymore posted a tweet which disrespected the memory of the 255 men and three islanders who died during the liberation of the Falkland Islands. It upset a lot of people and has taken us to this position. Everybody's got a right to hold an opinion and to voice that opinion. The issue with the tweet is that the words used, inferring that islands were thieved, we found disrespectful.

A number of people at the time asked Mr Collymore to apologise, which he refused to do. That added to the upset."

talkSPORT put the necessary plans in place to deal with any potential unrest on the day, but the protest passed off peacefully and without incident. "It was quite an emotional day," says Lauren Webster, who was in charge of talkSPORT's internal security team. "There were people laying wreaths outside. I remember someone coming to the door – we had been told not to let anybody in – so we were speaking through the speakerphone. We told them there was no comment from us, and they said, 'Fine, thanks very much,' and they left. It was all very, very peaceful and just very, very sad."

Remarkably, that was the second major Twitter row to engulf Collymore in just six months, coming as it did after his decision to quit the social media network in January 2014 and delete his account for a period of time, after he accused the site of failing to respond to racist abuse against him.

talkSPORT took the claims so seriously they took the decision to suspend all of their own accounts and ban any mention of the social network on any of their shows.

CEO Scott Taunton said in a statement: "We are dismayed at the lack of response and perceived inaction by Twitter. Racist or abusive messages of this nature are illegal and unacceptable.

"We have more than three million Twitter followers across our accounts but we will not promote these until we are satisfied that Twitter is doing its utmost to prevent abuse of this nature. We have a duty of care to all our staff and presenters and until I am satisfied that Twitter is treating this seriously we will no longer promote Twitter accounts or use tweets on-air.

"It seems inconceivable that a high-tech company with a market capitalisation of $30bn appears incapable of preventing racist and abusive tweets being broadcast across its platform."

It was a strong stand by talkSPORT and, coming as it did in the final week of the January transfer window, a potentially damaging one given that Twitter was a key platform for delivering news and generating engagement with its audience. But there was almost universal agreement it was the right decision.

Two people who were presenting a united front in Brazil were Mark Saggers and Dennie Morris. Four years earlier in South Africa, Morris had spent the whole tournament producing Mike Parry, and this time around he was on a one-man mission to bring out the best in Saggers.

Saggers is a brilliant broadcaster, as committed and passionate as they come, but that commitment and passion can also lead to occasional bouts of temper. His on-air spats with Collymore during their Monday night *Feist Night* show were must-listen radio, and sometimes those spats continued off air. It was often a delicate balancing act for the producers when they were around one another to ensure they brought the best out of each other on the radio, without falling out with one another off it.

In order to achieve that, Morris spent almost every waking moment with Saggers, as he explained: "He [Saggers] needs someone to be with him 24/7. He relies on you, and he needs that sort of close relationship. I love Mark and I think he's brilliant. There is nobody better at calling a game than Mark Saggers.

"It wears you down during the length of a tournament but it's never intimidating and as time passes afterwards you look back at it with fondness. But when you're in it, it's entirely draining. Every day you wake up and have to go and plan the show in a café, which is probably the same café you've been in the whole time. He desperately wants to keep you to himself, so you go to the same places and no one else comes along. It's like being a married couple."

Indeed, so possessive was Saggers in Brazil that on one particular morning as Morris took a call from his boss in London while they were having their pre-show meeting, Saggers grabbed the phone and announced: "He can't talk to you now, he's getting my breakfast." And promptly put the phone down.

But no one ever said managing a tournament was easy, and that was perfectly demonstrated on the day of the World Cup final as Germany took on Argentina in the Maracanã. It was clearly a huge game and the whole world's media wanted to be in attendance, meaning space was at a premium.

To that end, talkSPORT was able to secure only three seats in the commentary box for the final and they were taken by host

Mark Saggers, commentator Jim Proudfoot and pundit Stan Collymore. There were recriminations as this was the pinnacle of the tournament and the producer of the show, Dennie Morris, had no seat. Undeterred, Morris came up with the ingenious idea of pretending he had a seat and 'squatted' next to Saggers with his backside balanced on thin air. However, as the game progressed, his thighs gave way, around about the same time that FIFA security also realised what the cheeky producer was up to. A heated argument ensued which Morris lost and led to him being carried off, still in the squat position, with his aching legs now in seizure.

Morris was forced to watch the rest of the match from an observer seat and was angry and upset at having missed out on what should have been the highlight of his career in sports radio, producing a World Cup final. Meanwhile Bovill was being blamed by all and sundry for failing to solve a problem he could do absolutely nothing about – not for the first time in Brazil. And all of this came to a head in a not entirely unpredictable way later that night.

Despite knowing what was probably coming, Bovill insisted the presentation and production team should go out for dinner, because that's the kind of guy he is. When people talk about good tourists, they're talking about people like him, people who will do anything to help anyone at anytime.

The first problem was that Rio was packed to the rafters on that Sunday night. The city, and the country, had got the result it wanted. If Brazil couldn't win the World Cup – they had been embarrassed 7-1 by Germany in the semi-final – then all the locals cared about was that Argentina didn't win it, either. So Mario Götze's extra-time winner for the Germans had been celebrated almost as wildly as if Neymar himself had scored it. That meant the bars and restaurants around the Copacabana were absolutely heaving.

The best they could find was an Italian restaurant not far from the apartments, but which left plenty to be desired, both in terms of the food and the service. But hey, it was the night of the final, the tournament was over, a good job had been done by all over the course of the past six weeks and now was the time to enjoy a beer and look forward to going home. Only it wasn't.

All the frustrations of the presentation team came tumbling out, with Bovill copping it from all sides, so much so that, finally, he stood up, threw some cash on the table and stormed out. "The best thing he did," says Morris. "And while he won't know this, it was made funnier because the paltry amount he threw down didn't even pay for his starter, let alone his dinner, so the already annoyed team had to chip in to make up the difference. Bovill 1, The Team 0."

However, that wasn't the end of the drama. Not by a long way. The following day, as the circus left town, it was Bovill's job to get everyone to the airport on time before heading back to the apartments for a final sweep, make sure everything was in good shape and collect his deposit.

As he dropped Collymore off at the airport, he received a big hug and was told he'd done a great job and to not worry about what had been said the night before. Which was a nice touch.

Not such a nice touch was returning to the deserted main apartment, which had housed all the presenters and also been used as a studio, to discover a ramshackle mess of an apartment with strange odours coming out of all corners. He may have been there producing one of the most important tournaments of talkSPORT's history and one of the most senior members in the talkSPORT management team, but he had no choice other than to get out the bucket and bleach. Bovill 1, The Team 1.

He says: "Spending those final couple of hours on my hands and knees, scrubbing the floor while trying not to vomit, pretty much summed up my experience of the 2014 FIFA World Cup."

The only upside, if that is even possible, is that after the owner agreed to take some money to get the bathroom professionally cleaned, Bovill did at least get the rest of the deposit back.

The debacle of the meal the night before had not only left people with an unpleasant taste in their mouths, but in Morris's case with a particularly unpleasant sensation in his stomach.

Having seemingly been served undercooked chicken, he found himself being violently sick on the short flight from Rio to São Paulo, for most of the five-hour layover there, and then again for large parts of the journey from São Paulo to Heathrow.

To compound his misery, he was sat next to joker-in-chief Ray Parlour, which is normally a good thing given the raft of brilliant stories the former Arsenal favourite has to tell. But it's not ideal when all you want to do is curl up into a ball and sleep.

Little did Morris know at the time but he had caught a potentially lethal infection. Like most blokes, he chose to ignore the fact and spent most of the next six months feeling unwell until, on one night out, his old mate Mike Parry said to him: "Son, you need to go and get yourself sorted out. You're yellow, look at your eyes."

So in early January 2015 he went to the doctor and was sent straight to A&E where he was admitted immediately and didn't leave hospital until May. His liver had virtually packed up due to a rare strain of hepatitis. At one stage the doctors thought he might die, or that he would need a liver transplant.

Fortunately, just as in 2010 when Moz Dee announced "Dennie's dead," talkSPORT's very own Lazarus once more bounced back to full health and later would go on to be Programme Director on the new talkRADIO station.

'CLIPS OF THE WEEK'

The Top 20 All-Time Greats
#12

In this day and age of digital communications, getting in touch should be a simple process. But occasionally the presenters contrive to make it less than simple. Here's Keith Arthur on *Fisherman's Blues*, telling a caller, David, how to get in contact:

Arthur: The best thing to do David ... have you got email access?

David: I have.

Arthur: Yes? Well you can either email me now ... or Elliot may ... no Elliot's just gone to do something outside ... erm ... just go to talkSPORT.co.uk ... you can email me now and it will come through to the show ... or go to the presenters' page on the website ... email me through that ... I will get the email at home and we can converse that way.

Confused? You will be.

Chapter 8

Brian Moore's Butter Meltdown at the 2011 Rugby World Cup

talkSPORT has always been a station with balls, but it's not only those kicked around by the highly paid superstars in the Premier League and Champions League that showcase the station's talents and attract an audience.

Over the course of the past 20 years, as well as exclusive deals for major football leagues and tournaments, talkSPORT has also secured the rights to sports such as cricket, golf, rugby league, horse racing, NFL, tennis, boxing, UFC, rugby union and darts (yes, darts).

In fact, talkSPORT has been the exclusive home of several huge rugby union events, including the 2011 World Cup and the British and Irish Lions' tours of both Australia in 2013 and New Zealand four years later.

It was in New Zealand in 2011 that talkSPORT first made its mark on the oval-ball game, having surprisingly won the exclusive UK radio rights for the World Cup from under the noses of the BBC.

It was a massive coup, and marked the first time talkSPORT had ever broadcast a major sporting event exclusively. In the past the station had done World Cups and European Championship finals, but those rights had always been shared with the BBC. They had also broadcast coverage of England's overseas cricket tours in the early 2000s, but they were one-off events. This was a major global sporting occasion and the only place to hear it in the UK was talkSPORT. It was a genuine game changer.

But having outbid the BBC and persuaded the IRB (which later became World Rugby) to trust talkSPORT with the rights, they still had to get the tournament to air. And, not surprisingly, there were not going to be bundles of cash thrown at it.

In fact, remarkably, even though BBC Radio 5 Live was not the rights holder for the tournament, they had more personnel in New Zealand than talkSPORT! Those are the challenges the station has always been up against and, more often than not, has found a way to overcome.

So it was a small but happy band, numbering just five, who set off from London to Auckland. They were Mike Bovill and Matt Smith (responsible for all the production and logistics), Mark Saggers (main presenter), Brian Moore (lead pundit) and John Taylor (lead commentator). And that was pretty much it. There were reporters with the four home nations, covering the day-to-day stuff on tour, and then other people would be brought in on specific occasions, such as Gavin Hastings providing co-commentaries for Scotland games, for example.

But it was certainly a lean, mean broadcasting machine and the levels to which they were determined to keep a tight rein on the purse strings is brilliantly illustrated by the approach to the keys (or rather the lack of them) for their Auckland apartment.

One apartment. Five people. One key. And the responsibility for the key rested with Matt Smith who, despite some gentle persuasion, was not prepared to get any more keys because each additional one required the payment of a deposit of NZ$30 which, at a typical 2011 exchange rate, was about £15. And expenses could be hard to come by in those days.

Bovill says: "It was crazy. I even offered to pay out of my own pocket just to have a key of my own, but Matt was having none of it. So every time you wanted to leave the apartment, or get back in the apartment, you had to arrange to meet Matt or whoever had the key at the time. Luckily there were plenty of bars and restaurants nearby so it was never that hard to find each other."

Despite their limited numbers and resources, talkSPORT did a fabulous job of bringing the flavour of the tournament back to the UK. As anyone who has visited New Zealand will know, rugby union is a religion in the country. It dominates conversations and everybody has an opinion on the All Blacks and the strengths, or more often than not the weaknesses, of any touring opponents.

The Kiwis really wanted to show off their country and they wanted to show off what it meant to be a New Zealander. And of course they wanted the world to know how good their rugby team is. There would probably have been some kind of national crisis had they not gone on to win the Webb Ellis Cup but, of course, they did.

And talkSPORT tapped into that energy and enthusiasm of the host nation by devoting hours of airtime to its coverage. A widespread perception in those days was that everything the BBC did was brilliant and everything that talkSPORT did was terrible. What that tournament allowed the station to do, in terms of the way they covered a major sporting event, was show rugby fans that if you trusted them with the commentary they would repay you. The station ran wall-to-wall coverage in the way the BBC has never done, and cannot do because it does not have a 24-hour sports radio station. That's what talkSPORT did in New Zealand.

And it proved a real hit with the listeners, as did the on-air chemistry between Mark Saggers and Brian Moore. But off the pitch and away from the microphones, it wasn't all sweetness and light between the two. In fact, it would be fair to say there was something of a personality clash between the pair, probably because they are both far more alike than either of them would be prepared to admit.

Brian Moore is a rather gruff Yorkshireman who had a reputation for a fierce competitiveness on the rugby pitch, but who is also an excellent commentator on rugby. He famously trained as a solicitor and his media presence is that of a clever and erudite man. All the while there is an awareness you're never too far from the menacing player that battled it out in the front row for England and had the nickname 'Pitbull'.

Mark Saggers also likes to think of himself as a man of words, a man who dedicates himself to his craft, but who sometimes gives the impression he could also do a decent job in the front row for England. He certainly doesn't shy away from a verbal confrontation, if not necessarily a physical one.

And, at times at least, they didn't get on. It was that simple. The best example of the day-to-day tensions and the drip feed that culminated in their famous bust-up at half-time in the quarter-final between England and France was 'Buttergate'.

Both Saggers and Moore like to use real butter, but Mark likes to have his butter in the fridge and Brian likes his butter soft, so would leave the butter on the work surface. So Moore would walk into the kitchen, see that the butter was in the fridge, mutter darkly under his breath and take it out. He would then make himself something to eat, and walk away leaving the butter out. Saggers would then walk into the kitchen, see the butter dish out, swear not quite so quietly under his breath, and immediately put the butter back into the fridge. This went on for weeks, with the butter being ferried between the fridge and the counter on an almost hourly basis.

Bovill watched all this drama unfold with a wry smile on his face, and on telling this story to someone several years later, he was asked: "Why didn't you just buy two packets of butter?" That was something he admitted he had never even considered, although most of the producers will tell you that part of the fun of tours like this is witnessing the ridiculously petty power struggles that sometimes take place between some of the alpha male presenters.

But it was no laughing matter when the tensions between the pair spilled over on to the airwaves during one of talkSPORT's most infamous live commentaries.

England had performed badly throughout the World Cup, and there had also been the scandal of the dwarf-throwing escapades in Queenstown, but they got through to the quarter-finals where they played France. In the previous two World Cups, when England had won in 2003 and finished runners-up in 2007 – and arguably they had a better team in 2011 than they had had four years previously – they had dispatched France on the way to the final and the expectation was they would do the same again. That isn't how it worked out.

France absolutely spanked England during the first half and as the half-time whistle blew, Saggers said something along the lines of "now is not the time to over-react and over-analyse England's first-half performance ... but they were disgraceful and where was Jonny Wilkinson?" and it went on and on and on, and every time he asked Moore a question, he would then interrupt and carry on with his rant.

At this point it's worth noting that Moore lives every moment of the match when England are playing – every ruck, every maul, every scrum. You only have to hear him belting out the national anthem before the game to know how much it means to him. He still thinks he's on the pitch and he certainly wants to be, so that 40 minutes of rugby really hurt him. He was upset, he was angry and here he was at half-time in a World Cup quarter-final sharing a commentary booth with a ranting, purple-faced middle-aged man shouting in his face. Saggers was asking Moore to tell him why England weren't good enough but was giving him little time to respond without interrupting. During the heated exchange, Moore had already said he would tell him why England weren't good enough if he would "shut up a minute". But Saggers kept going in the same manner and Moore had had enough.

Unfortunately, he reacted as the man in the pub would if faced with a similar barrage, and as Saggers again pressed him asking, "You tell me why England aren't good enough," Moore cracked and shouted back, "I will do if you let me f*****g speak".

Only of course he wasn't in the pub. He was on air during a quarter-final of a Rugby World Cup being broadcast exclusively live on talkSPORT. It is worth pointing out here that talkSPORT normally works with a 'delay' button in place so that if anyone inadvertently or deliberately swears on air the producer has time to 'dump' what was said, before it is actually transmitted. The exception to this is during live sport where there is no delay, so on this occasion, back in the UK the nation was choking on its collective cornflakes as 'Pitbull' turned the airwaves blue.

Bovill, who witnessed the whole thing, says: "It was totally unacceptable. Everybody in the press box froze. I think we went to an ad break and we had to speak to both Mark and Brian to calm them down. Mark had to apologise on air and Brian was mortified at his lack of professionalism, one that could have had quite serious consequences for him.

"In the end we got through the rest of the game, got back to the accommodation quite late and called a team meeting for the following morning, where the two of them were still sniping away at one another. Matt Smith and myself had to make it very clear to the pair of them that this was a work environment, a professional environment, and that this kind of thing was simply unacceptable.

"We managed to get through the last couple of weeks of the tournament without any further major incidents, but it wasn't a great look for the exclusive national radio broadcaster to have to apologise for one of their pundits swearing on air during a match."

Fortunately the story does have a happy ending, although not for England who were dumped out in the last eight, resulting in coach Martin Johnson losing his job and not helped by a further demonstration of ill-discipline among his troops, when Manu Tuilagi threw himself into Auckland harbour.

At the same time as the Leicester Tiger was taking an unscheduled dip, the talkSPORT team was on a boat trip of their own to Waiheke Island, where the people who owned their apartment in Auckland had a winery. And it was during that afternoon that a slightly tipsy Saggers declared his love for Moore – and they kissed and made up after several bottles of Pinot Noir.

Two years later the pair were reunited in the southern hemisphere as talkSPORT secured another memorable rugby union turnover, this time winning the exclusive rights to cover the British & Irish Lions' tour of Australia.

It was another blow to the BBC as talkSPORT sneaked in under the radar to claim arguably the biggest broadcasting prize in rugby.

It was also the continuation of the transformation of the station under Dee, although he had departed from talkSPORT Towers by the time the tour came around. But deals of this kind were changing the perception of talkSPORT and the station was becoming a really serious broadcaster – Premier League football, UEFA Champions League, FIFA World Cups, UEFA European Championship finals and now, on the back of the success of the Rugby World Cup in 2011, the British & Irish Lions, another massive sporting institution.

It wasn't the first time talkSPORT had done a Lions tour, however. In 2001 they covered the Test series in Australia, alongside the BBC. Bizarrely, Chris Broad, the former England cricketer, father of fast bowler Stuart and now Test match referee, was the main host for that tour – very typical of talkSPORT back in the day. Why get a former rugby player to host your coverage when an ex-international cricketer will do? Obviously it made sense to someone at the time.

As was also usual at the time, the talkSPORT presence Down Under in 2013 was relatively thin on the ground. In fact, in the early weeks of the tour, there were just two of them – Mike Bovill and Andrew McKenna. 'Macca' had now taken over the main commentary duties, so the pair headed off to Australia and looked after the tour for several weeks before other people flew out to join them for the three-match Test series.

It made perfect sense to approach the trip that way, and allowed them to use pundits who were already out in the country to provide co-commentary of the early tour matches, including once more Gavin Hastings and, in something of a strange twist, John Taylor, the man who had led their commentary team at the World Cup two years previously. Taylor is best remembered as a commentator. He was the voice of ITV rugby when England won the World Cup in 2003, but before that he was a brilliant player and part of the Lions' squad in 1971 that remains the only one to win a Test series in New Zealand. So it's fair to say his credentials stack up against the very best.

His days as a marauding flanker for Wales were a thing of the dim and distant past, however, but one of his colleagues in the talkSPORT commentary box was of more recent vintage. So much so that, as he prepared to arrive in Australia, he was called away from the commentary box to take his place on the pitch.

The man in questions was Shane Williams, who had retired from international rugby only 18 months previously and was seeing out the end of his playing days in Japan with Mitsubishi Sagamihara DynaBoars. He was finishing his commitments there before heading out to Australia to join the talkSPORT team to commentate on the Test matches. At least, so everyone thought.

A fatal flaw in that plan for the station was the announcement by Lions head coach Warren Gatland that he had called the 36-year-old winger into his squad. So instead of flying in and picking up a microphone, he picked up a pair of boots instead, strapped them on and played for the tourists against the ACT Brumbies. It was great for talkSPORT, and great publicity to say one of their team had been called up by the Lions.

Williams, who had toured with the Lions in 2005 and 2009, said: "It was completely out of the blue. I was more shocked than anyone. I never thought I would ever get that opportunity again [to wear a Lions shirt].

"Rob Howley [Lions assistant coach] phoned me. I had been playing in Japan over the last 12 months, so fitness was not going to be an issue. If I had had any doubt whatsoever that I wasn't capable or good enough then I would have said no, because there is no way I would let the Lions down.

"I got into Sydney on the Monday morning, and I was training by about half past 10."

That certainly proved it was no idle boast on talkSPORT's part that they took the audience closer to the action than any other broadcaster.

The great thing about Lions tours is that, occurring in a summer where there is no major football tournament, more often than not they dominate the sporting landscape in the UK in a way in which rugby usually struggles, with even World Cups and the Six Nations always clashing with Premier League action.

With the relatively spread-out nature of the tour, it also allows for some much-needed downtime for those covering it. Brian Moore and Mike Bovill enjoyed a trip to the set of *Neighbours* and a tour of Ramsay Street, and Brian also had fun pretending to scrummage against a koala. He may have had a slight weight advantage.

Other highlights, according to those present, were Moore and Saggers squeezing into wetsuits to go surfing on the Sunshine Coast, and each sporting rather dubious swimming trunks at a hot spring.

On the field, the tourists were enjoying a successful tour and, off it, so were talkSPORT. And Moore was central to one of the lasting memories for those lucky enough to be in Australia – all because of what may seem to many onlookers as a slightly unusual friendship.

As we have previously touched upon, Brian is a very interesting chap. As well as being a qualified solicitor, when he retired from rugby he ran something of an unexpected venture, a nail bar in Soho. That's right, the man known as 'Pitbull' during his playing days is a trained manicurist.

And it was during those days that he met and became mates with James Dean Bradfield, lead singer of the Manic Street Preachers. Now the Manics are Welsh and famously huge rugby fans in a country where rugby isn't a sport, it's a religion. So, very sensibly, they had arranged a tour of Australia to coincide with the visit of the Lions, playing a gig in each of the three host cities the night before the Test matches.

The Manics even joined the talkSPORT team in the commentary box ahead of the second Test in Melbourne – ironically the only one they lost – but it made for some fantastic radio ahead of the game that then, sadly, turned out to be terrible.

That defeat for Gatland's men squared the series at 1-1 with the final Test to come a week later in Sydney. On the night before that clash, the talkSPORT boys joined the Manics backstage after their gig and a great time was had by all. Everyone was on their best behaviour – Moore and Bradfield probably realised their rabble-rousing days were behind them – and it was a great way to ease the tension ahead of what promised to be a huge game the following day (a game the Lions famously won 41-16 to wrap up the series).

It was a brilliant way for the tour to finish on the pitch, and the talkSPORT team were determined they would also bow out on a high.

The day after the Sydney Test, the last on tour, Saggers had arranged for the whole team to have lunch at a restaurant called

The kitchens at Hatfields were a daily hazard. This was a good day!

The English, West Ham supporting Ian 'The Moose' Abrahams 'running' the 2006 London marathon in a kilt and Millwall shirt after losing a bet with Alan Brazil. All for charity.

Former Irish international Ray Houghton watching former England international Ian Wright closely during the annual Drive vs Breakfast 5-a-side match with traffic on Hatfields at a standstill.

Jedward meet their match. It's hard to know which of this quartet was the most bonkers.

Alan Brazil and Ronnie Irani trying out new 3D glasses in the 'Green Room' at Hatfields.

Adrian Durham wears an Arsenal shirt outside the Emirates as part of a 12 Dares of Christmas Challenge.

A dishevelled but victorious Sony Award winning Station of the Year team at the Grosvenor House Hotel, May 2011. Alan Brazil was still in the kitchens somewhere.

Mark Saggers, Brian Moore and producer Mike Bovill take a breather during the British & Irish Lions' victorious tour of Australia in 2013.

The €400 lobster for Steve Archibald that used up the whole of the Champions League budget in Barcelona in one go.

Paul Hawksbee and Andy Jacobs meet the Haymaker.

Presenter Georgie Bingham, England World Cup winner Ben Kay and commentator Andrew McKenna on tour with the British and Irish Lions in New Zealand in 2017.

Alan Brazil explains to Sir Alex Ferguson and Ally McCoist how he missed yesterday's show at Cheltenham. As if they didn't already know ...

Last Day in Moscow at Russia 2018

Pictured (from l-r) David Walker, James Dodd, Jim Proudfoot, Ian Danter, Mark Saggers, Emma De Smith, Adrian Durham, Will Dowie, Declan McCarthy, Sal Ahmad, Kathryn Anastasi, Matt Holland, Stuart Pearce.

The talkSPORT team on tour of Sri Lanka, October 2018

Pictured (from l-r) Jarrod Kimber, Gareth Batty, Sal Ahmad, Darren Gough, Mark Butcher, Jon Norman, Kathryn Anastasi, Neil Manthorp, James Savundra, Adam Reed, Mark Nicholas, Andrew McKenna.

The 'studio' in Galle, Sri Lanka with Jarrod Kimber, Darren Gough and Mark Nicholas on air.

talkSPORT pundit Steve Harmison relaxes Goughie's shoulder tension as he gives some tips to Jonny Bairstow with Moeen Ali looking on at the 3rd test against the West Indies in St Lucia, Feburary 2019.

Alan Brazil and Rebekah Brooks cut the cake on launch day at the new studios.

England manager Gareth Southgate signs the talkSPORT visitors' board on launch day at the new studios.

If your name's not on a shirt, you're not playing!

The legend that is
John Motson in the
talkSPORT studios.
No sheepskin required.

Doyle's on Watson's Bay in Sydney. It was a lovely few hours and, just as they were sailing back into Sydney Harbour, Macca pulled a bottle of pink Champagne and some plastic glasses out of his bag and they toasted the success of the tour.

At that precise moment, however, Saggs received a phone call from Programme Director Steve Morgan telling him Colin Murray had been announced as the new presenter of mid-mornings on talkSPORT. And that somewhat ruined the mood as Saggers then spent the next hour complaining down the phone, wondering how the station could sign up the man who had replaced him at BBC Radio 5 Live. Oh well, every silver lining has a cloud. Normal service of Mark Saggers' disposition had been resumed.

In fact it was in the Land of the Long White Cloud where talkSPORT would next make its mark on the global rugby stage. By the time the 2017 British & Irish Lions' tour to New Zealand came around, the station was well established as a worthy competitor to the BBC having broadcast live Premiership action for several years and with a dedicated weekly rugby magazine show, *Full Contact*.

And having delivered a performance on a par with Warren Gatland's triumphant tourists in 2013, they were seeking a repeat having once again secured the exclusive rights to the tour.

British & Irish Lions chief executive John Feehan was confident the tour was in safe hands. "There is a huge appetite for radio coverage of the Lions and we are delighted that talkSPORT has been appointed as exclusive rights holder," he said. "They did an excellent job in bringing the 2013 tour alive for millions of fans and the addition of talkSPORT 2 [the second station which would launch in 2016] will take their coverage of the 2017 tour to New Zealand to another level." So no pressure then.

But by now talkSPORT was well used to dealing with high expectations, and the stellar team of experts and pundits they sent to New Zealand was a reflection of that, with England Rugby World Cup winner Ben Kay being named as lead co-commentator for all three Tests. Welsh legend Shane Williams was again part of the team (not the playing team this time!), along with Irishman Gordon D'Arcy and Lions legend Ian McGeechan, who toured as a player in 1974 and 1977, and was head coach in 1989, 1993, 1997 and 2009. Justin

Marshall, meanwhile, who played 81 times as scrum-half for the All Blacks, would provide the New Zealand perspective. If rugby union did five-a-side, that would have been quite the dream team.

talkSPORT's resident rugby experts Andrew McKenna and Russell Hargreaves were on commentary and reporting duty, and the main anchor and host was Georgie Bingham – the first time a female presenter had undertaken such a role on a major tour for the station. Indeed, at that time, she was the only female presenter on the station having joined in 2011 on her return from the United States, where she had been working for ESPN. Bingham has now been joined on the presentation roster by Natalie Sawyer and Laura Woods, and admits she feels like the "grand old Mama", although she's delighted there is a greater female presence on the station: "Both Natalie and Laura are utterly different to me, they are very, very funny and down to earth. They are perfect for the place."

Bingham felt it was a huge honour to be asked to anchor the Lions tour, particularly as rugby is one of her main sporting loves, along with golf. But she also knew it represented a huge challenge. "I've always wanted to do rugby and golf on talk-SPORT, which are my strengths, so the Lions tour was a really good chance to do that. I also knew I had to nail it otherwise I would never get the chance to host another Lions tour.

"And talkSPORT put together a great team. I didn't know Ben Kay before the tour but his agent told me he was the best rugby guy you could ever meet. I thought her hyperbole was maybe a bit strong but he was awesome to all of us and he was never 'Billy Big Boots'. We went out with him every night and I ended up out drinking with rugby players I loved and idolised growing up. It was very different to any football tournament or Olympics or anything like that I've previously been involved in. It was a lot of fun."

Considerably less fun for Bingham was the fact her tour could have been over before it started when she found herself at the centre of a Twitter storm following a social media post that upset the Lions management.

She was due to fly out to New Zealand ahead of the first Test and, at around that time, head coach Warren Gatland had called up six reserve players, four from Wales and two from Scotland, based largely on the fact they were touring in Australia, while England were in Argentina and Ireland were in Japan.

It was a decision that was met with widespread criticism, both among the media and the fans. Bingham expressed her disagreement with the decision on Twitter, but added a comment along the lines of Gatland being dry-humped by Welsh players. That tone upset the Lions management, who believed she, as part of an organisation that held the official radio rights to the tour, should not be putting out public statements of that kind.

talkSPORT has always taken the stance that presenters' social media accounts are their own and do not necessarily reflect the views of the station. That was made clear to the Lions management, as was the fact she wasn't criticising the Lions as an entity but was just making the very valid point that was being made by every other journalist – although she had attempted to do so in a humorous manner. Eventually it was agreed she would delete the tweet and apologise when she arrived in New Zealand, which she did: "I got out there and apologised and I was so nice to them. I think they hated me within two days and were really bored with me saying sorry."

With that issue safely put to bed, talkSPORT and the Lions could get on with the serious business of the Test matches. On the pitch, the Lions did magnificently to draw the series and, off it, the talkSPORT team threw themselves into the local culture like a group of excited and adventurous backpackers.

They went night skiing, bungee jumping and jet boating, played golf at the top of a mountain, and even did a SkyWalk around the rim of the tallest building in Auckland. But one other experience nearly ended the entire tour – and worse.

Bingham says: "On one trip, this guy took us in this amazing adapted Land Rover-type vehicle up a river – it was where they filmed the iconic scene in the second *Lord of the Rings* movie where the wall of water comes down the river. It was a really cold day and he said we were going to go up to where they filmed one of the famous mountain battle scenes.

"As we were making our way uphill I was saying, 'That's a lot of ice'. He [the driver] was insisting it would be fine but he got us halfway up, and the wheels locked as he moved into first gear from second and the car started to slide back down. It slid down sideways until it was literally hanging off the side of the road.

"Everyone, even Ben [Kay] who is the coolest guy, was quite scared because we really thought we were going to fall off the side of a mountain. Of course we didn't. The car was stopped by a verge and we had to try to get it out, which we couldn't do. The road was so icy that when we got out of the car to try to help get it back on the road we were all sliding around everywhere, ten or 15 feet back down the road. You couldn't possibly have pushed the car because of the extraordinary amount of ice under your feet on the road.

"People with specialist equipment had to come out to help us, but this guy who claimed to have done about a million tours was like, 'It's all fine'. We really didn't think it was fine at all! We could have died. After we'd managed to get back down the mountain and a few drinks later, it was funny with hindsight. At the time, it definitely wasn't."

Near-death experiences don't just happen Down Under, but also much closer to home.

Scotland, in fact. And more specifically, St Andrews.

'CLIPS OF THE WEEK'

The Top 20 All-Time Greats

#11

Getting sports people's names wrong is the scourge of news-readers and presenters alike. Here's Ian Danter reporting from Wimbledon in 2013 on giant killer Sergiy Stakhovsky.

"Let's reflect on Federer's departure to the qualifier ... Sergiy ... Shit-off-ski."

Chapter 9 ⚽

Brazil Serenades Westlife's Brian McFadden in Gleneagles

There was also a near-death experience for another talk-SPORT presenter during the station's first foray into golf in the summer of 2000 when a team that was sent up to St Andrews in Scotland to cover the Open Championship was rewarded with a Sony Silver Award – a huge feather in the cap for a station that was barely six months old.

The talkSPORT team on that occasion, alongside Alan Brazil, included commentators Richard Boxall and Robert Lee alongside Andy Gray, the Sky Sports football pundit (Kelvin MacKenzie thought his presence would attract listeners not necessarily known for being golf fans), and American reporter Bob Bubka, while Sarah Sanderson and Rupert Bell roamed around the course, reporting from each playing group as they went hole to hole.

As well as it being talkSPORT's golfing debut, it was also Rupert Bell's. Rupert was more often found on the racecourse as talkSPORT's horse-racing correspondent. He was recruited having said on air one day that he had played golf at Michael Owen's course near Chester races. It was immediately assumed therefore that he had a widespread knowledge of all things golf. And despite the fact that in those early days he didn't, the poshest man on talkSPORT has been a staple of the station's golf coverage ever since.

So posh, in fact, is Bell, that his brother, Michael, is a trainer of the Queen's racehorses. And Rupert was on the end of some strange looks from Her Majesty while covering Royal Ascot in 2009 when, following a fall in the weighing room, he was left with eight stitches in a facial wound and a quite spectacular black eye. On spotting him, Queen Elizabeth remarked to one of her racing managers: "What is the brother of my trainer doing? Has he been drinking?" Good job he hadn't been 'out on the gallops' with Alan Brazil!

But Brazil had his own problems, and that brings us back to that near-death experience. Also along for the ride at St Andrews – quite literally as it turned out – was reporter Andy Clarke. His main job was to chaperone Brazil, a thankless task for any man, and his duties included delivering the Scot from the station's living quarters to the on-course studio each morning. He did that in a golf buggy but, unbeknown to anyone at the time, Clarke didn't have a driving licence. Nor could he properly pilot the buggy.

On the first morning as he raced along the pathway next to the course, he failed to slow down as he approached a mini roundabout and took the turn basically on two wheels nearly wiping them both out. That was the last time Brazil got in a buggy with Clarke.

And it was a good job, too, because the following day, as Clarke was leaving the media compound, he somehow failed to notice another buggy in front of him, forcing him to swerve wildly to avoid it, sending him flying straight into the side of a catering stall.

The following year talkSPORT was back at The Open, this time at Royal Lytham & St Annes, although Clarke's buggy was conspicuous by its absence on this occasion. But the talkSPORT crew still needed to hitch a ride on that particular mode of transport from their rented house to their studio overlooking the 18th green. Actually, it was less a studio, more a motorhome. Actually, it was less a motorhome, more a caravan. And actually, it didn't overlook the 18th, but the car park. Maybe if they had won gold at the Sonys the year before the bosses would have splashed out for a better spot …?

Alan Brazil and Mike Parry were presenting the breakfast show from the course throughout the tournament, and this was the scene of another famous Brazil disappearing act, although on this occasion booze was not to blame.

The plan was for the big man to follow his fellow Scot Colin Montgomerie around the course, kitted out with a radio microphone and a backpack with an aerial poking out of the top in order to bring the audience an up-and-close personal feel for the action.

As it had been cold and wet when Brazil rose from his slumbers at 5am to present that morning's breakfast show, he was very sensibly decked out in full waterproof gear but, as the morning wore on and the sun came out, he was beginning to feel the pace. By now he had walked around five or six holes and, with lunchtime approaching, was starting to flag.

It was at this point as he was walking along the fairway towards the next hole that he spotted the back of the talkSPORT house on the other side of the fence. Having been told earlier in the day by producers that he would be unable to get radio reception on some parts of the course, he sensed an opportunity to duck out of his duties.

Having enlisted the help of a couple of spectators to aid him getting over the fence while laden with his heavy equipment, it was a simple enough task for him to cross the railway track, navigate one more fence and then he was safely back in his bedroom in time for an early afternoon power nap.

While all this was unfolding and Brazil was getting ready for bed, he could hear producer Claire Furlong over the radio mic yelling furiously about getting engineers out on the course, complaining she knew the equipment wouldn't work properly. What's more, she was fretting about how Brazil would go mad when he found out he was slogging his way around the course but that they had no way to get him live on air.

As he emerged smiling to himself from his pre-nap shower, Brazil bumped into reporter Clarke, who was just heading out to begin work, so he handed him the radio kit and asked him to take it back to the caravan while he got his head down.

As he arrived at talkSPORT's broadcast operation centre (or caravan, as it was otherwise known), Clarke could hear Furlong still screaming at engineers and berating them for their overall ineptitude. As she continued to rant and rage, he calmly strolled over and handed back the kit, explaining that Brazil was now happily in the land of nod.

That forced Furlong into some furious backtracking with the engineering staff but, as was so often the case, Brazil got off scot free, explaining to Furlong a little while later, as she prepared to give him a thorough rollicking, that he had seen the house and simply given in to temptation. He then handed her a glass of bubbly, prompting her and the rest of the breakfast crew to burst into laughter, and continued to enjoy the rest of the day in the Bollinger tent in the company of his old mate Parry.

Surprisingly for him, Parry had been keeping a relatively low profile at Lytham and was not his usual ebullient self. This was because a couple of months earlier on the breakfast show he had criticised Lee Westwood for pulling out of the Masters to stay in the UK to be with his wife, who was expecting their first child. Apparently, the golfer had not been too pleased to be branded a 'wimp' for taking this decision.

It was said Westwood was on the lookout for Parry – he should have tried the Bollinger tent – but it was the unfortunate Adrian Durham who eventually fell foul of his ire. Westwood had not performed as well as expected in his first round and in an interview with Durham he was being deliberately unhelpful, giving monosyllabic answers and generally trying to make life as uncomfortable for his inquisitor as possible. Durham is not a man to take a step backwards so responded by asking Westwood what he thought the cut score would be. Apparently, it's considered poor form to ask this question after only one round, however, and Westwood flounced off in an ever increasing huff with all things talkSPORT, while his agent laid into Durham for his insensitive line of questioning. Meanwhile Parry, the architect of all this unpleasantness and ill feeling, was happily quaffing Champagne on another part of the course.

Golf has continued to be a major part of the station's sports coverage ever since, leading to some unlikely partnerships, including Bob Bubka and Geoffrey Boycott. They were paired to cover a tournament in Germany where Tiger Woods was to make a rare appearance at a European event. But American Bubka had no real idea what to expect from Boycott having been told only, "He's an English cricketing legend with a bit of an ego".

And that became apparent very quickly when, having watched Woods practising on the driving range for all of a minute, Boycott announced to his surprised colleague that he had seen enough. That stunned Bubka and, as the pair made their way away from the driving range, he asked Boycott what he thought of the world's greatest golfer.

Even for Boycott, the reply was remarkable. "Absolutely incredible," he gushed. "Unbelievable. What an amazing athlete that guy is, reminds me so much of myself."

Bubka is rarely lost for words, but that definitely knocked him off his stride. He recalled: "I said to him, 'Well, Geoffrey, they told me you had a bit of an ego, but I didn't think it was that big'."

Another slightly surprising coupling, so to speak, came about at the Ryder Cup in 2014. The event was staged at Gleneagles in Scotland and the talkSPORT crew found themselves sharing a house with former Westlife front man Brian McFadden and Peter Jones from *Dragons' Den* who were there as guests of the company who had arranged all talkSPORT accommodation.

The breakfast show was being broadcast live from the house each morning and McFadden would wander down and watch the show. No one minded, of course, and everyone was getting on famously. So much so that when Alan Brazil went into a bar one night, he found McFadden was already there, leading to the magnificent sight of the former lead singer of one of the world's biggest-selling boy bands and a former Scottish international striker performing karaoke together, at one stage leading the whole bar in a rousing rendition of 'Flower of Scotland'. Brazil says: "Brian is a very good golf player and does all the pro ams and stuff like that. We'd been for a bevvy down to the local hotel pub and we were actually singing at a wedding that was going on in the hotel."

The pair spent the evening drinking together, but the one-night bromance didn't quite end at closing time. As producers Jon Norman and Izzy Minter arrived at the house in the wee small hours of Saturday morning to get ready for *Weekend Sports Breakfast*, they found Brazil, Champagne bottle in one hand, Champagne flute in the other, serenading McFadden.

"What are you doing here?" asked Brazil. "We're here to produce *Weekend Sports Breakfast*," they replied. "What time is it?" he asked. "It's 5.15am." "Ooooh," he said. "I'd better go to bed." And that is Alan Brazil in a nutshell.

'CLIPS OF THE WEEK'
The Top 20 All-Time Greats
#10

As noted elsewhere in this book, The Moose is one of the most tenacious reporters for getting those insightful interviews with the big names – but sometimes it just doesn't quite happen. Here he is at Wembley grabbing another scoop:

Moose: The Manchester United players are just literally walking past me right now. In fact, let's see if we can grab a quick word with Carlos Tevez ... Carlos, good luck this afternoon.

Tevez: Thank you. [walks quickly away]

Moose: Carlos Tevez there, saying thank you to me for wishing him luck.

Chapter 10

talkSPORT Upsets Aggers and Wins Award for Sri Lankan Cricket Coverage

Accommodation is always an issue on any outside broadcast or overseas tour, and arranging it is often a thankless task for the individual whose job it is, as Jon Norman found when making arrangements for talkSPORT's long overdue return to live international cricket in the winter of 2018.

The station had not broadcast an overseas tour since England's trip to the West Indies way back in 2004, but they had won the exclusive commentary rights to England's trips to Sri Lanka in late 2018 and to West Indies in early 2019.

That decision was met with widespread derision among stick-in-the-mud traditionalists who were aghast at the thought of no longer having their cricket brought to them by the BBC's *Test Match Special* team.

No one was more sniffy at the prospect of cricket on talkSPORT than *TMS* stalwart Jonathan Agnew ('Aggers'), who took to social media to highlight some of the negative responses that had been generated following the announcement of talkSPORT's rights acquisition. And boy was middle England upset.

Apparently talkSPORT would be responsible for the death of cricket. Among the measured responses posted on social media were the following:

- Bollocks to this! @Aggerscricket @philtufnell @GeoffreyBoycott @Swannyg66 @MichaelVaughan TMS is by far the best. Talk sport is shit even for football
- Can't think of anything worse – you will f*** this up!!!!! Arlott, Johnston et al will be turning!!!
- Dear Talksport, everyone that listens to TMS is extremely upset that you have won the rights. Their coverage is untouchable. I for one won't be listening and I call on all TMS listeners to do the same. The only way you can hurt them is by switching off. Let's Geoffrey Boycott!!!!
- "Would rather listen to static interference on a battery powered LW transistor, and pretend that TMS will crackle through at some point. Not sure how this will go down with your usual overnight listeners (doggers, burglars, etc) as the audience you've gone after now hate you"
- This is just another nail in the coffin of test match Cricket. Ads in between overs, promotion of betting etc. @bbctms is an institution of our game.
- I'm totally gutted. In fact I'm almost in tears. It will be like losing a personal friend next winter.
- I won't be listening to your tinpot coverage. You're not fit to lace @bbctms's boots.

All of this, of course, before any details had been revealed about what the coverage would sound like or who would be part of the commentary team. And as noted elsewhere, coverage that would win one of the top industry awards. Further unexpected accolades appeared once commentary had started when none other than *The Spectator*, the highbrow political and cultural magazine of the establishment, called talkSPORT "cricket's new radio stars". Full of praise for the talkSPORT team, Roger Alton's article said: "You underestimate Talksport at your peril. It is fresh and original, but also highly knowledgeable …"

Mind you, in Agnew's defence, he had played three Tests and three ODIs for England, amassing a total of seven wickets in an international career that spanned 12 months. How talkSPORT was supposed to compete when Darren Gough had taken only 464 wickets (including an Ashes hat-trick, in Sydney) in his 217 international appearances across 12 years is anyone's guess. The criticism must have kept Goughie, Steve 'Grievous Bodily' Harmison and three-time Ashes winner Matt Prior awake at night throughout the tours.

Darren Gough gives his perspective: "I've got a lot of mates there at the BBC. And everyone I know has said what a great job we were doing. That we'd lifted it [cricket commentary] another level and that they realised they had to up their game. When you read these responses it's almost like schoolboy texts. And I don't get that. I don't believe in slagging off the opposition. We offer two totally different services. They are more traditionalists who do it like they always have done. There's no difference to how they do commentary now, to how they did it 20 years ago. We do it totally differently. Loads of energy, loads of fun, and express ourselves. We don't talk about tea and cakes. I find it pathetic some of the tweets. You get tempted to respond to them but I just won't. It's ridiculous."

But before they got to the point where they could begin broadcasting to the nation, talkSPORT had to find places to stay. And that proved particularly challenging.

It was decided that the best option would be to book accommodation online through one of the apartment rental sites.

Norman knew there were going to be issues when he went out there a month or so before the tour was due to start, to do a final recce, dot the i's, cross the t's and make sure everything was in order. It was not.

On arrival in Galle he found out the accommodation they had booked had changed ownership six months previously and the new owners had no record of the booking. In Kandy, he discovered the place they had booked had been turned into a school. And when he got to Colombo he found he had booked accommodation that was not going to be built until the following year.

Perhaps not ideal for a commentary team embarking on their first commentary of live Test match cricket since 2004 and with the irate *TMS* following and other 'establishment' figures waiting to pounce.

However, those issues were dealt with and alternative accommodation booked, but that still wasn't the end of the problems. When they arrived in Kandy on the actual trip, at the accommodation Norman had gone to see a month previously, he was confronted by the owner, who actually owned four properties, and informed him there had been a double booking and the guy was trying to palm them off into one of his other places. That was all taking place at 5.30pm on the evening they arrived to stay there for a week. Suffice to say, talkSPORT was not for backing down. Darren Gough comments:

"It was a good team on that trip. There was a lot of things we have to learn from. Like turning up to hotels and nothing being booked. And the road journeys were just horrendous. The worst thing for me was when we had to get from Galle to Kandy, Sky offered me a lift in their private plane. So they said they had one spot for me but then I felt bad because Mark Nicholas couldn't be on it and, me being a team man, chose to go in the car instead. And it was the worst eight hours of my life! After two hours I wish I could have taken it all back and said, 'F*** team spirit, I'm going on that plane.'

"Sky were all teeing off at Royal Kandy Golf Club about 45 minutes after they'd left and I had eight hours in a car with Mark, who never spoke a word because he had his earphones on for the full eight hours."

Later on the trip they arrived in Dambulla in the middle of the monsoon season to find all of the wildlife in the neighbouring area had decided to seek shelter in the house they had booked. So as they walked in they were confronted by frogs hopping around and about a thousand bugs flying about the place. One of the assistant producers was woken that night by insects falling from the ceiling on to his face, probably crickets.

To add insult to injury, when they gathered in the kitchen the following morning for breakfast, they found the cooker wasn't attached to the gas so didn't work, and there was no cutlery, no bowls, no plates, nothing. That was a short-lived stay.

And as if having to deal with sub-standard living conditions wasn't bad enough, when it came time for the cricket they were hit by another blow they could do nothing about – the weather.

Scheduling an ODI series in monsoon season on the subcontinent was always going to present issues, and so it proved, as did the on-site conditions in which the team was expected to work.

It would be fair to say that covering an overseas cricket tour is not the same as covering a football World Cup or European Championship finals. With the greatest respect to both Sri Lanka and West Indies cricket, they are not run in the same way as organisations such as FIFA and UEFA.

At a World Cup, for example, once you're at the stadium, you could be anywhere on the planet inside that carefully constructed world where people and facilities are on hand for you as an official broadcaster. Cricket is very different, and not always for the better.

For instance, no one who has worked at a major football tournament for talkSPORT in the past 20 years has ever found themselves broadcasting from a roof in the middle of rainy season as was the case for the team on one occasion in Galle. Every stadium presented its own challenge, not least the almost constant threat of thunder and lightning.

Colombo's R. Premadasa Stadium is a modern venue but, despite that, the talkSPORT team was forced off air just five minutes after the game finished because there was so much water flooding into the commentary box there was a real fear of electrocuting everyone. It was like a fountain cascading on to the equipment.

The second stadium in Colombo, the Sinhalese Sports Club, has a very small commentary box and, for some reason, there is a concrete pillar in it. This resulted in producer Sal Ahmad having to sit on a raised platform just so he could see the pitch. Unfortunately, he had the air-conditioning unit right above him so in 33-degree heat he had to wear jeans and a hoodie.

But all of those problems paled into insignificance alongside the one that confronted Norman on the first morning of the team's first broadcast at the first one-day international at the Rangiri Dambulla International Stadium when, because of a miscommunication, talkSPORT had set up their kit in the wrong room. So with just five minutes before they were due on air, Norman was in the office of the chief executive of Sri Lankan cricket pleading with him not to turf them out of the ground.

Luckily, that was an argument he was able to win, but no one could beat the elements. After just an hour of play, the heavens opened, leaving talkSPORT with five further hours of live cricket to broadcast … but with no actual cricket. Normally in a situation like this, management would take a decision probably to return back to the London studios after an hour or so of no play and broadcast the normal programme schedule. But as the station had a crack team in place and had paid a lot of money to be there, they took the decision to keep broadcasting, eventually returning to London after five hours. In a strange way, however, Norman reckons that difficult start paved the way for what would turn out to be a hugely successful tour.

He says: "What was different to a World Cup or any other football tournament is that for those events you use people from within the building, but on this tour we were using people who didn't work for talkSPORT. So it was 11 or 12 people who kind of knew each other, but not everyone knew everyone all that well. The production staff knew each other but we'd never toured together, and we all had to come together quite quickly. And in a weird way the rain on that first day helped because everyone had to rely on everyone else to pull off five hours of broadcasting … with no play."

Goughie picks up the story: "To have our own commentary was such a proud moment but, when it started, the first two days were rain. We talked for five hours without a break. It wasn't a problem for me as I like talking but I think that's one of the reasons we ended up winning the award [from the Sports Journalists' Association]. We talked so much cricket and so much good stuff about the game, with so many different voices, whether it was Nasser, or Athers, Mark, or myself, and whoever was on that day. It was an amazing listen for fans. What you found was that most players, who would normally go out of the studio when not broadcasting, actually stayed in the room to listen because it was fascinating."

Norman continued: "Later that evening we went to the hotel where Goughie, Mark Nicholas and Mark Butcher were staying and we all had dinner together. Goughie has been in football circles for ten years but here he was surrounded by cricket people, and so all the stories he couldn't tell a football crowd came tumbling out. With all of Goughie's stories he adds 10% tax and everyone was having a little drink and he held court, telling stories for about three hours. Spirits were really high and it was an amazing night. It really set the tour up."

The fun for the team had really started the day earlier in Dambulla, the day before the first ODI. Despite their professionalism at delivering the action on the pitch over the airways, some of the talkSPORT commentary team fancy themselves as rather handy cricketers. Pretending they can play can lead to embarrassing moments, as happened to talkSPORT's professional commentator and dad-rock enthusiast Andrew 'Macca' McKenna. Whilst milling around the practice areas and getting interviews and content for the shows, he had been joining in to field the odd rogue ball coming out of the nets. When called into action, he'd been fielding like a god and bounding around like a 15-year-old trying to catch the skipper's eye as a sizeable local crowd watched on. He scooped up every ball that strayed out of the nets like a steroid-assisted ball boy. But one ball was to ruin Macca's reputation, as well as his pride and dignity. The ball that ultimately led to Macca's loss of pride was a very simple floater: a leading edge from one net popped up, and straight away everyone called either 'heads' or 'catch it' to the assembled throng of journalists and broadcasters on the pitch. Macca called the ball early, and he ran for it. He did so, with every single person in the nets watching. Ben Stokes, Trevor Bayliss, Sri Lankan net bowlers all craned their necks around to see this beautiful (not so svelte) amateur cricketer stride purposefully towards the ball, and set himself under what is now deemed as a 'dolly'.

But it was clear that Macca didn't quite get set right. He was moving too excitedly in anticipation of demonstrating his cricket prowess to the assembled international squad. As the simple-looking chance came down to earth, he was all over the shop – not the smooth-fielding pimp of earlier in the day.

Then came the noise. It sounded sickening, like a small dove being crushed by a giant ogre paw. It was a squelch and pop. Ben Stokes' face wasn't one of contempt, but of actual disgust. Either at the noise, or the drop, we will never know. Macca bravely went on, threw the ball back and returned to the talkSPORT group with a battered ego, and a bleeding hand. The ball had decimated his fingernail and bent the finger in all sorts of directions. There he was, in the middle of Dambulla, bleeding, and pretending it wasn't a big deal. But he was in real excruciating pain. He was forced over to the England physio to get treatment and a professional job was done of putting the cricketing 'wannabee' back together.

Gough recalls. "We'd waited so long to get the rights. Getting cricket back on talkSPORT was like winning the lottery and a great opportunity. And our first man on the ground is Macca. So keen to impress. He loves cricket – it's his dream job as well. He's there representing talkSPORT. And the first nets session he breaks his finger dropping a catch. I immediately sent him a message as soon as it happened saying, 'Oh my God. You've embarrassed talkSPORT. You've let talkSPORT down.'"

But the show must go on. Minutes afterwards, Macca had to interview Mark Wood whilst it felt like a nest of scorpions were attacking his bandaged finger. Such was the intense physical pain, not to mention the emotional embarrassment, that he couldn't remember any of his questions. But he soldiered on to create one of the most discombobulated interviews on tour, with Wood, very politely humouring his incoherent interrogator. He was watched on by a wincing but appreciative local crowd, and thereafter they referred to him a 'The Hard Man of Dambulla'. His hand might have fallen apart but the man never did – well, not entirely.

A sense of camaraderie was enhanced by the fact the touring party travelled around Sir Lanka together in a mini coach – whereas at a football tournament requiring multiple commentary teams, individuals teams are dispatched to different parts of the country, meaning the whole team is very rarely all in the same place.

However, something was needed to relieve the boredom on the roads, and to take people's minds off the fact that, as is so often the case in that part of the world, you have to ignore the perils of seeing buses hurtling towards you on the wrong side of the road, or rounding corners to discover several elephants blocking your path. So producer Sal Ahmad came up with the idea of each member of the touring party creating a playlist that could be enjoyed by the whole group. And it would be fair to say tastes were eclectic.

There was some classic 'dad rock' courtesy of McKenna, whose final choice was a track from one of talkSPORT colleague Ian Danter's albums, while Ahmad himself accused the rest of the bus of being chin-stroking music snobs for not fully embracing his choice of Kylie Minogue. Elsewhere, the young assistant producers inflicted Justin Bieber on their unsuspecting colleagues. It made for quite the soundtrack to the tour.

The weather continued to play havoc with the one-day series, with all five matches being interrupted by rain, leading to some very uncomplimentary media coverage about the scheduling of the series slap bang in the middle of monsoon season. Ironically, if every ODI had been arranged for 24 hours later, the sun would have shone and they would have got a full series. It was just bad luck all round.

Fortunately the weather was much improved by the time the Test series got under way, and England performed admirably on the field to clinch a 3-0 series whitewash. Also performing admirably was talkSPORT who, by now, had silenced a good many of the doubters with their slick, informative and entertaining coverage.

The mix of cricketers like Mark Nicholas, Matt Prior and Gareth Batty, alongside respected cricket journalists Neil Manthorp and Jarrod Kimber, had proved a winning formula. And then, of course, there was Darren Gough.

Goughie has been a fixture on talkSPORT for the past ten years as the regular drive-time co-host alongside Adrian

Durham, and he was in his element, providing some of the tour's most memorable moments. None more so than during the tense last-wicket partnership in the final Test in Colombo as Suranga Lakmal and Malinda Pushpakumara threatened for a time to chase down the 327 runs they needed to claim an unlikely victory. At this point, Goughie had been on air for 30 minutes when the call of nature arrived. As the tension mounted on and off the pitch, Goughie refused to hand over the microphone and could be heard on air exclaiming, "And I need a wee!" as the excitement levels increased.

Mind you, as his producers know, you can't mess with Goughie and his bladder. The larger-than-life Yorkshireman nearly always has a smile on his face, but he can get a bit grumpy if he's hungry or needs a wee. So the trick is to make sure you're never too far from a restaurant or a toilet.

There's no doubt Goughie brought a real energy and expertise to talkSPORT's live cricket output. Indeed, so well received was the coverage of the Sri Lanka tour that it earned talkSPORT the award for best Radio Sport Live Broadcast at the prestigious British Sports Journalism Awards in February 2019 – much to the dismay of the Twitter trolls. And presumably a former Leicestershire bowler.

It was a terrific accolade. National Controller Liam Fisher reflects: "Winning the award was a real testament to the hard work of the on and off-air team. We had a brilliant line-up and, to paraphrase Frank Sinatra, we did it our way. Brilliantly. The coverage deserved that recognition. And as the official broadcaster of England's major overseas tours until 2021 there's plenty more cricket to come."

By the time the talkSPORT team was collecting that award, the second part of its winter of cricket was well under way in the West Indies.

For ex-England fast bowler Steve Harmison, who had been added to the commentary team for the tour of the Caribbean, working with Goughie was a dream come true.

"Growing up when I first got in to cricket, my hero was Darren Gough. To work alongside him in the West Indies, was everything.

It was brilliant. I enjoy his company. I enjoyed being around Goughie again. I was fortunate to play alongside him and to share the commentary box with him, hotels, airports, all that stuff. It meant everything. Sometimes you get told not to meet your heroes. Well, not in my case because I played alongside mine and I've now commentated alongside mine.

"And he'll always be my hero. And that's Darren Gough for me. Brilliant man, fantastic commentator and knowledge of the game. He should be on a lot more and he's somebody I can't wait to start working with again."

The West Indies tour proved less of a logistical challenge than Sri Lanka, with better accommodation on offer throughout the Caribbean and better facilities at the grounds, although the number of flights on small aircraft between the islands didn't go down too well with cricket editor Jon Norman, whose fear of flying is well known among his talkSPORT colleagues.

It all came to a head on a pit stop in Grenadine with the great and the good – Norman, Goughie, Harmison, Batty et al. – squeezed on to a small propeller plane en route to St Lucia. With the plane on the tarmac awaiting more passengers, the heat in the cabin became stiflingly hot and Norman's cool evaporated.

To the surprise of the team and his fellow travelling commentators, the normally very mild-mannered and unflappable Norman was soon seen high-footing it out of the plane and across to the departure gate. He'd requested a beer to calm his nerves and when told there was none on board had told the surprised steward that "either I get a beer or I'm getting off the plane".

The quick-thinking steward sized the situation up quickly. Either he sorted Norman out with a couple of cold Caribs or the flight would be delayed as Norman and his luggage were put in a van with the men in white coats. Norman reappeared minutes later with two cooling lagers in his mitts and the show could go on.

The show almost came to an abrupt halt though when wet-behind-the-ears young producer Sam Ellard was almost killed by a marauding cow in Sri Lanka. In fairness to him, the near-death bovine experience was not his fault. Jarrod Kimber described the story that occurred in Galle:

"So we were in the tuk-tuk on our way back to the hotel and there was a bunch of what we thought were cows on the side of the road who then started to come on to the road. Our driver expertly drove around them. Except that one wasn't a cow. It was a bull and it had its eyes set on the cow nearest our tuk-tuk. It just launched itself and slammed into the cow's back. The cow wanted none of this and made a sideways move like Messi. The problem being, that's where our tuk-tuk was. The driver, a hero to us, then just swerved, as I can only imagine 500kg plus of this Messi cow was about to destroy young Sam who was leaning his leg out of the tuk-tuk.

"I still don't know how the Messi cow missed us. I'm pretty sure Sam's thigh had cow drool all over it. And he found a new animal in Sri Lanka to be afraid of."

For all his naivety, however, Ellard's natural charm means he's also capable of putting an arm around Mark Nicholas, who can by accounts be prickly at times, ruffling his hair and eliciting a positive response. Something few people would be advised to try. "I'd been warned by the guy who had done my role before I arrived on tour that Mark could sometimes have a bit of temper, but maybe he felt sorry for me," says Ellard. "I had a very good relationship with him. And his hair is magnificent."

Ellard has this infectious enthusiasm that rubs off on people, and within five minutes in his company you're usually laughing, probably because he's said something ridiculous like, "What's a male cow called?" But occasionally his speak first, think later approach can land him in sticky situations, which is exactly what happened towards the end of the Sri Lanka tour when he decided to challenge Matt Prior to a contest.

Prior, who retired from professional cricket in 2015, had enjoyed his first tour for a few years and admitted he needed to get back home, work out and shed some pounds. This was not least because he would be attempting a gruelling charity bike ride in July 2019 when he and his cycling teammates were due to tackle all 21 stages of the Tour de France.

On hearing this, Ellard, not the most svelte young chap in the world, bet Prior he could lose more weight than the former

England wicket-keeper, an ex-professional athlete used to a strict regime of fitness and nutrition. Not only that, but that he would do it over the Christmas period back in the UK before they reconvened for the West Indies tour in January 2019.

So the bet was struck, with the loser promising to treat the winner to a slap-up meal at one of the most exclusive and expensive restaurants in Barbados – Lone Star, where a starter will set you back 50 quid. Alarm bells should have been ringing for Ellard when, upon hearing of their wager, Gareth Batty offered to foot the bill for the entire touring party if the youngster managed to beat Prior. It was never going to happen and, of course, it didn't.

In his naivety, however, even at that stage Ellard didn't really think the bet counted. He figured you shook hands but then forgot all about it, and never imagined for one minute Prior would go through with it. But when he discovered there was to be a weigh-in on the final day of the Sri Lanka tour, he realised this was serious and began to appreciate the error of his ways on entering into a wager with a professional sportsman, former or otherwise, for whom the competitive juices never truly stop flowing.

In fairness to Ellard, on his first few days back in the UK he did have a bit of a go at instigating a diet and fitness routine and even managed to shed a couple of pounds. But then came Christmas and the wheels fell off in spectacular fashion. So while Prior was working out, sending through video messages of him on an exercise bike or a treadmill, Ellard was pigging out on chocolate and sausage rolls.

And when it came to the second weigh-in on their first day back on tour in the West Indies it surprised no one that Ellard had lost the bet. Mind you, they might have been a little shocked that not only had he predictably come a distant second in this particular two-horse race, but he'd even managed to put weight on.

But fair play to Ellard, he stepped up to the plate and treated Prior to an enormous steak at the luxurious Lone Star restaurant. Fortunately for him, Prior was not drinking as he prepared for his cycle ride that summer – so at least that saved Ellard a few quid. Even so, the two courses Prior tucked away still cost the youngster a whopping £120.

At that point, you'd think Ellard would have learned to keep his mouth shut, but there were still more lessons to be learned, and painful lessons at that.

Gareth Batty, the fiery ex-Surrey County Cricket Club captain, was at a bar with Steve Harmison when Ellard started going on about Batty's inability to drink as much as Harmison. Batty takes up the story:

"He was banging on that I was getting on a bit, losing my hair, that kind of thing. I half-jokingly said I'd knock him flat off his bar stool if he didn't wind his neck in. But he kept going. And going. And going. Eventually I launched himself at him and rugby tackled him off his lofty perch. He stopped banging on about stuff then."

All sorts of unforeseen problems can occur on tour. The former England fast bowler Steve Harmison had been booked to appear at a Barmy Army event during the Test match in Barbados. But on arriving at the venue, the local doorman refused to allow him entry. Harmison tells the story:

"I got asked to do a Barmy Army event in the Caribbean and me and my 'partner in crime' Sam Ellard walked into the front reception and the guy on the desk just looked at me and said 'Where's your ten quid?' And I just said, 'Eh, excuse me'. And he said. 'Yeah, it's a ticket event'. So I said, 'Oh, I've not got a ticket'. 'Ah,' he said, 'well, it's ten pounds on the door'. So I said, 'Well, what's going on tonight?' to which he replied, 'We've got a question and answers session with Steve Harmison'. I said, 'Oh, alright' and then I said, 'Is that him there on the picture?' At this point Harmison pointed to a full life-size cardboard cut-out of himself right beside the door but still the guy was none the wiser.

"Now, I know I'd put a few stone on since I'd finished playing but I was quite alarmed that this guy couldn't recognise me from a photograph of me playing for England, so that was worrying. But as it happens, I now wasn't going to be allowed into my own Q&A event. It could have been quite a long night for people who did pay a few quid if I was still standing outside."

The guy on the door was simply not budging. Eventually, after standing around in the rain for 20 minutes, Harmison managed to persuade the guy to fetch a member of the Barmy Army who vouched for him and he and Ellard were finally allowed into his own event.

He might have got in that night, but Ellard was very nearly kicked out of his first tour match during the first leg of the winter in Sri Lanka, having been in the country for only three days. It was day three of the first Test in Galle and Ellard went for a stroll with Batty, down to below the pavilion where the non-playing members of the England squad were congregated. They were having a chat with a couple of people and had been there for quite a while, leading to Ellard losing his bearings somewhat. So as he took a few paces to his left, he was slightly startled to hear Stuart Broad yelling at him, "Where are you going, mate?"

He looked up and Jos Buttler, who was at the crease batting, had taken a step to his left and was waving frantically and everyone on the pitch and in the crowd turned around and looked at him as he realised he was right behind the bowler's arm! People in the crowd were moaning at him and at this point Broad warned him, "If he gets out next ball, I'm going to knock the s**t out of you," while giving him a withering glare which he held for several seconds, leaving Ellard ashen faced, before breaking into a big grin and laughing, "Only joking, mate".

And so the youngster swiftly power-walked out of there and back to the commentary box, hoping and praying no one from talkSPORT had seen what he'd done. But of course Batty had witnessed it all first hand and the next time he was on air he couldn't wait to tell the story about how talkSPORT 2's young producer, who had been on tour for only a little more than 72 hours, had managed to stop play.

Unbelievable from the young man. Further evidence that no one does sport quite like talkSPORT ...

'CLIPS OF THE WEEK'

The Top 20 All-Time Greats
#9

Sometimes in the fray of presenting, unintentional innuendo will pop up ... so to speak. Here's Mike Parry speaking to *Fisherman's Blues* presenter Nigel Botherway:

Nigel: I've got an email from Jean. "I want to marry a fisherman," she says. Great shout. What do you reckon, Mike?

Mike: Well, there's still a vacancy for the first Mrs Parry – so I'd better get me rod out!

Chapter 11 ⚽

Joey Barton Rows with Collymore, Who Says 'Au Revoir' at Euro 16

Euro 2016 would turn out to be as challenging a tournament as any for talkSPORT to cover. England, Wales, Northern Ireland and the Republic of Ireland had all qualified meaning meticulous planning was required to ensure that the production team could cover the wealth of stories and news coming out of the respective camps.

The tournament would be remembered for tension, conflict and dramatic exits – not just on the field. It would be played out against a backdrop of the two worst terrorist atrocities in French history.

In January 2015 in Paris, the offices of French magazine *Charlie Hebdo* were attacked with gunmen killing 12 people. And in November in the same city, gunmen and suicide bombers left 130 dead and hundreds wounded in a series of co-ordinated terror attacks, including a mass shooting at the Bataclan concert hall.

So it was a nation on high alert that was preparing to host Europe's biggest football party just a matter of months later. There were a lot of concerns for fans and broadcasters alike, particularly around safety at airports and other major transport hubs.

Senior producers Laurie Palacio and James Dodd were dispatched on a recce six months or so before the tournament started, which essentially involved travelling around the nine host cities in seven days, checking into a hotel, and then visiting the airport, train station and stadium, and plotting the best and most convenient routes in order to move the commentary teams around.

But heaven knows what would have happened had the pair been stopped by the authorities and asked to explain why they had detailed plans and photographs of every stadium and airport, and the quickest means of moving between one and the other. Finding themselves at the centre of a terrorist investigation would have been a first, even for talkSPORT.

Of course, no one knew at the time that the greatest threat to anyone's safety would be caused by marauding Russian fans fighting with their English counterparts. But that wasn't the only conflict talkSPORT would have to confront in France, however. There were other warring factions much closer to home to deal with.

In the build-up to the tournament, talkSPORT had signed up Joey Barton to its commentary team, adding another assertive and uncompromising voice to a stable that already included the likes of Stan Collymore and Stuart Pearce. This was certainly a formidable trio of very opinionated presenters, but by bringing them together had talkSPORT potentially bitten off more than it could chew?

Barton, much like Collymore, is not afraid to speak his mind and while that made for some great content on air, there was also the possibility it would lead to tensions behind the scenes.

And the first hint of that came on the very first day of the tournament, with the pair clashing in a heated exchange on drive-time in the build-up to the opening game between France and Romania.

In a nutshell, Collymore took umbrage with Barton's view that, while both Wales and Northern Ireland had done brilliantly to qualify for an expanded finals that now included 24 teams instead of the historical 16, neither had a chance of winning it (no one at that stage envisioned what the Welsh would achieve) and were therefore merely 'padding out' the tournament.

This is how it played out:

Collymore: It was a little comment Joey made earlier about the competition being padded out. Not everyone can win anything. There would be no point having a Barclays Premier League if everyone went into it, and we as fans thought everyone had a chance of winning it. That's not how football now works, unfortunately. But in terms of Wales and Northern Ireland ... Northern Ireland won their [qualifying] group. Wales finished behind, and they took four points off the best team in the world in Belgium. So I don't necessarily buy the fact that because the tournament has been expanded ...

Barton: The best team in the world?

Collymore: Well, they're ranked number one in the world, Belgium.

Barton: Yeah, but come on. You can read whatever you want into rankings. I mean, Stan, look, I get your point ...

Collymore: Would you say they're a good side, or not? Would you be happy playing in a team ...

Barton: Do you want me to speak, or do you just want to shout at me?

Collymore: No, I'm going to ask you a question, I'm going to ask you a question. Would you be happy to play in an international side that went to Brussels and got a 0-0 draw against the likes of [Romelu] Lukaku, [Eden] Hazard, etc., etc., and then beat them 1-0 at home?

Joey: Listen, they've done phenomenally well, let's not get away from that, but the likes of [David] Vaughan, [George] Williams, [Dave] Edwards, I've played against them all this year and they're not even the top of the Championship, they're smack bang in the middle of the Championship. Wales' team is full of players like that. You're talking about elite level football, a major European Championship where the best in Europe ...

Collymore: And they finished second in the group ...

Barton: Credit to them, they've had a really good campaign, but this is where they'll be tested. Wales have done really well, I'm not trying to knock Wales, but I'm being realistic about what's going to happen. There are players pinching themselves, this is the pinnacle of their footballing careers ...

Collymore: Yeah, but is it not patronising to suggest they're going to walk out on to the pitch and be taking selfies and what have you?

Barton: We'll see won't we, we'll see ...

Collymore: I mean with the greatest respect to you and me, Gareth Bale has won the Champions League a couple of times now, he's playing with the biggest club in world football, which is better than what either of us have done, so we can't sit here and pontificate, can we?

Barton: OK, Stan. I'm not pontificating at all, I'm talking about being realistic. Obviously you've got a bit of a bee in your bonnet so let me explain this to you. You should know this, having played at the level you've played at, or the way you're talking, Gareth Bale, when he plays club football, is a phenomenal player. But he's surrounded by superstar players as well, really good players at domestic level, when he plays for Real Madrid, when he played for Spurs, he's surrounded by quality players, top-drawer players, opening up spaces and creating things for him. This is not the case with Wales. He's in an inferior side to the England side, or the teams that are in the group. When he plays for Real Madrid he's in a superior team with superstars all around him. Gareth Bale is a phenomenal player, don't get me wrong, a phenomenal player.

Collymore: Would you say Bosnia & Herzegovina, that were in the last World Cup, and had a lot of quality through their side, their golden generation if you like, Wales finished four points above them ...

Barton: Stan, I'm not knocking Wales. They've qualified, they deserve to be here, they've done really, really well, but what I'm saying to you is ...

Collymore: Well, I'm not getting the point you're making about the padding out of the tournament. They haven't finished third or fourth.

Barton: It's gone from 16 teams to 24, so the tournament's been padded out, so let's not get away from that, the objective data says the tournament has been padded out, it's got bigger.

Collymore: Yes, it's been padded out ...

Barton: So the quality's been diluted ...

Collymore: Well, it's not ...

Barton: Of course it has ...

Collymore: How is it if you finish first or second [in your qualifying group]?

Barton: Because Northern Ireland ...

Collymore: First or second has always been the qualifying criteria ...

Barton: Northern Ireland have done phenomenally well. Look, we can stay here and debate this about football all day, I'll quite happily do this with you. I've got an opinion, I believe in it, you're a very opinionated man, you believe in yours. We disagree. That's football.

Collymore: Yeah, but you can't disagree when the criteria for virtually every international tournament since the inception has been first or second qualifies, and Wales and Northern Ireland have finished first or second.

Barton: And they've done phenomenally well, no one is saying that. But I don't think you realistically, even you in your argumentative tone at the minute, you do not believe Wales or Northern Ireland can win this Euros either.

Collymore: I don't believe England can either, so by that criteria ...

Barton: I never asked you that question, Stan. I asked you, do you believe Wales or Northern Ireland can win the tournament? Do you believe they can?

Collymore: We could go through every team ...

Barton: OK, we'll agree to disagree ...

Of course, that was merely a minor tiff compared to what was to take place later that night and the following day both before and after the opening Group B clash between England and Russia. Rival fans were fighting in and around the Old Port area of Marseille, with Adrian Durham at one stage broadcasting live into the *Sports Bar* show the night before the game at the same time as people around him were being sprayed with tear gas.

It certainly leant an extra edge to talkSPORT's coverage of the match, with the team in the Stade Velodrome already in a state of nervous excitement – not least because it was England's first match of the tournament; not least because of the trouble that had taken place the previous night; and not least because Collymore and Barton were now sat together in a commentary box just a little over 24 hours after they had argued so vociferously on air. If Carlsberg did powder kegs ...

Of course, the fact Russia equalised two minutes into added time to cancel out Eric Dier's opener and ensure the game ended 1-1 only added to the unnerving atmosphere inside the stadium. But when a firework sent up from the Russian end merely drifted up into the air before tamely fizzling out, it seemed there was little to be worried about.

But as England supporters greeted the damp squib firecracker with a rousing rendition of "What the f*****g hell was that?" it became apparent that, although it wasn't an act of aggression, it was the signal for co-ordinated acts of aggression.

Palacio says: "A couple of minutes later the whole stand behind the goal that had the England and Russian fans side by side turned into total carnage. I've been to football matches my whole adult life and never seen a stand clear in that way as 20, 30, 100, I don't know how many there were, Russian fans stormed the England fans.

"We saw kids being thrown over barriers, and young lads innocently turning around to see what was going on only to be punched in the face by fellas in balaclavas and full paramilitary gear. It was total chaos."

But one show team nearly didn't make it to Marseille.

The best-laid plans can sometimes go awry and no amount of planning and preparation can sometimes make up for a very simple old-fashioned 'cock-up'. Cue producer Ian Morris who was with Darren Gough and Adrian Durham in Chantilly where the England team were based, about an hour or so north of Paris. The drive-time duo had been doing lots of stuff from the England camp in the build-up to their first game against Russia. The team had been there for a week before the tournament and were now going to fly from Paris down to Marseille where the game would be played on the Saturday.

Morris had booked the flights for early Friday morning, and the drive-time show, the last one before England would open their account, would be broadcast from Marseille – it would be a big and important show. Everyone was fired up, excited and keen as mustard to get down there and start experiencing the atmosphere and match build-up.

Morris had printed off the boarding passes on the Thursday evening, booked the car to give them plenty of time to get to Charles de Gaulle Airport and set off at 5am saying "Airport" to the driver. However, the first hint that all was not well came shortly into the journey. Goughie picks up the story. "[I said to Morris] 'You do know there's two airports do you?' Ian looked at us and said, 'No.' I said, 'Well, one's about an hour away and the other one's about 40 minutes further on. Which airport are we going from?'"

Morris had assumed it was Charles de Gaulle Airport and, as he fumbled around to check the tickets, the driver asked which terminal they were going from. "Terminal B," Morris replied.

"Terminal B, monsieur?" said the taxi driver. "Es-tu certain? Il n'y a pas de terminal B à l'aéroport Charles de Gaulle. Il s'agit du terminal un, deux ou trois. Il n'y avait pas de Terminal B à Charles de Gaulle." As the conversation unfolded the driver said that there was indeed a Terminal B but that would be at Orly Airport, the other side of the city, as Goughie had just pointed out. Morris asked what were the chances of getting to Orly on time. To which the driver replied with a sly smile, "Comment dites-vous en anglais ... eh ... vous avez two chances. No chance and f***-all chance."

Durham and Gough were fuming beside him. The last drive-time show before the start of a tournament is always a big flagship show that they were both desperate to do. Adrian is meticulous in his planning, particularly when on tour. And both were really pumped up and ready to do the show. Here they were, heading to the wrong airport with little prospect of getting the flight and therefore doing the show.

Goughie says: "Adrian, being Adrian, when he loses it like that is on the phones, emailing and texting everyone."

Durham had got straight on the phone to the studios in London asking them to look up alternative flights, routes. Anything. But it was looking bleak as lots of fans were flying down that morning. This was a disaster before the tournament had even started. The taxi driver had a brand new Mercedes so the worried presenters told him to put his foot down and get to Orly as fast as he could. It was like the scene out of *The Bourne Identity* with the driver at breakneck speed weaving in and out of rush-hour traffic and up and down slip roads.

Goughie says: "He got us there. It was like being on an F1 track. It was peak hours and we were going in between everything to get there."

By some miracle, the driver made it and they hopped on the plane seconds before the steward removed the boarding ladder.

Morris says, "I'm not saying it was connected but not long after that I was moved off drive-time to *Weekend Sports Breakfast*. The irony is that on the way back from Marseille, Air France was on strike so we took the train everywhere and this became our preferred method of transport. And in a double irony, as I left the show it posted its highest ever audience so I must have been doing something right."

The trouble at the England vs Russia game in Marseille gives context to what happened next to thrust talkSPORT back into the media spotlight, with Collymore again leading the charge – quite literally this time.

Given what had transpired in Marseille, the fact that Russia were playing their second game in Lille just 24 hours before England were to face Wales in Lens – a distance of less than 25 miles – always had the potential to lead to more violence. And so it proved. But it also led to one of the defining moments of the entire tournament.

As Russian fans rampaged through the streets of Lille, where many England supporters had based themselves because of the lack of available accommodation in Lens, a small town with a population of only 250,000, Collymore decided to wade into the centre of it. As with Darren Gough at Euro 2012, Collymore has to be commended for his bravery, but probably condemned for his stupidity.

Palacio says: "I remember sending him a text as the boring health and safety side of me kicked in, bearing in mind I was notionally in charge of this group of people, saying something like: 'Dear Stan, for health and safety reasons I must advise you not to go down there. It's for the best.'"

Collymore chose to ignore those words of advice, however, and what followed was extraordinary as, broadcasting live via his mobile phone on Periscope, the footage immediately went viral as he filmed the violence, while shouting *"journaliste, journaliste"* at local police, to make it clear he was a witness to the trouble and not a perpetrator. It was truly remarkable stuff.

Also having a remarkable time at the England vs Wales game for different reasons were some of the talkSPORT sales staff and 50 of their clients, although that trip won't necessarily be remembered for all the right reasons.

It had started to go wrong from the very beginning when the coach to take them to the ferry port failed to arrive at the pick-up point at the talkSPORT studios on London's South Bank at the allotted time of 5.30am. Laura Cork, the PA to the sales team, attempted to contact the travel company they were using but, unsurprisingly, no one was answering the office phone at that hour of the morning. Fortunately she had the coach driver's mobile number. But when she got hold of him she discovered he was still in Basildon and, according to his timetable, he was not due to arrive until 6.30am.

That delay meant they missed their scheduled ferry and also forced the cancellation of the plush lunch they had arranged at a restaurant in Lens. But by this time no one was too bothered about that because they'd all had a few drinks on the Channel crossing and had also loaded the coach with booze which was stashed in with the luggage underneath the bus. Unfortunately, en route to Lens the coach was then stopped by the local police and all the booze was confiscated. At one point, the officers even enquired as to whether or not a couple of members of the talkSPORT party would mind helping them remove the alcohol from the bus. Safe to say, that particular request was met with a very firm no. They did eventually make it to Lens close to kick-off time, but the driver couldn't find the stadium meaning the entire group of 60 people had to walk, jog and sprint the last mile to the ground.

The game was enjoyed by all, but still that wasn't the end of the problems. After arriving back at the hotel and getting changed for dinner, Cork telephoned the local restaurant where they had made a reservation for the evening only to discover the restaurant had no knowledge of the booking, and that they were full. At the end of an already trying and tiring day this was not the news Cork needed to hear and she was practically slumped exhausted over the hotel's reception desk as the guests began to gather for dinner. They did manage to find a local eatery that could accommodate them and a fine night was had, helped no doubt by the fact they basically drunk the place dry.

But there was yet more drama to come the following morning when one of talkSPORT's guests somehow got locked inside his room, meaning they were once again an hour late departing and once again missed their scheduled ferry.

So it was an eventful sales trip to say the least. But not as eventful as what, unbeknown to talkSPORT's team on the ground, was about to happen that would lead to a parting of the ways with one of the station's biggest names.

Ironically, while Collymore's mobile-phone videos on the streets of Lille brought him nationwide coverage, it was other video content he was producing in France that was to lead to his eventual departure from talkSPORT.

Collymore had been filming himself inside the stadiums before matches, something that had seemingly not attracted too much attention during the group stages.

But, as the tournament reached the last 16 and the knockout stages, Managing Director Macaulay was informed one Saturday evening by rights holders UEFA that they had been made aware that Collymore had apparently been doing live transmissions from his Twitter account, via Periscope, during the Wales vs Belgium quarter-final match in Lille. This was against all terms of the station's broadcast contract with no filming from any venue allowed and particularly not from within the areas exclusively accessible by media/rights holders. The problem was further compounded by the fact that his footage was associated with a betting company – a very sensitive element for UEFA. There was a real threat that if this continued then talkSPORT's accreditation could be withdrawn and the station would not be able to finish the tournament. The message was crystal clear: he stops now, or we stop you now. The message was duly relayed to the production team who were in the commentary box in the Stade Pierre-Mauroy.

That phone call prompted Collymore to have the mother of all meltdowns and he was raging, ranting and raving in the press box, shouting and calling people every name under the sun, all the while as the other assembled journalists looked on in stunned silence, as he refused all efforts to pacify him and was threatening to quit the tour.

Commentator Mark Saggers says: "A call came through from London and we were told to tell Stan to stop filming. That's never an easy thing to do, but when we were told UEFA were monitoring it, Stan was told at half-time he had to stop. And at full-time he started [trying to film] again. That was Stan. If he wanted to do something, he would do it. We tried to stop him, and told him we didn't want to lose our accreditation, nor him to lose his, and told him if we break the rules here there could be serious repercussions, not only for this tournament but for future tournaments as well.

"I told Stan he had to stop, and he went into a rant beyond a rant in an open press box for everyone else to hear for half an hour. That was unfair on the rest of the team and he stormed off. Producers Sal Ahmad and James Dodd were really shocked, particularly at everyone else being around us, and they were brave in their own way and said they would have to report it. And we all did, and Steve Morgan knew we had to be backed on that one. There was a real danger of us never being accredited again."

Several days later, Collymore quit the tour, and that marked the beginning of the end of his days at talkSPORT.

He was persuaded to stay on and be part of the commentary team for the quarter-final between France and Iceland. But by this time, he wasn't speaking to anyone from the station apart from Palacio, and he was only communicating with him because he was the man sorting out all his travel arrangements. And it was Palacio who was the last to see him in talkSPORT colours, so to speak.

As they were making their way back into the centre of Paris following Les Bleus' victory over Iceland, the French fans were celebrating by doing laps of the Arc de Triomphe, flying their flags and beeping their horns. Collymore was loving this, so instructed Palacio to join the throng of cars and mopeds while he filmed it on his phone. It took about 20 minutes to do a solitary lap of one of the most dangerous roundabouts in Western Europe, which has 12 different avenues leading into it. Then Collymore insisted they go around one more time. In the spirit of keeping the peace Palacio acquiesced before, at the end of lap two, Collymore ordered him to pull up on the side of the road. He then got out of the car, took his bag out of the back and walked off into the night. And that was the end of Stanley Victor Collymore's talkSPORT career and the last time anyone from the station saw him.

It marked the end of a turbulent era but, for all their frequent arguments, Saggers, who knew Collymore as well as anyone having worked so closely with him over the years, believes that parting of the ways was sad for both parties.

He says: "He had gone to talkSPORT before me and I knew at some stage we would work together and there was this opportunity for 'Monday Feist Night', as we called it, and it really was edge-of-the-seat radio. We started by clearing out all the problems he had had – the dogging, the issues with Ulrika Jonsson, and such like. He could have gone all the way, he could have presented *Match of the Day*, but then the demons got in the way.

"There was always a wrestle with Stan between wanting to be famous and the main man in everything. This was completely at odds with how he'd looked after his dear mum. Here was this complex character with different personalities at different times.

"But without his energy we would never have put together one of our greatest moments when, in 2015, we won an SJA British Sports Journalism Award for Radio Sports Documentary for a programme on mental health issues. That sort of show would have been unthinkable on talkSPORT a few years previously.

"He did some incredible work on that, and we respected each other as broadcasters. Could he have been that broadcaster without the other side [of his personality]? Probably not. I don't think he would have been that footballer either. Whoever you are, if you spend your whole working life talking into a microphone in front of nobody in a studio, and listening back to yourself, it's a strange world to live in.

"We knew each other inside out, it was like a father-son relationship. We had row after row after row, and then we also had loads of great moments. At times it was part of the greatest radio I've ever been part of."

Of course, amid the carnage and controversy in France, there were plenty of lighter moments, with Hawksbee and Jacobs enjoying a very different travel experience to that of Palacio driving Collymore around and around roundabouts.

Hawksbee and Jacobs were offered the chance to fly by helicopter from Nice to Monaco – but Chelsea fan Jacobs was none too keen on the idea, having been put off the idea of helicopters for life following the death of Chelsea vice-chairman Matthew Harding in a crash in 1996.

Instead, it was decided that, in a nod to *Top Gear*, they would race the 13-mile distance, with Hawksbee and their producer, David Walker, going by helicopter and Jacobs taking the train.

Things started badly for the latter when the taxi driver took him to the wrong station in Nice. Once he eventually got to the right one he struggled to work out how to buy a ticket and, once he had negotiated that problem, he discovered his train was delayed. All the while, he was sending increasingly angry texts to his radio partner. At this point, Hawksbee and Walker had basically got the cigars out as they waited for a chopper, only to realise they had just missed one and would have to wait at least half an hour for the next one.

By then Jacobs was on the train and off and running, sending happier pictures through by text as he raced around the coast. Meanwhile, on arrival in Monaco, Hawksbee and Walker still had to get from the heliport to the hotel, where they walked in to find Jacobs sat in the bar with a large glass of wine in front of him. Victory to the man who couldn't stop moaning about things just a couple of hours before.

Rewinding slightly, Jacobs' food snobbery had once again come to the fore in Nice when he suggested they visit a restaurant he had previously dined at with his wife – although it turned out he had an ulterior motive for wishing to return to this particular establishment.

On the previous occasion he had been there, his wife had fallen down the stairs and he was hoping to recreate the scene and send her a photograph. Well, nothing says 'I love you' more than being reminded of the time you tumbled down some steps! The restaurant was run by a fierce old woman who didn't look like she was up for a laugh. But after keying his rather strange request into a translation app on his phone, they allowed Jacobs to lay himself at the bottom of the stairs and take the picture he wanted. How very accommodating, although at about £100 a head for dinner they should have been.

Less accommodating was Jacobs with the night producer Walker, who fell foul of his temper. And once again the problem was watching football in a bar. Andy, by his own admission, hates watching football in pubs but, when you're in a foreign country for a tournament, it's often the only option. But in a pub you're surrounded by noise and a cacophony of other people's (mainly unwanted) opinions.

On this particular evening in Bordeaux, England were playing Slovakia in their final group game, needing a win to top the group, and the chaps had been agonising all day over where to watch it. They had done their show from an Irish pub in the middle of town, but they were keen to go somewhere else for the England game. Everywhere was really busy with fans from all different countries congregating in various restaurants and watering holes.

They eventually found this place that was reminiscent of a Spanish tapas bar, and managed to get seats at the counter from where they could watch the match on a small TV high up on the wall.

Andy was relatively happy with this situation, but Paul was less thrilled as he was hoping to see the game on a bigger screen, preferably with English-language commentary. Walker had spotted a pub a little further down the road when they had arrived, so he decided to go and take a look and see if that might provide a better alternative. And he decided it did, as they had a massive screen at one end of the pub, several other screens dotted around the bar and there were places to sit.

He returned to the tapas bar to relay that information, and the three of them subsequently moved down the road. But as soon they walked in, Andy took one glance around and announced: "Oh, for f***'s sake, look at this place. I can't watch it in here."

In the few minutes it had taken them to move from one venue to the other, the second one had got a bit busier and there was now nowhere to sit. All that meant in reality, of course, was they would have to stand up to watch the game with a couple of beers, rather than be able to rest their weary rears.

But Andy insisted they return to the Spanish place by which time, of course, they had lost their seats at the bar, leaving them with no alternative but to return to the lively pub. And this time Jacobs did not hold back. Walker says: "It was one of the first times I'd ever really been bollocked by Andy. If you fall foul of him sometimes, no matter how much he likes you, he'll absolutely go for you. All I could say really was, 'Sorry, I just thought the screen was bigger'. It was a difficult few moments."

Jacobs wasn't the only member of the talkSPORT team to encounter a problem with a pub full of fans in Bordeaux although, in fairness, this particular issue certainly didn't provoke such an angry outburst from the man in question, Matt Holland.

The ex-Ipswich and Charlton midfielder is a former Republic of Ireland captain and something of a legend in those parts and the plan on this particular day was to get him to engage some Irish fans in a series of challenges for some video content for a sponsor.

The problem was, as Holland and the video team rounded the corner, heading for the Irish pub Hawksbee and Jacobs were using as their broadcast base, they were confronted by an absolute sea of green. There were several thousand Ireland fans in attendance, happily drinking and singing the afternoon away ahead of their game against Belgium the following afternoon.

Holland took one look at the size of the crowd and announced that he couldn't go down there because he would get mobbed. He had a point. There were so many of them that the Irish had taken it upon themselves to erect temporary road blocks to stop any traffic wishing to drive past the pub, which is situated on one of the main routes through Bordeaux. And no one minded. The contrast between the Irish fans on that trip – both from the north and south – when compared with, say, their English and Russian counterparts, could not have been greater.

But back to the afternoon in question and it was decided to divert Holland down and around a couple of back streets (where they even managed to find a few Irish stragglers to take part in a keepy-uppy challenge to fulfil the sponsor's needs) and take him in through the rear entrance of the pub where he was also due to give an interview to Irish TV.

All went swimmingly until a couple of fans caught sight of him through an upstairs window, and then it was bedlam as the fans began serenading him with cries of "One Matty Holland" until he went out on to the balcony to greet them. It was a bit like a papal audience at the Vatican.

Of course, it was all very good natured and Holland was loving it, but it did create one significant problem – how the hell were they going to get him out of the pub?

In the end, in scenes not dissimilar to Hawksbee and Jacobs using The Moose as a human shield in Rio, Mike Bovill stepped up to the plate. In his younger days, Bovill was a pretty decent prop forward, so he's not the smallest of blokes, and his ample frame provided the perfect barrier for Holland as the pair barrelled their way through the crowd.

Also having fun with the Irish fans at Euro 2016 (those from the north this time) was Colin Murray who, together with Keith Gillespie, the ex-Northern Ireland player, embarked on an epic adventure that involved a lot of laughs … and even more lager.

There was a fair amount of randomness involved, particularly in the initial part of the tour when it was just Murray and his producer, Kathryn Anastasi, creating colour content. They embarked on a Citroen 2CV tour of Lyon, went on a wine tour of a local vineyard and also took in the Korean ballet at the amphitheatre in the town. Sadly for them, they missed out on seeing Radiohead playing there as they were out of town on those couple of nights, although apparently the Korean ballet was "alright, actually".

So at this stage it was fairly sedate, then Gillespie arrived. That's when it started to go wrong. Or, depending on your point of view, when it started to go right. What was clear was the pair were going to have a grand time together.

Essentially, they worked hard and partied just as hard, but they created some brilliant on-air moments, particularly from within the stadiums during Northern Ireland games where it had been arranged that Murray, Dundonald-born and a massive fan of course, would sit pitch side behind the goal and provide analysis from there into the live match commentary. It was not something talkSPORT had ever done with one of their main presenters before and it worked a treat.

And that reached its peak during the match against Ukraine in Lyon, a game the Northern Irish of course won. On the morning of that game Murray had put out a call on Twitter for Northern Ireland fans to join him in the restaurant from where they were broadcasting that day's show in the build-up to kick-off later that afternoon. He invited 20 or so of the respondents to watch the show and then they all made their way to the stadium together, where Murray took up his spot behind the goal. Despite the rain – Murray had to use bin bags to protect his sound equipment from the elements – the team was winning, the fans were lapping it up and Murray was even conducting the singing from his enviable vantage point. You could barely hear the commentary above the chorus of "Will Grigg's on fire ..."

That evening, having got the tram back into town with all the fans, he and Gillespie joined them in a bar, with the night ending with the former Manchester United, Blackburn and Newcastle winger, who had also won the small matter of 86 caps for his country, crowd surfing through the place. There will be a fair few fans from inside that bar that night telling that tale to their grandkids.

It's probably not the best idea to advise any budding young footballers to follow Gillespie's diet, however. Fruit and vegetables don't feature at all. Even on a burger he would insist on any sauce being taken off before he would eat it. It's less of a vegan diet, more of a beige one.

From Lyon they made their way to Paris where Northern Ireland were to play their third and decisive game against Germany, and moved into the rented flat that had recently been vacated by Alan Brazil, who had returned to the UK after the first week of the tournament.

The apartment boasted breathtaking views of Paris, and Brazil must have loved that view so much because, apart from a visit to a local bar/restaurant down the road and a trip to undertake a spot of Champagne-tasting, he didn't set foot outside it. Not even when Paddy Power offered him full, five-star hospitality at the opening game between France and Bulgaria at the Stade de France. "Ah Paddy, I cannae be bothered. Open another bottle of Pinot," was pretty much how that invitation was greeted.

To be fair to Brazil, Murray and Gillespie didn't venture too far afield from there either. The flat was above a shopping precinct that had a bowling alley in the basement, and the pair went there every night they were in Paris. Never mind the sights and sounds of one of Europe's most enchanting cities. Maybe they liked the shoes ...?

Another former international enjoying himself as part of the talkSPORT team was Danny Gabbidon, who won 49 caps for Wales between 2002 and 2014. He was still really close to many of the Welsh players, and was even asked by one or two members of the squad to smuggle fags and booze into the otherwise locked-down camp.

As a recent former professional, he still kept himself in good shape and avoided too many beers and late nights. But on one evening he was fairly keen to drown his sorrows, the night Wales lost to England in the group stages in Lens. For some reason, rather than book a train for him and his producer, fellow Welshman David Williams, to take them back to their base in Dinard, talkSPORT had arranged a taxi for the pair – a journey of around four and a half hours.

Sensibly, the pair had grabbed a few beers before leaving the stadium but it was only when they were on their way that they realised they didn't have a bottle opener. Their driver spoke only French so, after a bit of Google translation action, they managed to find a service station where they bought what looked like a bottle opener, only for it to promptly snap as soon as they tried to use it. They eventually worked out that a seat-belt buckle would do the trick, but only after they had been travelling for around three hours.

Wales' remarkable run to the semi-finals took everyone by surprise, not least midfielder Joe Ledley. He had booked his wedding in Ibiza for the day before the final, seemingly safe in the knowledge the Welsh would be nowhere near it. So as they prepared for their last-four date with Portugal, he was facing the prospect of cancelling the ceremony to play in the final instead. Sadly, of course, the Welsh were beaten by the Portuguese, but at least that meant the wedding could go ahead.

And that left Gabbidon, due to be one of the main guests at the ceremony, facing a difficult choice, having been asked if he would like to be part of talkSPORT's commentary team for the final in Paris. Eventually, having returned to Dinard, he discovered he could get a seat on a private plane to Ibiza for the wedding, so that was pretty much decision made. For Williams, unfortunately, that meant no ticket to the final for him, nor was he able to swing an invite to the nuptials in the sun. So very much a lose-lose situation for the talkSPORT man.

Of course, Collymore's departure from talkSPORT wasn't the only dramatic exit that took place in France in the summer of 2016 as England unwittingly staged one of their own in the last-16 clash against Iceland. It was a game the Three Lions had been expected to win handsomely and, when they didn't, all hell broke loose.

And nowhere more so than in the talkSPORT commentary box where Mark Saggers launched into a rant so furious that, when the audio was used in a video posted on the station's Facebook site, it was viewed more than six million times in less than 48 hours.

This was the sound of a very, very angry man:

"Pack your bags, Roy Hodgson, we've had enough of you. We've had all the talk, we've had all the chat, we've had all the promises, we've had all the excuses, and it's never, ever, ever changed. You, Ray Lewington, Gary Neville ... pack your bags.

"Wayne Rooney, we've had enough of you, too. You've never delivered on the highest, the most important stage. Some of these youngsters will have to come again, but my word, how far short did England fall? And you know what, the whole of this tournament will be quite happy that England's going home because our reputation, on and off the field, is as low as it gets right now.

"The players might have sunk to their knees, the likes of [Daniel] Sturridge, probably crying his eyes out, you want to feel like we do watching you playing for England, week in, week out. Raheem Sterling and Daniel Sturridge ... 'Go easy on him,' said Sturridge about Sterling. 'He'll come good, he'll come right, don't you in the media blame him, it's not his fault.' England collectively, as a squad, were a disgrace. They have been, yet again, not only a side that has short-changed the good fans. You can hear what those fans think. It's alright you wanting to put your hands up, Kyle Walker, and applaud them, they're answering you with, 'You're not fit to wear the shirt'. That's what they think of this England side.

"We were a shambles coming into this tournament, we were a shambles during it, we haven't got a clue who should be playing where, we haven't a clue what formation, you [Roy Hodgson] hadn't a clue who you should be picking, you hadn't a clue who should be left out, it was absolutely, start to finish, an absolute load of rubbish."

It was spectacular stuff from Saggers and captured the feelings of the nation perfectly.

And it was that sort of broadcasting brilliance that led to talkSPORT winning the Radio Sport Live Broadcast award at the 2016 SJA British Sports Journalism Awards, the first time the station had scooped top prize in the category. It was a huge achievement.

While there had been some significant awards down the years, not least the Sony Station of the Year Gold in 2011, this one really felt as though it had been earned 'on the ground', so to speak, with the tireless efforts of the presentation and production staff both in France and London being suitably recognised.

'CLIPS OF THE WEEK'

The Top 20 All-Time Greats

#8

Continuing on the innuendo theme here's Toby Gilles reporting from Wimbledon:

"At Wimbledon, Jo Konta is through to the third round joining fellow Brits Harriet Dart and Dan Evans there. Roger Federer though, has just knocked another one out."

(Ooh, er, missus.)

Chapter 12 ⚽

talkSPORT International Launches and the Queen Becomes a Fan

With the station now firmly entrenched in the UK's live football scene, the next opportunity saw talkSPORT expand into new areas that would have been unimaginable previously.

In 2012 someone spotted that the international radio and audio rights for the English Premier League had effectively gone unutilised for a number of years, meaning the chance was there to take talkSPORT to a truly global audience.

It was felt that if talkSPORT could acquire those rights, they could be packaged up and built into their apps for worldwide distribution, while also being syndicated on to other overseas radio groups on a territory-by-territory basis.

CEO, Scott Taunton says: "I think that deal helped us further cement our relationship with the Premier League and positioned us, albeit in a small way, on a global stage as someone who had aspirations to build our sports broadcasting outside of the core we had in the UK."

It was certainly an ambitious project, and an even more ambitious timeline. Having acquired the rights in April 2012, the service was to begin in August that year at the start of the Premier League season.

But having committed to providing live commentary of all 380 matches in not one but three different languages (English, Spanish and Mandarin), talkSPORT then had to build both studio space and commentary teams. And ensure the space was fully operational and the teams were fully trained. All within just three months.

It was decided the lower basement floor at Hatfields was the perfect venue for the new operation. At that stage it was where all the office stationery was kept, doubling up pretty much as a warehouse and dumping ground. Within 12 weeks, it needed to be reinvented as what became rather grandly known as the International Broadcast Centre.

In truth, it was a hugely impressive facility, kitted out with dozens of individual broadcast booths. For years talkSPORT had been unfairly criticised for supposedly providing all its commentaries 'off tube', something that was most certainly no longer the case, but there was no pretence that there was any other way to do it for an international audience.

In fact, it was the only practical way to do it, with commentary teams in London and the crowd effects coming in live from the actual stadia. Doing it otherwise would have meant getting all the Premier League clubs to accommodate three additional commentary teams broadcasting in multiple languages at three additional commentary positions at each ground. Achieving that outcome was never practical and it was never going to happen.

So with the rights secured, the studio build well under way and the clock ticking down to the start of the season, the only remaining task was to assemble the respective commentary teams. And what a task it was.

With a little under three months to create teams capable of broadcasting every Premier League match in English, Spanish and Mandarin, the question was where to start, particularly for the latter two. After all, this was London, not Barcelona or Beijing.

Laurie Palacio remembers Moz Dee saying to him at the time: "You were born in Spain, you speak Spanish, I'm making you Spanish Editor. Build the Spanish department."

Meanwhile, the task of creating a team of Mandarin speakers fell to Oliver Zheng, who had been recruited from a leading sports digital and media group, and who had also previously played the role of a Chinese interpreter in the 2011 film *Johnny English Reborn* alongside Rowan Atkinson. Also recruited was Tom Rennie, an experienced radio and football broadcaster, who would be in charge of the English-speaking commentators.

It was rumoured around talkSPORT Towers that waiters were being approached in Soho's Chinese restaurants to see if they knew much about Premier League football. It would be fair to say that the first two questions asked of budding broadcasters were: "Do you like football? Do you speak Mandarin?" And if you answered yes to both of those questions you had a very strong chance of making it into the inaugural Chinese commentary team.

While that may have seemed rather far-fetched, the reality is that it wasn't all that wide of the mark with on one occasion at least Oliver Zheng (editor) and Hongtao Lui (now editor) entering a Thai restaurant to track down football-loving waiters after a new broadcast contract had been secured in Bangkok.

Nowadays, as the international service has grown in stature the team has more tried and tested hunting grounds for top overseas talent.

But back to 2012 and Palacio's task was also far from straightforward. The economic crisis in Spain at the time meant a lot of journalists had come to the UK looking for work. He was able to unearth a pool of talent willing to be part of this exciting new venture. By August he was quite pleased with himself that he had managed to assemble a large enough group of commentators, although he now admits that initially some were quite close to the edge of what you would deem acceptable.

With the respective teams now in place, an intensive period of training took place to get the fledgling John Motsons fully up to speed in readiness for the start of the new season and the launch of the new service.

One of the big problems that was encountered early on, particularly in the Mandarin section, was that all the commentators shared one major interest. They did one pilot game where all ten teams in each language would commentate on the same match in order for them to be given feedback and tips to improve the coverage. And all the Chinese guys turned up in Manchester United kits.

Despite the obvious partisan bias, it was explained that a more impartial commentary style was needed, a message that eventually got through.

Editor Tom Rennie recalls recruiting to fulfil commentary obligations in Arabic:

"One of the Arabic commentators we recruited when we first did the deal with a station in Bahrain was a policeman in Forest Gate. Before his first shift on the station he had been up patrolling the streets all night until about five in the morning and then he was in with us doing the Tottenham game at midday. He's a real Tottenham fan and speaks Arabic with a bit of Cockney accent. He'd flit between proper Arabic tones to 'norff Landan' Cockney and drop in some English words. We were slightly concerned, but the clients loved it as they felt it created real authenticity."

It was a crazy period of time, but the end result was something quite staggering to behold. With the English commentary team occupying one area of the basement, the Spanish and Mandarin teams shared another. And so you could stand in the doorway of this sealed glass room, in between, effectively, Spain and China, and you would be met with a cacophony of sound (and the odd recognisable player or stadium name) as anything up to six or seven Premier League games were being broadcast at the same time on a Saturday afternoon. It was an incredible buzz and would have the hairs on the back of your neck standing up as the Spanish commentators particularly would "sing a goal" (as it is called) for up to a minute. More recently, with the addition of Arabic commentary, the melee has grown, with the Arabic commentators outdoing their Spanish counterparts in the top trumps of noise.

For those with limited language fluency outside English it wasn't always easy to make sense of exactly who was saying what, and that certainly presented a challenge for the station's multi-award-winning creative team, led by Peter Gee, who would have the task of building packages and trails to promote the games without being able to understand a word of it! It was all done by interpreters having to clip bits of commentary, including goals or other major incidents, and then Gee and his team working their unique brand of magic.

There were some amusing asides resulting from all this new-found cultural awareness. One morning the staff arrived at talkSPORT Towers to discover new signs in the toilets throughout the building instructing people "not to flush paper towels down the toilets as they would cause blockages". With all these signs in English, Spanish and Mandarin.

Many superstitions surround Chinese New Year, one of which is that having your hair cut during the first lunar month of the new year will bring bad luck, especially to your maternal uncle. As a consequence, many young people either get their hair cut before the New Year, or on the second day of the second month after New Year. But as current Editor Tom Rennie explains:

"Back at the start of talkSPORT international, this was not something we knew and one day the whole Mandarin-speaking team turned up having completely shaved their heads. So the guy with the side parting was no more. The guy with the crew cut was no more. It made it extremely difficult for a period to recognise who was who. It was a bit like it was for John Motson in the 1998 World Cup when the entire Romanian team bleached their hair blond.

"One of the Mandarin commentary team once brought us in a whole tray of 40 Chinese tea eggs as a 'gift'. These are eggs that are boiled, the shell cracked and then steeped in a tea and spice marinade. A really common street snack in China.

"But to bring and consume 40 eggs in talkSPORT International's basement studios, with no windows, no air and only one air-conditioning unit, was maybe not the wisest decision. The studios smelt of eggs for the next three weeks."

While the various cultures were being integrated into Hatfields, the money men at the station set about turning the rights into readies. In stepped International Sales Director Kurt Edwards whose job it was to try and sell the rights to overseas broadcasters in individual territories.

For Edwards though, globetrotting was not to be in the style of James Bond, as the fledgling station was operating on tight budgets. Such was the frugality that Edwards managed to plan a whole four-day trip to Zimbabwe, Botswana, Uganda, Kenya and Chad without staying in a hotel once. When we say 'managed' we mean 'was made to'. It was simple logic by management that if he was always travelling by night he could sleep on the plane, so saving on accommodation.

But saving cash wasn't on the agenda the day he left in a taxi from Harare International Airport heading to a meeting in town. The driver shot out at breakneck speed along the road into the city and about a minute later managed to smash into another vehicle. Edwards emerged dazed but still standing and phoned back to the London office to say, "I'm not getting paid enough," along with a photo of the damaged taxi. As the fair-haired Edwards stood in the burning heat of the African sun with the taxi driver arguing furiously with the other driver, Edwards became very conscious of his vulnerability as a crowd had begun to emerge, perhaps sensing rich pickings from the man dressed like 'The Quiet American'. He gathered his strewn belongings together and got ready to get on the move. But to add insult to (his considerable) injury, the taxi driver was now demanding payment from Edwards to cover the repair costs following damage to his car as he had no insurance. Edwards thrust a wad of dollars into the agitated driver's hands, flagged down a passing taxi and hot-tailed it to the safety of the city. Well, the apparent safety of the city. By the time he arrived he had to go straight to his meeting with no chance to freshen up so he sat down at the restaurant table to meet his client with clothes soaked with sweat. And unfortunately for Edwards his client had chosen to do business over a curry. It wasn't the best of starts to his five-country trip.

Edwards was a colourful character having been brought up as the son of Scandinavian parents who during his childhood allowed him to bear witness to many risqué model photo shoots taking place in his house. He recounts the tale of him as a child, ready for school with his shorts and cap on, innocently munching on his cornflakes at the kitchen breakfast table while various naked women wandered past getting ready for action in the living room next door.

The vagaries of doing business internationally would often confront Edwards as he travelled to the far reaches of the continents.
In Singapore, he had met a potential business contact for lunch in
a very respectable 'restaurant' in a very residential-looking street
with nice boutiques, a Waitrose and a shopping precinct that you'd
expect to find in Croydon. Across the road, families were sitting
with their children, nursing cappuccinos. Once inside it became
apparent that all was not quite as it seemed. There were girls
around. Hundreds of them. His potential client told Edwards not
to make any eye contact with them as, once you do, they want
money from you as they think you're now 'trading' with them.
Edwards spent the next 40 minutes not once looking at his laptop,
but with his head down, eyes firmly fixed on the floor. Later he
would find out that he had been dining in the infamous Orchard
Tower, known colloquially as the 'Four Floors of Whores'.

A similar fate befell his successor Rob Tomalin in equally
'salubrious' surroundings. The first business meeting he did in
Malaysia was with a client who chose the Kuala Lumpur Beach
Club Café as the venue to meet at midday. But as Tomalin sat
down with this potential client, the Kuala Lumpur Beach Club
Café had a live shark in the middle, an ABBA tribute band going
at full pelt and hundreds of women trying to catch Tomalin's eye.
But a true professional, Tomalin persevered with his Power-
Point sales pitch before escaping into the daylight an hour later.
The US Embassy not long after issued a statement warning its
citizens to stay away from the club.

Back in London, the talkSPORT International production
team would often receive delegations of interested visitors from
the various stations across the globe where deals had been done.

In 2013, Voice of Vietnam, a state-run radio station, signed up
to carry talkSPORT's live Premier League commentaries. But as
a communist state, there was lots of anxiety from the station officials as to who the station was recruiting to provide the on-air
Vietnamese commentary. The fear was that given an open mic,
they could broadcast anti-government propaganda to the listening audience. A delegation of secret service agents were duly
dispatched to talkSPORT towers to 'vet' the commentators. But

bizarrely the 'interrogations' took place over lunch at the nearby Oxo Tower Brasserie. One by one the commentators would be taken aside by the secret service to a separate part of the restaurant where all that seemed to happen was that they ate pistachio ice cream and smoked Marlboro red whilst declaring undying love for the regime.

In a nutshell, however, talkSPORT International continues to thrive, with the global rights deal secured until the end of the 2021/22 Premier League season. Over the years, aside from English, Spanish and Mandarin, the team has also commentated live in Thai, Vietnamese, Bahasa Malay, Arabic and even Swahili. Now you try finding Swahili football commentators in London.

It continues to be profitable and is recognised around the world for outstanding performance. Not only that, it also has the Royal seal of approval after being named as one of the winners of the 2016 Queen's Award for Enterprise – the UK's highest accolade for business services. That's right, the Queen is a talkSPORT fan.

And if it's good enough for Her Majesty …

'CLIPS OF THE WEEK'

The Top 20 All-Time Greats

#7

Liz Saul's news-reading skills were brilliantly captured earlier. Here's newsreader Daisy Gray going even one better. Try and make sense of this!

"Manchester City surrendered a two-goal lead to draw 2-2 with Tottenham in the Premier League's late game. It means they're now nine points behind leaders Chelsea, who play tomorrow. Earlier, Wayne Rooney became the best … one-all … record. And Sir Bobby Charlton. That's the latest. I'm Daisy Gray."

Chapter 13 ⚽

Laura Woods Gets Sir Alex Ferguson to Do Karaoke at Cheltenham

The Cheltenham Festival is one of the highlights of the talk-SPORT calendar – in more ways than one.

For starters, it's lucrative commercially for the station with book-makers climbing over each other to get advertising space and airtime during what is one of the most important weeks of the year for them.

It's also arguably the most important week of the year for some of the talkSPORT presenters, with Alan Brazil more often than not at the front of the queue.

As retold earlier in this book, one escapade at Cheltenham, in 2004, very nearly ended his talkSPORT career and it was back at the scene of that crime, in 2010, where he once again fell foul of the station's senior management.

In the intervening six years he had, broadly speaking, kept his nose clean and he had re-established a relatively clean slate when it came to being forgiven for any misdemeanours. And that was probably a good job given what followed over the course of the next four days.

Having said that, asking him to broadcast live from a bar for all four days of the festival was like putting a kid in a sweet shop and expecting them not to rot their teeth. Suffice to say, had he been a youngster he would have been knee deep in chocolate. Instead, it was the black stuff that would cause the problems.

The situation was not helped by the fact that Brazil had been suffering from a bad throat for several weeks in the build-up to Cheltenham, and his voice was far from its best when he turned up at The Front Rooms on the Tuesday morning, the first day of the festival.

For the first couple of days all was well with the world, but by the third morning events of the previous 48 hours were beginning to take their toll. Well, two full days and nights at Cheltenham will do that to any man, even one with the remarkable constitution of Brazil.

The show that Thursday morning was not his finest hour – or four hours to be more accurate – and the station's bosses were not impressed. So much so that they issued instructions to The Front Room bar staff not to serve Brazil any alcohol during Friday morning's show.

On learning of his booze ban, which he only discovered at around 7.45am on Friday morning as he ordered a pint of Guinness, Brazil came to a swift and simple conclusion – if he couldn't drink on air, he would drink off it. And that was the end of his participation in that morning's show.

His reaction didn't come as a total shock to the production team, who simply juggled things around a little with co-host Ronnie Irani now taking over as the show's main anchor and guests simply being asked to hang around for a little longer. As luck would have it, former Cheltenham Town manager and talkSPORT regular Martin Allen turned up early for his slot, and was happy to fill in alongside Irani for the final one hour and 40 minutes of the show. At the same time, Brazil was happily enjoying himself over a few pints at the bar with his mates.

Sadly for Brazil, the talkSPORT bosses didn't have blinkers on and they wasted no time in coming down hard on their main man, and he was immediately suspended for his refusal to complete the show. There were also widespread rumours that he had been fired again when he failed to present the show on the following Monday morning, but once disciplinary enquiries had been concluded he was back on familiar territory behind the microphone.

Brazil was also indirectly responsible for one of talkSPORT's most memorable Cheltenham moments of recent years, although at the time he probably didn't even realise it.

Laura Woods, who was relatively new to the station at the time, was at Cheltenham for the first time as part of the breakfast team. Woods is one of the new generation of talkSPORT presenters, appearing regularly on *The Alan Brazil Sports Breakfast* and also hosting the full-time phone-in every Saturday. She epitomises where talent, tenacity and hard work can get you, having started off doing work experience on Sky's *Soccer AM* and then progressing through the ranks to present *The Debate* on Sky and reporting from pitch side on *Super Sunday*. But none of that experience quite prepared her for a day at the races with Alan Bernard Brazil.

At the end of the first breakfast show at Cheltenham she was planning on making her way back to the hotel and getting her head down for a few hours of much-needed sleep before the racing began. Brazil, of course, had other ideas and almost before she knew what had happened Woods had been whisked away to the Guinness tent where there was already a pint on the bar with Brazil's name on it. Well, not literally, but you get the picture.

The following morning, with Woods feeling a little delicate after the excesses of the day before, history began to repeat itself as they returned to the Guinness tent post-show. Fortunately a chink of salvation arrived when Brazil announced he and his wife were having lunch in this particular VIP tent and invited Woods to join them. Well, at least that would get her out of the Guinness tent for a while.

They arranged to meet at around 12.30pm but, when Woods arrived, there was no sign of either Mr or Mrs Brazil. She told the girl at the entrance her name would not be on the list but that she was there to meet Alan Brazil, and she was duly shown to a table where there were three spare seats. The room was full of stars, a genuine who's who of the British sporting world. And there she was, all alone.

She says: "Everyone was wondering who I was and why I was there on my own, and I told them I was meeting Alan Brazil and everyone was fine. I was texting him, ringing him, trying to find out where he was, but he wasn't responding. So I just settled in and had some more Champagne but it got to a point around two or three hours later, by which time I'd had quite a lot to drink, when he sent me a text to find out where I was. It turns out they were in a different VIP tent, and he had told me the wrong one."

So quite brilliantly, and whether or not intentionally, Brazil had VIP tickets for not one Cheltenham lunch that day, but two. Well, there's nothing like hedging your bets at a big race meeting like that.

Eventually Woods went to meet Brazil in the 'other' VIP tent, where she found him and Ally McCoist chatting with Sir Alex Ferguson. Brazil says: "We met Fergie in the owners' and train-ers' restaurant in the paddock. Fergie was there with Ronnie Wood and Ged Mason who owns a lot of horses. We ended up with McCoist, me and Fergie chatting away all day. It was a great day. Fergie loves his horses."

Woods remembers simply sitting there in awe of them, unable to think of a single question that would be worthy of Sir Alex's time. Maybe a few more glasses would help ...

The afternoon dragged on into the evening and to the pub and then to a stately manor. By now Woods had plucked up the cour-age/had enough Champagne to be bold enough to ask Sir Alex about his career and his life. There was karaoke going on in the room and everyone was trying to get Ferguson to have a go but he was having none of it. Cue Woods:

"I asked, if he did do it, what his song would be. He said, 'Leaving on a Jet Plane' so I sloped off and thought I was doing this really quietly but in reality I probably marched right up to the people organising the karaoke and shouted the song in their faces. I then took the microphone back to Sir Alex, and he stayed sat at the table but sang the song. It was brilliant. There was real joy in his face.

"I only know him like everyone else as this strong, iron-fisted Fergie but he had this big smile on his face. He was in his element.

It was an amazing experience. I turned up to work the next day and all the production boys were asking me where I'd got to last night and I told them I was doing karaoke with Alex Ferguson. You don't get that at many places other than talkSPORT."

The festival is also a firm favourite of Hawksbee and Jacobs who, although they both admit to not being racing experts, nor even great racing enthusiasts, have both grown to love Cheltenham.

Their first broadcasting experiences at the course actually came outside of the March festival when they used to go to the November meeting as part of the show's sponsorship deal with bookmaker Paddy Power.

They would go on the Friday of that week – Countryside Day – and the first time they went, it quickly became apparent that no one had really thought about where they could broadcast from. So eventually they ended up in the catering section of the main stand, in what was effectively a large storage cupboard.

They christened it Lord Vestey's cupboard (Lord Vestey being the long-serving former chairman of Cheltenham racecourse), joking that while Alan Brazil was quaffing Champagne in Lord Vestey's box, they were stuck in his cupboard.

The breakfast show broadcast from Lord Vestey's box for a number of years and Brazil recalls getting up to mischief while he and Parry were broadcasting. "At Cheltenham, we always open Champagne at 8am and it was Mike Parry's turn to bring two bottles for the show. But he forgot. We were broadcasting from Lord Vestey's box at that time so I said to him, 'Get your arse under Lord Vestey's table where all the stash is'. There was Petrus, Bolly, Dom Pom. He's under there saying, 'I can't, I can't find any,' and I'm saying, 'You can, it's nearly 8 o'clock. Get your arse under there, there's loads. Go in a bit deeper.' Then this bloke in full morning suit and bowler hat opens the door and walks in and looks at me, just as Parry pops up from underneath the table, triumphantly saying, 'I've got two, Al, let's get these ... open ...' So Parry is on his knees looking up at this bloke [presumably thinking it was Lord Vestey himself] and is saying, 'Lord, Lord, I am so sorry. I promise you that at

10 o'clock I was going to replace the Champagne.' The bloke just sighed and said, 'Mr Parry, I'm Lord Vestey's butler. Please get up.'"

It was a very bizarre set-up in that cupboard for Hawksbee and Jacobs, and they remember that while they were on air that first year speaking to racing royalty like Jenny Pitman, Henrietta Knight and Sir Peter O'Sullevan, staff would be wandering in and out to retrieve hams and such like from the industrial-size fridges that were also residing in the cupboard.

Since 2013, however, they have been very much part of the Cheltenham furniture, happily no longer stuck away in a cupboard but very much on show in Paddy Power's box. And they love it.

"It's an amazing experience," says Hawksbee, "albeit the same experience every year. It's déjà vu, the whole thing. We play the same games, tell the same jokes and do the same things each year. We could probably play last year's shows and people wouldn't know the difference – apart from the names of the horses."

Indeed, so set in their ways are they that even their journey to Cheltenham each year is the same as they set off for Gloucestershire after finishing their show at 4pm on the Monday before the start of the festival. They get the train from Paddington, but before boarding, Andy Jacobs insists on having a Burger King burger, he then chats to Richard Scudamore on the train (this actually happened twice!), they play 'Laurence Llewelyn-Bowen cricket', getting runs for spotting any look-a-likes, get to the hotel where they always eat on the first night even though the staff are terrible, just like the food, before walking out to the Queens pub for a pint. That's been day one for the past seven years, and will be for at least the next seven if they have their way.

Although Andy now admits to thoroughly enjoying Cheltenham, he wasn't quite so keen on being there on the night Chelsea were playing Steaua Bucharest in the second leg of a Europa League last-16 tie in March 2013. A huge Blues fan but, as noted earlier, with a natural aversion to watching football in pubs due to the noise and number of people around, he was naturally keen to watch the game. As they were walking back from the course to the local pub, Paul suggested they watch the game in there. Andy wasn't too struck on that suggestion, however. "It will be horrible in there, we'll be surrounded by idiots." So Paul suggested they watch it in the hotel, but Andy wasn't happy with that either. "I don't want to watch it in there, it will be boring, there's nobody there." So Paul asked him where he wanted to watch the game, to which Andy replied: "I just want to watch it at home." Unfortunately, he was about two hours and 90 miles away from his lounge in west London.

He was unhappy once more at Cheltenham two years later when he again just wanted to be left in peace to watch Chelsea, this time in the Champions League against Paris St Germain.

On this occasion Ray Parlour was with them and, shortly before kick-off, a load of Arsenal fans who were presumably going to the races the following day, turned up in the bar. They spotted Parlour and were getting on famously with him, and then they caught sight of Andy who was in his Chelsea shirt with '10 Jacobs' on the back.

Chelsea were not playing well (they eventually drew but were knocked out on away goals) and the Gooners were becoming increasingly rowdy, although without really aiming it in Andy's direction. But he was taking it personally and at the final whistle he simply got up, told them, "You can all f*** off, the lot of you," and stormed off. Unfortunately, as he did so, he tripped over the TV.

It's rare, however, that Andy finds himself as the butt of the joke. More often than not the boot is firmly on the other foot as he puts it in on an unsuspecting soul, usually one of the production staff, and more often than not, the same one.

Andy will enjoy a pint or two, but he is also very well behaved and, no matter how the evening unfolds, he will always take meticulous notes. And that means that come 1pm the following day, anyone is up for ridicule in the opening section of their show.

And on more than one occasion that "person" has been producer David Richards, lovingly known as 'Barman Dave'. He's a terrific bloke and liked by everyone, but as Alan Brazil's producer for many years he was always in danger of making a bit of a fool of himself at Cheltenham. After all, surely no one could be expected to keep up with Brazil all day and then still be compos mentis late into the evening. But he would try. So he'd start drinking with Brazil at 10am, turn up at Paddy's box at 4pm, and then go out with H&J and their producers in the evening. So essentially, two days out in one.

On one memorable occasion at dinner after another long day out trying to keep up with Brazil, he ordered scallops and an espresso. Nothing else. That was it. No one at the table had ever seen that before, or has ever seen it since. Another night they were in a Thai restaurant in Cheltenham when he stood up to go to the toilet and promptly fell head first into the table in front of him. Fortunately, the diners who had been sitting there had just left and the table had been cleared, otherwise he would have totalled the lot. Mind you he has form for this sort of thing. At the prestigious British Sports Journalism Awards, as everyone was standing solemnly in silence remembering those in the profession who had passed away that year, Barman Dave managed to connect his knee to a table full of empty glasses which came crashing down, just as the name of talkSPORT's long-time cricket commentator Jack Bannister came up on the roll call, shattering the silence.

He had also upset Andy Jacobs the previous year when he had joined them at dinner but had fallen asleep at the table. Not to be deterred, however, when the waitress came over to take their order he perked up, raised his head a few inches off the table and said he'd have a pint! Tottenham had lost in the Europa League earlier that night and, as Spurs fans, he and Paul Hawksbee were at one stage attempting to discuss that but all Dave could say was: "But Paul, how much would we get for Lamela now? £10million? £12million." And he kept repeating that over and over and over again until eventually Andy barked: "Dave, will you shut the f*** up about Lamela and just go home."

It's not just the talkSPORT crew who sometimes get a little carried away at Cheltenham, though, and what Hawksbee and

Jacobs often see are a lot of famous sporting faces, particularly footballers, who turn up in Paddy Power's box incognito.

One particular Premier League team arrives each year en masse, but everyone is sworn to secrecy because the boss doesn't know they go. In fact, to those in the know, it's often possible to spot a correlation between a player who's had a good day at Cheltenham and his performance in the Premier League the following week as was certainly the case with one member of England's World Cup squad.

Similarly, there is the great tale of the Premier League striker who had a three-day bender at Cheltenham – on one of those days escorted by two beautiful ladies – and then had a 'mare' at the weekend.

But those stories pale into insignificance alongside the remarkable time in 2014 when one bloke disgraced himself so badly he was banned from Cheltenham. He was in the Paddy Power box, and apparently he was a guest of a guest. Even Paddy himself wasn't quite sure how he'd managed to get himself in there, but by all accounts he wasn't a particularly nice fellow.

Now one of the highlights of being a guest in Paddy's box at Cheltenham is that legendary jockey Ruby Walsh makes an appearance each day to give people the benefit of his experience and a bit of inside info – who he expects to go well, which horses have looked good in training, that sort of thing.

But on this particular day, this chap felt the need to take umbrage with Walsh and interject that he didn't agree at all and that trainer Nicky Henderson had given him completely different advice. Not surprisingly Walsh was slightly taken aback by this and responded with words along the lines of: "If you want Nicky Henderson's advice, ask f*****g Nicky Henderson."

That seemed to upset the guy still further and he proceeded to get increasingly drunk and increasingly obnoxious, at one point loudly and gleefully informing Hawksbee and Jacobs, who were in the middle of a live broadcast, that he had been invited to a very exclusive party they would not be allowed into. "He was vile," recalled Jacobs.

But it's safe to say the 'gentleman' in question never made it as far as his fancy post-racing soirée, because shortly after his outburst there was a kerfuffle in the Royal Box that was right next door. Apparently this bloke had got in there having spotted Nicky Henderson and was planning to berate him for giving him bum advice – it turned out Ruby Walsh had been right all along.

No one is quite sure what happened next, or how it happened, but the stroppy bloke took his trousers off in the Royal Box, was wrestled to the ground by Her Majesty's Secret Service and was banned from Cheltenham forever more. As Jacobs added: "It couldn't have happened to a nicer bloke."

It just goes to show you have to be careful who you upset at Cheltenham, something Jacobs himself almost fell foul of one year. It was the year when he first started taking notes during the evenings and, on this particular night in the Queens, he spotted this fella passed out on a sofa. And for once it wasn't Barman Dave.

This guy was huge, about 6ft 7in, and certainly didn't look like the sort of bloke you'd mess with. Anyway, despite that, Andy thought he'd capture the moment with a photo but, unfortunately for him, as he did so the flash on his mobile phone went off startling the guy awake.

He jumped up, squared up to Andy – Paul remembers it looking like Dave Courtney was about to attack his co-host – and demanded to know why his photograph was being taken. Brilliantly, Andy's response was simply to turn his back on his would-be assailant and hope he would go away quietly.

That was one lucky escape for Jacobs at Cheltenham, and he and his colleagues were fortunate to enjoy an escape of a different kind at the festival on another occasion. An obvious hazard of broadcasting and working at Cheltenham is you end up chasing your money because you don't know what you're doing. You get tips from all quarters and whispers about this horse, that horse or the other horse. Some of which turn out to be better whispers than others, of course.

This can often find people desperate at the end of the day because they've lost so much money. And that was the case for

H&J and their team one year, but they were bailed out by Stephen Hunt, the former Reading and Republic of Ireland winger, who gave them a tip that had come via his dad for a horse in the 6.15pm at Huntingdon.

Andy went down to place his bet, and the bookie in question was very dismissive of his going 'off course', but Andy didn't give a jot about that. He'd done a packet 'on course' and was quite keen to try to recoup some of his cash. And he and his colleagues did so in some style, totally cleaning up and wiping out all their losses for the entire week.

Sometimes, that's how easy it is to clean up. And fortunately it's usually also relatively easy to clean up any on-air issues that might arise at Cheltenham when a guest may say something he or she shouldn't, having possibly taken a little too much refreshment. That's why the producers have a 'dump button' which allows them to erase anything dodgy or defamatory before it actually gets to air.

And one such occasion when it came in particularly handy involved talkSPORT legend Mike Parry, who joined H&J live on air from Paddy's box at around 1.15pm and was perfectly lucid and his usual slightly bonkers but charming self.

But when they got him back on air shortly before the end of the show at 4pm, he was speaking Spanish! He memorably cast treasonous aspersions against the Royal Family for their part in the death of Princess Diana, although he did caveat it slightly by claiming, "That's what Mr Brazil always says". Praise be for that dump button.

'CLIPS OF THE WEEK'

The Top 20 All-Time Greats

#6

Micky Quinn is a stalwart of the talkSPORT team and a Scouser by birth. He was a prolific centre-forward and played for, among others, Portsmouth, Coventry and Newcastle. He also had a spell in Greece with Thessaloniki, but never played in France. Here's why, as revealed during a conversation about clothes, as he is reading off a cue sheet:

"And off the back of Sagger's man bag we heard that producer Scagsy wore a pair of Ugg boots ... what are they? Ugg boots? on Boxing Day. He took 'em back the next day after getting so much abuse from his mates. We want to know what's your biggest fashion ... er ... fox paz."

Did you mean faux pas, Quinny?

Chapter 14

'Romford Pelé' Interviews the Real Pelé and Callers Phone in with Fishy Tales

ootball fans in the UK are among the most passionate people in the country. As legendary Liverpool manager Bill Shankly once said: "Some people believe football is a matter of life and death. I can assure you it is much, much more important than that." And there can be no doubt those sentiments are shared by a great many talkSPORT listeners.

That passion regularly comes across over the airwaves with supporters calling the station to have their say on the key issues involving either club or country, but sometimes confusion reigns.

Take this Liverpool fan, for instance, who called them on *Sports Bar* in February 2019 in the wake of the Reds' 0-0 draw at Anfield in the first leg of their Champions League last-16 clash with Bayern Munich. He remained very confident his side would still go through, but his logic was somewhat wide of the mark …

Caller: Will we go through? Well, you know, a draw in Munich will do us and we'll go through. So we don't need to win. We can just draw. If we score a goal, they need to score one, or two, so you know, remember one thing Andy, away goals count double.

Goldstein: Yeah.

Caller: So if we score a goal in Munich they'd have to score two.

Goldstein: Yeah.

Caller: We score two, they'd have to score four. So, you have to remember that we're still in a very good position.

Goldstein: I think three ... I think [laughing] ... I think if you score two away goals, they'll only need to get three. I mean it's, it's not, it's not actually double! You know it's not actually, like, if you score three away goals, they don't have to score six [laughing]. Oh my God! 'If we score three, they've got to score six!' [laughing]. Oh my God! That is the most amazing thing I've ever heard. Ever.

The most amazing thing Andy Goldstein has ever heard? That is really saying something, because he's heard a lot of weird stuff on his show over the years. But you always have to be ready for the weird and wonderful when you're working at talkSPORT. Presenter Matt Smith discovered this in October 2016 when he was standing in for Jim White and received a call from a confused Arsenal fan who was particularly upset about the lack of game time being given to German star Lukas Podolski:

Smith: Are you happy with how things stand? You're top of the league.

Caller: No. At the end of the day it is not good enough. We are top of the league for the moment. It's October. Will we still be there when it comes to February/March time? Honestly, will we still be there?

Smith: I don't know, you might be.

Caller: [fighting back tears] What would give you the impression to see that? Alright? Twelve years and we haven't even challenged, we haven't even come close.

Smith: But aren't you ...

Caller: [still fighting back tears] We fall apart.

Smith: Aren't you closer now then you have been in the last ten or 12 years?

Caller: Maybe. Maybe, I don't ... but at the end of the day, at the end of the day look at the talent we have in Mesut Ozil, Santi Cazorla ... [Alexis] Sanchez is playing up front for the moment but other than him, who have they got up front? Where's [Lukas] Podolski? Where's Podolski?

Smith: Well he left, a while ago.

Caller: Of course, cos [Arsène] Wenger doesn't play him. Where's he gone? Why's he's not playing him?

Smith: Well, he's in Turkey now. He's playing his football in Turkey because he couldn't get into the Arsenal team.

Caller: Is he?

Football fans have long memories and are not quick to forgive. If their team has been wronged, you can be sure they will still be talking about it years later. Max Rushden was in the hot seat in the mid-morning show alongside ex-Arsenal player Perry Groves when this classic call emerged from a caller who wanted to have his say after Argentinian superstar Diego Maradona had invited former England goalkeeper Peter Shilton to meet him and bury the hatchet more than 30 years after his infamous 'Hand of God' goal at the 1986 World Cup finals. But his anger quickly turned to another subject:

Caller: I would go as far as getting Shilton to get his two fingers up, photocopy it, send it to him in a letter with a kiss underneath it. Why would he want to shake a fat Mario Brother's hand? The man's a cheat. Do you know what I mean?

Rushden: It was 31 years ago, I think, and people have forgiven each other for more than that.

Caller: Mate, seriously, seriously, 31 years ago I was getting over the fact that me dad set fire to me Womble and I still hold a bit of a grudge about it now.

Groves: You've never forgiven your dad? There's a Womble feud. Was it Orinoco, or Madame Cholet?

Caller: Orinoco, mate. I had it for years. He said: "You're too old for that now" and set fire to it. You're going to get me emotional, Perry.

Rushden: Did he set fire to it in front of you?

Caller: Yeah. He said: "You're too old for it now, son" … I was ten.

Groves: That's like a scene out of *The Wicker Man*. Was there like, a funeral pyre?

Caller: Mate, I was having counselling until I was 22. Just the vision of his eye falling out of its socket.

Rushden: This isn't about Maradona, is it? This call is about the Womble.

Caller: Sorry, but I just needed to share it, get it off me chest.

That sense of injustice is inbred into football fans, and no one would ever want them to lose that passion and desire. But sometimes it's hard for them to keep their emotions in check. And that was definitely the case for this long-suffering Liverpool fan who rang in to 'Call Collymore' towards the end of Brendan Rodgers' time at Anfield:

Caller: Good evening, Stan. How are you doing, mate?

Collymore: Very well, thanks. Talk to me about Liverpool, your club. What needs to happen next?

Caller: [fighting back tears] I'm broken-hearted about 'em, mate. I've got to be honest, Stan. I've been supporting 'em since I was six, I'm 41 now. I think they've gotta get rid of [Brendan] Rodgers, and bring in either Joachim Löw or Jürgen Klomm [sic] and let them demand the players they want to make Liverpool the great club, the best team England has ever had.

Collymore: How upset are you this season?

Caller: [sobbing] I am more than broken-hearted, Stan. Liverpool fans are so wonderful. You couldn't want for better fans and when you're getting players like [Raheem] Sterling moaning and groaning, you know, surely there's wrong things happening there and it needs to be sorted out.

Collymore: How much do you love this club? I can hear it in your voice ...

Caller: [balling his eyes out] Oh Stan, I'd die for Liverpool because they're absolutely God on earth, they really are. I love 'em to pieces. Liverpool fans are just outstanding, the history they've got. I mean you look at 'em all, I mean Liverpool and Manchester United have got the greatest history in this country and they haven't had to buy it. Chelsea and [Manchester] City have had to buy it. We haven't had to do that, we haven't had to do that. Arsenal are holding up there at the top, you know, why can't we do that? I mean you played there, Stan, you know the score, mate.

Collymore: I hear the passion and upset in your voice and there's not much more I can add to that.

That's what happens sometimes, the emotion just gets too much for people – that's why pictures of supporters crying are flashed all over TV screens, newspapers and the internet when their team gets relegated.

A case of mistaken nationality created surely one of the greatest calls of all time in the talkSPORT archives as a Hearts fan rang former Manchester United and Scotland full-back Arthur Albiston on a special Scottish football phone-in to bemoan Antti Niemi's lack of international recognition:

Caller: I'm phoning about Craig Brown's selection for the Scotland squad.

Albiston: Yep.

Caller: He must know that Hearts have got a good team. We get Colin Cameron in the squad, Steven Pressley, but I don't know why for at least three seasons he's been ignoring Antti Niemi.

Albiston: Antti Niemi?

Caller: Aye. I don't know why he doesn't get a game.

Albiston: For Scotland?

Caller: Aye.

Albiston: He's from Finland.

Caller: He's what?

Albiston: He's Finnish, isn't he?

Caller: He's not finished. He's only 28.

Albiston: No, not finished ... he's from Finland.

Caller: What do you mean?

Albiston: His nationality is Finnish. He's from Finland.

Caller: He's not Scottish?

Albiston: No.

Caller: Oh, I thought he was Scottish.

That's one of the beauties of talkSPORT: you never know quite what's coming when callers are live on air. Having said that, it's not always the members of the public who generate mirth among both talkSPORT staff and listeners. Sometimes the presenters and pundits contribute in their own unique way. For instance, you would struggle to find a funnier exchange than the one that took place when talkSPORT's very own Ray Parlour was given the opportunity to interview Brazilian legend Pelé. What followed was comedy gold:

Assistant: Hi, Ray.

Parlour: How are you doing, you OK?

Assistant: I'm good. This is Theresa, I've got Pelé here for you.

Parlour: Brilliant. OK. Alright. I'm gonna ask him a few questions, is that OK?

Pelé: OK.

Parlour: Hi, Pelé, how are you, you OK?

Pelé: Everything's OK.

Parlour: Ah, brilliant.

Pelé: [muffled noise]

Parlour: Sorry, mate.

Pelé: [muffled noise]

Parlour: It's just cutting out.

Pelé: I can hear you.

Parlour: You can hear me OK, yeah?

Pelé: Yes, I hear you. Nice to talk with you.

Parlour: And you, too. I'm just gonna ask you a few questions, Pelé, if that's OK.

Pelé: OK, OK.

Parlour: OK, here we go.

Pelé: Sorry, my English is not the best but I try to understand you.

Parlour: My English is not the best either, Pelé, don't worry [laughs]. Anyway. OK, Pelé, great to speak to you, it's Ray Parlour here. Do you think England can win the European Championship this summer?

Pelé: Football, everybody knows is the box of surprise, but of course I think, England, the level of the team, they have a possibility to win the tournament, no doubt. You can catch them by surprise, the best team. Of course England have the opportunity to win the tournament, no doubt.

Assistant: Hi, Ray, we're running out of time now.

Parlour: OK, yeah. Umm … well, Pelé, my nickname, believe it or not, is the 'Romford Pelé'. I played for Arsenal and England. Did you ever see my winning goal in the 2002 FA Cup Final?

Pelé: No, I don't see, I'm sorry. I don't have a TV.

Parlour: Hahahaha … OK, thank you anyway, Pelé. Thanks for your time. *Obrigado.*

It would be fair to say wires were slightly crossed in that exchange, with poor old Pelé clearly desperately trying to think of an excuse for never having seen Parlour's Wembley wonder strike.

But perhaps the most extraordinary calls into the station have been courtesy of a relatively new feature on the station, 'Midnight Train to Madness' which runs in *Sports Bar*, presented by Andy Goldstein and ex-Chelsea, Spurs and Ipswich player, Jason Cundy. Goldstein explains the feature's origins.

"The show runs every weekday night from 10pm until 1am. The hour after midnight was always the Achilles heel of the show ever since *Sports Bar* began way back in 2008/9. Trying to get people to stay up past midnight seemed to be more difficult than making it through the three hours without Cundy ever coughing, spluttering or sniffing.

"In the past we'd tried everything from a look 'Inside Tomorrow's Back Pages' to 'Cundy's Question Time'. The latter worked for a period, with the premise being that at midnight we'd ask a stupid question (e.g. if you had a bicycle with the wheels as big as the London Eye, how long would it take to cycle round the world?) and people call in with possible answers … It worked brilliantly, but bizarrely we ran out of stupid questions after a couple of months.

"'Wheel of Cundy' was another item we tried that worked for a bit but ultimately ended up on the scrap heap because of the finite amount of 'Player A' stories that Cundy had stored in his (tiny) brain.

"So, one night me and producer Pat [D'Angelo], knowing just what kind of person was still up listening at that time of night (usually drunk, but definitely bonkers), decided that we'd try something we did years ago (but packaged up slightly differently) and allow people to call up and talk about anything they wanted apart from sport (and later, politics, religion and nothing too serious). It was the first time ever that we'd got a full switchboard, at midnight, in under two minutes. It was bonkers.

"After that show we discussed if we should only roll it out once a week to avoid killing the idea. We decided to give it one more go the following night and if the results were the same we'd continue it until it followed a similar fate of previous items at that time slot. After a week I told the listeners it was here to stay but we needed a name for it. Lots of listeners tweeted in ideas, included one that read, 'Why don't you call it "The Midnight Train to Madness?"'

"It's still the most popular thing that people stop me in the street to talk about, mainly down to the emergence of talkSPORT's social media feed that sends out a video of the most popular (bonkers) calls. Whereas before, a call at that time of the night would get a relatively small audience, some are now getting over 2 million views."

Such is the power of 'The Midnight Train to Madness' (and maybe something to do with the fact that the pubs have shut by then) that the presenters, as well as taking calls from the mad, the funny and the insomniacs have also become a sounding board for relationship advice. Take this recent call from listener Matt who phoned up with a problem, perhaps looking for a sympathetic bloke's view but ended up with Cundy and Goldstein taking opposing sides – all of this played out live on air:

Matt: Look, I've got a bit of a dilemma, boys, and I don't know who to turn to at this time of night.

Cundy: Well, you've come to the right place.

Matt: I've just crept out the bedroom. And I've got my missus in there next door. And a text has popped up on her phone ... um ... and it's from a Terry. Now she said that she was out for drinks last night with a few friends from work. Everyone she

works with are girls and this text has come through and it's ... it's
... taken me by surprise.

Goldstein: What does it say?

Matt: Well it says, "Thanks for last night. It was lovely to see you.
Hope to see you again."

[Production team plays cliffhanger music motif effect.]

Goldstein: Can you text back.

Matt: I don't know the passcode.

Goldstein: Matt, I want you now, live, to go and wake her up and
go, "You've just got a text from Terry. Who's Terry?" And I want
to hear what she says.

Matt: OK, OK.

Goldstein: I want to hear this though, Matt.

Matt: OK, OK one second. [shuffles back into the bedroom] Babe ...
babe ... wake up ... Who's Terry?

Girlfriend: [confused] What?

Matt: You've got a message from Terry.

Girlfriend: [even more confused] What? What are you talking
about?

Matt: You was out with the girls last night weren't you.

Girlfriend: Yeah.

Matt: Was it with Terry, or ...?

Girlfriend: Terry's one of the girls

Matt: Ah ... are you sure?

[Production team plays laughter track and Goldstein signals to
them to turn it off.]

The call then developed and Goldstein asked the caller to pass
the phone on to his girlfriend so he and Cundy could talk to her.

Goldstein: How are you?

Girlfriend: Fine. You?

Goldstein: Yeah good, you have a good night last night with the girls?

Girlfriend: [laughs nervously, still no idea what's going on] Yeah.

Goldstein: [mischievously] Just the girls was it? No boys? You didn't
speak to any boys?

Girlfriend: Er ... there was a few boys out. Yeah.

At this point, in a role reversal, instead of being on the side of a bloke who saw a text from a potential love suitor, Cundy decides that she should now dump Matt for going through her phone, saying "there's no trust". He talks directly to the girlfriend who is still on the phone.

Cundy: Matt's just phoned up OK? And he's phoned us for advice. He's gone through your phone. Do you know what, I'd get rid of him. He don't trust you. Get rid of Matt. He's been going through your phone. He's phoned up national radio.

Goldstein: He didn't say that.

Cundy: He's going through her phone. Na na na, he's tried to use your thumb print when you were asleep.

Girl: What is going on?

Cundy: Dump Matt.

Goldstein: No don't dump him.

Cundy: No, honestly, Matt's got to go. He's got to go.

Goldstein: Is Terry a boy?

Girlfriend: No. No, Terry's a girl. What's going on?

Goldstein: Why is she calling you at twenty past midnight?

Cundy: There's no trust. Get rid.

Goldstein: Why is she texting you at twenty past midnight?

Girlfriend: I don't know, I was asleep.

Cundy: Dump Matt. Hashtag dump Matt.

Matt joins back in and Goldstein and Cundy encourage each side to dump the other one first. The girlfriend disappears (presumably out of the room) and Matt reveals that she has previous, having cheated on him years ago. The girlfriend comes back on. An argument ensues and the final word goes to Jason with a great timely intervention.

Cundy: If you can't patch it up can I suggest talkSPORT Singles.com?

'The Midnight Train to Madness' has attracted some brilliant calls over the time, none more so than what is now known as the 'Schmeltz Herring' call. A boy (who must be a creative genius) who says he's called Kevin phones up and, as he is under 16, Goldstein asks him to get his mum or dad on to get permission. Kevin goes off to get his dad whose name apparently is Schmeltz Herring. And more apparently sounds just like Kevin putting on a slightly older voice. He is apparently a 'shopkeeper' but then it turns out he works in Tesco by the tills. Cundy then quizzes him about his wife and her name. "Hannah Herring," says Schmeltz.

Hannah comes on and sounds uncannily like Kevin putting on a very high-pitched voice. Says she's from South America, Brazil actually, and more specifically São Paulo. The call carries on in this vein and ends up being seven minutes of comedy gold. Whoever Kevin is, he deserves an Oscar and the call deserves the following full transcript and Goldstein's assessment that this is the finest call ever:

Goldstein: Let's speak to Kevin.
Kevin: Hello
Goldstein: Hi, Kev, you alright?
Kevin: Yeah, very good and you?
Goldstein: Are you home alone at the moment?
Kevin: Er, no.
Goldstein: Kev, how old are you?
Kevin: Er, 15.
Goldstein: 15. Legally you need permission from the bill payer, your mother or father. Are they in at the moment Kevin?
Kevin: Er, can I do my older brother?
Cundy: I'd rather you didn't. Rather, speak to your mum or dad.
Kevin: OK.
Goldstein: Are they asleep?
Kevin: No.

There's a bit of silence and shuffling at the other line as 'Kevin' goes off to find his 'mum' or 'dad'. Then Kevin's 'dad', who sounds uncannily like Kevin, just with a slightly deeper voice, comes on the line.

Kevin's 'Dad': Hello.

Goldstein: Hello, who's that?

Kevin's 'Dad': This is Schmeltz Herring [immediately both presenters are smelling a rat and smiling].

Goldstein: Is that not just Kevin putting on a deep voice?

Cundy: Are you Kevin's dad? Are you Kevin's dad?

Kevin's 'Dad': [pause] ... Yeah ... [in a very deep voice].

Cundy: What's Kevin like as a young boy, as a son?

Kevin's 'Dad': He's a very good boy

Goldstein: Are you both there? Are you both next to each other?

Kevin's 'Dad': No, he's just outside the room

Goldstein: Can you get him so he's next to you, Schmeltz Herring? [a bit of silence and shuffling in the background] Can you get him so he's next to you ... Is he there? Are you together?

Kevin's 'Dad': Er ... one second.

Goldstein: [aside to Cundy as by now their suspicions are fully aroused] Very bizarre this is. What was his name?

Cundy: [smiling] Schmeltz Herring.

Goldstein: Wow, how did he come up with that? Fair play. Schmeltz, are you there?

Cundy: Schmeltz or Kev.

Kevin's 'Dad': Hello.

Goldstein: Who's that?

Kevin's 'Dad': Schmeltz.

Goldstein: Is Kevin there? Kevin Herring?

Kevin's 'Dad': Yeah.

Goldstein: OK, so you're both next to each other, yeah?

Kevin's 'Dad': Yeah.

Goldstein: OK, just both at the same time count to ten for me, off you go.

Kevin: [in odd voice starts] One ... two ... [then says] Hello.

Goldstein: OK, both count to ten for me at the same time.

Kevin: [young voice] Hello.

Cundy: Alright, Kev.

Goldstein: Both count to ten. You and your dad, Schmeltz, can you count to ten for me both at the same time?

Kevin: I don't know my numbers.

Cundy: You don't know your numbers? What's your dad like, is he a good dad?

Kevin: Er, yeah, he's tops

Cundy: What's the best thing about your dad … Schmeltz?

Kevin: Um …

Goldstein: Is he German?

Kevin: What?

Goldstein: Where's he from with a name like Schmetlz?

Kevin: Holland.

Cundy: He's Dutch. That's fair enough.

Goldstein: What have you phoned up for then, Kev?

Kevin: Er …

Goldstein: Oh hold on, I just need permission from your dad. Put Schmeltz back on and we'll get permission.

Kevin: OK, one second.

Goldstein: Yeah, we'll wait.

After a pause, Kevin's 'Dad', Schmeltz, comes back on with an even deeper voice than before.

Kevin's 'Dad': Yeah, hello.

Goldstein: Yeah, Schmeltz. Hello, you OK?

Kevin's 'Dad': I give permission [in a deep authoritative voice].

Goldstein: How do you know I was going to say that?

Kevin's 'Dad': Kevin just told me.

Goldstein: OK, what do you do for a living, Schmeltz?

Kevin's 'Dad': I'm a shopkeeper

Goldstein: OK and what's in your shop?

Kevin's 'Dad': Oh, I'm in Tesco.

Goldstein: [looking at Cundy and laughing] You're in Tesco, you're not a shopkeeper, then, you work in Tesco?

Kevin's 'Dad': Er … up by the tills.

Goldstein: Ah, OK, up by the tills. You're on the checkout.

Cundy: Are you married, Schmeltz?

Kevin's 'Dad': Yes.

Cundy: What's your wife's name?

Kevin's 'Dad': Hannah.

Cundy: Hannah Herring. Hannah Herring. [now in uproar and laughing incredulously] Hannah Herring. Amazing. Hannah Herring. Can we speak to Hannah Herring?

[Goldstein in the background muttering, "Oh, please say yes".]

Kevin: Er, yeah.

Goldstein: Oh we can [excitedly], excellent stuff.

[Goldstein in the background saying "This is amazing".]

Cundy: We're speaking to all the Herrings. Hannah, Schmeltz and Kev.

Goldstein: Let's find out.

We hear some grumbling down the line and then duly on comes 'Hannah Herring' in a voice that's similar to Marge off *The Simpsons* but twice as high.

Hannah: [high-pitched] Hello.

Goldstein: Hannah?

Hannah: [high-pitched squeal] Yes.

Goldstein: [laughing now] How are you Hannah, are you good?

Hannah: Yes I am.

Goldstein: We were just talking to your husband.

Hannah: Oh that's nice.

Goldstein: Yeah. Eh, where are you from? You've got a different accent to him.

Hannah: Er ... South America.

Cundy: Oh whereabouts?

Hannah: Er ... Brazil.

Goldstein: Whereabouts in Brazil?

Hannah: São Paulo

Goldstein: Oh I know it well. Where, whereabouts?

Hannah: Er ... what? Where do you know?

Goldstein: Where are you from?

Hannah: Er ... er ... er ...

Goldstein: Long time ago you grew up there?

Hannah: Yes.

Goldstein: OK, your son has phoned up, Kevin Herring, and has asked to talk on the show but we need permission from either you or your husband.

Hannah: I give permission.

Goldstein: OK, what do you do for a living, Hannah?

Hannah: Er, nothing.

Cundy: OK, so your husband works on a till at Tesco's and you don't do anything.

Hannah: Yeah.

Cundy: I mean lazy, Hannah, lazy from you. Honestly he should get rid of you. If Schmeltz is listening, divorce Hannah, divorce her. Schmeltz?

Kevin's 'Dad': [grunts] Yeah.

Goldstein: That was quick. [laughing] The phone went back quick!

Cundy: She's lazy. She's lazy. Why don't you send her out to work? She could do something. She could stack shelves.

Kevin's 'Dad': She does the cooking.

Cundy: But she doesn't put any bread on the table.

At this point Goldstein and Cundy are cracking up with laughter as this call unfolds and Kevin keeps up the pretence. There's a bit of a silence and then they ask for Kevin to be put back on.

Kevin's 'Dad': OK, one second.

Goldstein: [mocking the voice which sounds like Harry Enfield's Kevin from *Kevin & Perry*] OK, Mrs Patterson. [laughing]

Kevin: Hello.

Goldstein: Hi, Kev, you alright?

Kevin: Yeah I'm good and you?

Goldstein: Yeah, Kev, we've run out of time I'm afraid.

Cundy: Weird family, mate.

Goldstein: What were you going to say, what did you phone up for?

Kevin: Er ... I missed a lesson.

Goldstein: You missed a lesson? Jason and I are back on tonight from 10pm. Will you phone back then?

Kevin: [Ums and ahs, and then says] No

[Cundy and Goldstein erupt in fits of laughter.]

Goldstein: Fair enough, Kev. You tell us straight, Kev, I like it. Good work. Kev, you might just be my favourite caller to the show ... ever.

Kevin: OK.

Goldstein: I might just want to hear Kev's story. [Looking at producer who's signalling they're running out of time] Kev, phone back tonight, please. And we'll speak to the rest of the Herrings again. Will you promise me that?

Kevin: No.

Both presenters collapse into laughter and finish the call by getting the rest of the Schmeltz family back on. Schmeltz sounding even more like a deep-voiced Kevin and Hannah even more like a high-pitched Marge.

Callers. You can't live with 'em, you can't live without 'em.

'CLIPS OF THE WEEK'

The Top 20 All-Time Greats

#5

Sometimes Alan Brazil goes a bit too colloquial when he gets talking about stuff up in Glasgow. Here, Neil Warnock unceremoniously pulls him back on track.

Alan: I was going to say it's a Glasgow derby but St Mirren are up in Paisley now, aren't they? I say now, they've always been out there. In fact, that is probably closer to Ibrox than Parkhead, I think. Well, Love Street used to be right up from Glasgow airport, so it was nothing – just a flick from Ibrox to Love Street. I don't know where St Mirren Park is now. Someone will text or email me … Oh six miles, is it? So that would be … would that be … I was going to say that would closer. I don't know. Parkhead's not that far from Ibrox …

Neil: Listen, I'm not really bothered, Alan. Can we move on?

Chapter 15

Big Names, Big Egos, Big Trouble

talkSPORT – the very name of the station suggests opinion and debate. And that's never in short supply. Away from the arguments and calls from the listeners, the presenters are never averse to getting stuck into each other and to the sports stars occasionally. Some belting rows have erupted on air over the last 20 years because you have opinionated presenters who are very rarely backward when it comes to going for-wards in a verbal joust.

One of the most famous of these was when then Liverpool player Jamie Carragher was listening to the station as Durham and Micky Quinn discussed his early retirement from international football. England were in the middle of a difficult qualifying campaign and Durham felt Carragher was letting the team down but also that, rather than fighting for his place in the team, he had bottled it. The phone lines lit up for an hour and Durham repeatedly called Carragher a bottler. Carragher then phoned the studios and spoke to fellow Scouser Micky Quinn as the station had gone to a break. "What is that dickhead going on about me being a bottle job? I'll get his arse to the training ground and we'll see who is a bottle job." Quinn said to Carragher he should come on the show, but couldn't swear. Durham got back in the studio and thought "Oh s**t" but as he says, "It's easy just to sit there talking about someone when they are not there. But when they confront you, you've got to learn to deal with that." After the red on-air light flicked on the following exchange took place:

Durham: Someone has said, if Jamie Carragher called you up, what would you say to him? Well, we'll find out because Jamie has called up. How are you doing?"

Carragher: Yeah, I'm alright. I'm just on my way from training and listening to your show this afternoon, normally a good show until you started rabbiting on about me being a bit of a bottler. It'll be interesting to see if you've got any bottle and come down to Anfield or Melwood and say it to me and we'll see what happens.

Durham: I'd say it to your face and I'll say it to you now.

Carragher: Oh would ya, mate? Tell you what, come down to Anfield for a Champions League game or whatever then we'll see then won't we?

Durham: Yeah we will.

Carragher: You can say other players are better than me, everyone's entitled to their opinion, but don't ever call me a bottler in front of thousands of people that are listening!

Durham: So why are you thinking about quitting international football?

Carragher: Because there's that many people who he [then England manager Steve McClaren] has played ahead of me. It's a game of opinions but when you're at my age, they're all younger than me and they're all going to improve which maybe I won't at that age. I played in a Champions League final. There's not much more you can do in football. He [McClaren] played Ledley King who is a top player but he's been injured all season so how would you feel in my situation, what would you do?

Durham: I'd feel like proving myself and getting a stomach for the fight going and going for it.

Carragher: Proving yourself? I'm 29 and I've been doing it for eight years and obviously I haven't proved it enough. So it's not going to change now is it? It's not as if I just got in the squad and jumped out. So when you talk about proving yourself ... And who's the other fella going, "Oh, he's probably got his contract at Liverpool worth a hundred grand a week". Who's he?

Durham: He reads our sports news bulletins [it was Andrew McKenna].

Carragher: Is that ...

Durham: Hang on, Jamie, he's a football fan. An England fan who's entitled to his opinion.

Carragher: None of yous are more of a football fan than me so don't try and make out that I'm more interested in the money than playing football.

The call lasted more than ten minutes. Carragher was excellent, managed to not lose his temper or swear, and finished the call by repeating his rather challenging 'invitation' for Durham to get up to Liverpool. The call hit the nationals, and Durham and Quinn did accept the 'invitation', going up to Liverpool to do a special broadcast which would coincide with the launch of Carragher's book. They shook hands for the first time since 'Bottlergate', with Carragher guesting on the show for an hour. They even posed for photos for the *Liverpool Echo*, both with boxing gloves on. Since then the pair have actually stayed in touch with Carragher writing the foreword for Durham's 2013 book *Is He All That? Great Football Myths Shattered.*

However, some on-air exchanges do not end so amicably.

It's not often that Chris Eubank Sr is left lost for words. But that's what happened when he was confronted by Joey Barton on *The Alan Brazil Sports Breakfast*, with the former Manchester City and Newcastle midfielder keen to get to the bottom of why Eubank's son, Chris Eubank Jr, was fighting on a relatively obscure TV channel:

Barton: My biggest disappointment is I almost missed Chris Jr's fight [at the weekend] because it was stuck away on ITV Box Office, which I didn't even know existed. He's the kind of fighter which I think if he's fighting, when I watched yourself fight Chris, it was on ITV, but it was on the normal TV, it didn't have pay-per-view. These big fights with big British boxers, we've got to get them back on easy to view sources.

Eubank: Remind me of your name again, sir.

Barton: Joey Barton my name is, mate.

Eubank: Joey?

Barton: Yeah.

Eubank: You'll get over it.

Brazil: Ha! Get over it.

Barton: Get over what?

Eubank: Over not, or nearly, missing him fight.

Barton: No, I managed to catch it. I'm just saying I'd like to see him fight. I've seen him a few times but I'd like to see him now, when you're saying he's in the prime of his career, I want to see him on the big channels.

Eubank: The world is what it is today and we have to go with the times. And the advanced technological era in which we live, you have to buy the fight on pay-per-view, and I don't see why not. The man has spent 14 years in a gymnasium and he's asking you for £10, two beers. I'm sorry, pay the money or don't.

Barton: That's fair enough, I'm just saying it's a shame he can't build a huge fan base because if he was on terrestrial TV, or if he was on Sky, a lot of people would be more aware of him. You look at the likes of Callum Smith, George Groves, Carl Froch selling out Wembley, Anthony Joshua selling out Wembley, you know, he doesn't have the same pull because he's stuffed away on ITV pay-per-view.

Eubank: No, he's not stuffed away.

Barton: Well, I'm a boxing fan and I didn't know he was fighting that night. I knew Anthony Crolla was fighting that night, and I knew there was another domestic clash that night, but I didn't know he was even fighting because there was no real publicity about it. Now are you getting a fair shake in the media, are you getting enough exposure, are you getting enough publicity?

[Silence]

Brazil: Oh, he's gone, he's gone.

Barton: He's not happy with me line of questioning it seems.

Joey Barton upsetting someone? Surely not.

One man seldom lost for words is drive-time host Adrian Durham. People don't always agree with what he says, but he has strong opinions and he's not afraid to air them. And even the fact people accuse him of "only saying this stuff to get calls" doesn't bother him.

"Of course it doesn't," he said. "I'm just a very opinionated person, especially about sport. If others aren't so opinionated, that's up to them. The show is about encouraging people to express opinions. But nobody forces anyone to call in. What's wrong with someone speaking up and having a view? The critics sometimes assume that all callers must be inferior to them simply because they pick up a phone. It's a superiority complex they cannot substantiate I'm afraid. I spoke to someone from the BBC recently who said he didn't like phone-ins because he didn't care what a random fan had to say. I couldn't quite understand why fans should be excluded from the conversation."

Another stick always used to hit Durham with is that he has an agenda against Arsenal – despite the fact his wife supports them! But it's true the north London giants are often in his cross-hairs. Take his views on why Arsenal's 'Invincibles' side of 2003/04 are nothing more than a myth:

"OK, here are the facts shattering the myth that the Arsenal Invincibles were that special. First of all, they got 90 points. Chelsea's champions got 95 the following season, so who was better? Arsenal's Invincibles lost crucial games that season. They lost Champions League group-stage games to Inter Milan and Dynamo Kiev, they lost home and away to Middlesbrough in the semi-final of the League Cup – they put out a decent side Arsenal, as well – they lost to Man United in the FA Cup. Not exactly Invincible then, were they?

"The most painful defeat, though, was second leg Champions League quarter-final to Claudio Ranieri's Chelsea. Wayne Bridge scored the winner to knock Arsenal out at Highbury. Well, that defeat opened the door for Mourinho to win the Champions League with Porto, get the Chelsea job and keep Arsène Wenger in his pocket for years. Now, had Wenger managed his squad better he'd have won that second leg versus

Chelsea. But he was obsessed with going unbeaten ... so obsessed he didn't even try to win games as the season came to an end. He was happy to draw, four draws out of the last six, including home to Birmingham.

"Well, throw in the Pires dive at home to Portsmouth to steal an undeserved draw – Arsenal's Invincibles actually cheated – and the bullying of Van Nistelrooy before, during and after his penalty miss in the goalless draw in September at Man United. Then add on the fact you can go unbeaten and get relegated – 38 draws equals 38 points and you're going to go down with that – and you'll realise how anyone saying the so-called Invincibles were the best ever has lost their mind completely. It's desperation. Chelsea in 2004/05 got more points.

"The most significant moment of that season was the Champions League defeat to Chelsea and it let José in to lord it over Wenger. And it meant Arsenal gave Chelsea that prize of first London club to win the Champions League years later. That's why my friends, and you cannot disagree with any of that, the Invincibles were a myth."

Maybe he thinks you cannot disagree with any of that, but one man certainly does have an alternative view when it comes to the regularly posed question of which team was better: Arsenal's Invincibles or Manchester United's treble winners of 1999. And that man is Durham's sometime co-host on *Drive*, the equally outspoken Piers Morgan.

Here is the pair debating the point in January 2019:

Morgan: The Invincibles did something that was completely unique, which no team is ever likely to replicate and in a hundred years' time we will still be talking about that Arsenal Invincibles team with a magic to it. I don't think you get that from winning a Champions League.

Durham: The problem you've got is that only Arsenal fans really care about the Invincibles tag. Nobody else really values it. Arsenal only value it because they can't shout about the Champions League or the treble, or they can't even shout about being back-to-back title winners.

Morgan: You don't think fans of other Premier League teams want to go a season unbeaten? Don't be ridiculous.

Durham: I think they want to win the title. Chelsea did it with five more points the next year. That was better.

Morgan: Look at the reaction of [Manchester] City fans and Liverpool fans [this season] when they lose a game in the Premier League and realise they can't replicate it. They know how difficult it is.

Durham: Do you know what the most painful thing for you though is? When you lost to Chelsea in that quarter-final, to a Wayne Bridge goal; they then lost to Monaco who then lost to Porto. What an easy route to win the Champions League title by the way. And what happened after that? [José] Mourinho, after having won the Champions League, then got the Chelsea job, which he wouldn't have got if Arsenal had beaten Porto in the final and he completely destroyed [Arsène] Wenger's legacy.

Morgan: None of that I disagree with you about. But in terms of you trying to trivialise the Invincibles and trying to diminish what they achieved and try to bring in the '99 United team, which got incredibly lucky with that [Ryan] Giggs goal (in the FA Cup semi-final). It was incredibly lucky at the Nou Camp, because I was there.

Durham: Were they lucky when [Dennis] Bergkamp missed a penalty?

Morgan: Well, Bergkamp should never have taken a penalty, he was no good at penalties.

"I'd have to say I thoroughly enjoy working with Piers," says Durham. "He's opinionated and loves it when I challenge him. On air he's an opinionated loudmouth. Off air he's charming and good company. We have a lot in common."

And while Durham may love baiting Gooners, he knows where to draw the line from a professional standpoint, as was evidenced following an exchange that occurred around the time 'The Daily Arsenal' feature became a regular on his drive-time show.

He says: "The beginning of the end of the Wenger years led to a regular stream of stories of Arsenal calamities. It was happening way too frequently to ignore so the idea stemmed from the long slow painful end of Arsène Wenger at Arsenal Football Club. The clincher was an article I wrote for the talkSPORT website which was forensically researched, legally sound, and full of facts, quotes and details about Jack Wilshere's lengthy lay-off when he missed the whole of the 2011/12 season.

"Arsenal Football Club demanded the right to reply, and asked if their PR could come on and address my points. He was given the option of a live or pre-recorded interview on the phone and he chose the latter. We had barely got started when he made a claim that I easily proved incorrect with quotes from Wilshere and Wenger. It stopped him in his tracks, and he stumbled over his words, and said that he wanted to stop the interview. So I stopped, and said goodbye, he put the phone down, and we were left with a tape of a representative of Arsenal FC making himself look a bit foolish. The question was – should we run it on air? We would have been well within our rights to do that but chose not to. The view was that Arsenal FC had seriously underestimated talkSPORT, but to belittle the club in such a way would be unfair. So we didn't run it."

Despite the claims of his anti-Arsenal bias, the truth is Durham is quite happy to have a go at anyone and anything when he thinks it's the right thing to do. He's even been known to rant and rave about his beloved Peterborough United.

The listeners love it when the presenters go nuts about stuff. After all, everyone listening is a fan, so it makes sense that those behind the microphones are also fans. And they're equally as passionate as the men, women and children who fill the stadiums up and down the country each week.

Take Joey Barton, for example, a lifelong Everton fan who is desperate to see his boyhood club do well. And he was very unhappy with the appointment of David Unsworth as caretaker manager following the sacking of Ronald Koeman in October 2017. What he had to say on talkSPORT about it ended up creating a storm in the press and his comments were all over the back pages – it was explosive stuff. He claimed Unsworth was "a glorified PE teacher" who "makes Alan Brazil look like an athlete". He predicted Everton would be relegated if Unsworth remained manager.

This sparked a war of words with former Crystal Palace chairman Simon Jordan, who called Barton's words a "disgrace". Describing him as "a bang average Premier League player", Jordan said that he would pick Unsworth over aspiring manager Barton any day. Barton's response was to label Jordan "a failed footballer" who "clearly doesn't know an awful lot about the game".

All great stuff, and there was even more to come when Barton, who had advocated Sean Dyche, Sam Allardyce and David Moyes as all being better qualified for the Goodison job than Unsworth, clashed with Jim White on the same topic:

White: Is there a bit of history between you and David Unsworth?

Barton: Absolutely not, other than that I had to endure watching him play [for Everton] for long periods. It was abysmal.

White: It sounds as if there is. I mean, I've got to say, I think he's trying his very best, he's in there on an interim basis.

Barton: But he's chirping himself up for the job, Jim. He's saying, "I'm the man, I can take Everton on".

White: Clearly there's history between you and him. To be honest I agree with you and some of the names you've mentioned, Dyche. I think Marco Silva would be a great candidate with all due respect to Watford, and with all due respect to Burnley, they are bound to be shortlisted, I'm sure of that. Sam Allardyce as well.

Barton: Would you give Unsworth the job?

White: It's not down to me.

Barton: I'm asking you, would you give Unsworth the job?

[This was left unanswered.]

White: There is clearly history between Joey and David Unsworth.

Barton: I've never had a conversation with David Unsworth. There is no history at all. I'm telling you as a football man who knows football, if you appoint him it's only going to get worse, it's not going to get better. Look, Unsworth has had two games in charge. The tactics and the game plan were incorrect. He's lost both of his games.

White: Did you see the game at Stamford Bridge the other night? He went about that absolutely brilliantly.

Barton: But they lost the game.

White and Barton went on to row further about what White perceived as a personal insult to Unsworth by calling him overweight,
a point which Barton continued to defend vigorously:

Barton: Obviously you've got to have the requisite skill but it's important as the leader of a group of athletes that you set the right
tone. If you don't have the self-discipline to set the right example
from the top then how can you demand that players are fit, that
they're in shape and they run hard when you aren't yourself?

White: How would you feel if you were David Unsworth this morning and he turns his radio on in his car?

Barton: Slightly body conscious?

That sort of passion jumps out of the speakers and there was certainly no more passionate man in the office than Stan Collymore,
and he was particularly vociferous about his beloved Aston
Villa. Collymore is a broadcaster who says it as he sees it with no
sitting on any fence. He is passionate and no more so than when
Villa's relegation from the Premier League was confirmed in
April 2016. This came just weeks after Joleon Lescott had accidentally 'pocket tweeted' a picture of his expensive sports car.
Collymore couldn't disguise his rage, particularly as Lescott
had once again taken to social media to describe suffering the
drop as a "weight off the shoulders". This is how Collymore
reacted on his *Call Collymore* show:

"I would love Joleon [Lescott], or any other Villa player to
call me up. In all seriousness, I'd like any Villa player, particularly Joleon Lescott, to come on and first explain about the
non-tweeting tweeting car [picture].

"This is a senior international footballer in the modern era.
'Now confirmed, maybe it's a weight off the shoulders.' Why is it
a weight off the shoulders? It should hang on your shoulders in
Dubai, in Marbs [Marbella], with the gold bottle with the ace of
spades on it when you and Gabby [Agbonlahor] and Leandro
[Bacuna] are all going to be laughing, when your agents go and
tout you to other football clubs. That's where the weight of the
world should be, on your shoulders.

"And also the Villa staff. There's the real weight on their shoulders, the people that are getting made redundant, that have been there for 20 years, who don't know where the next pay cheque might come from, that's what the performances have done. Now confirmed, maybe it's a weight off the shoulders and we can give these fans what they deserve, some performances.

"Now I was crap at Villa, I was crap. Considering where I'd come from at Liverpool, and particularly before that at Nottingham Forest, I was crap. But I was crap having played in every game for a club winning a record amount of games – I think it was 11 or 12 games. I was crap scoring in the quarter-final of a European club competition and firmly top half of the table, and I was crap at Aston Villa. So what does that make you, Joleon? And Leandro? And many of the other players that were wearing yellow today, and that was the most apt colour those Aston Villa players could have worn. The colour yellow. Go and check out what it actually means. You have a big yellow stripe running through every single one of you. You've all talked the talk all year about staying up, wanting to stay up, wanting to keep the club up, and none of you have done it.

"I saw Bacuna at Birmingham Airport at six o'clock in the morning, having been beaten at Southampton, going around on his hoverboard. You're a disgrace! Joleon Lescott, you've won [trophies] and hid behind players like [David] Silva and [Sergio] Aguero. When it mattered today with your hometown club that you profess to support, you couldn't be as crap as me and keep us in the top half of the table or play in Europe, you've helped them go down.

"So if you're listening, Joleon, if you're listening, Micah [Richards], if you're listening, Brad [Guzan], if you're listening, Leandro [Bacuna], give us a call and instead of tweeting and putting on Instagram that Collymore's this and Collymore's that, come and tell us about your season and about the weight of the world on your shoulders."

Maybe having the weight of the world on their shoulders was what was affecting the Scotland national team as their 2-2 draw in a World Cup qualifier in Slovenia in October 2017 meant they missed out on a place in the play-offs and the chance to qualify for a major finals for the first time in 20 years. Not that his players would have been able to carry the weight of the world on their shoulders as manager Gordon Strachan bizarrely blamed genetics for the failure, claiming his squad was simply too small to compete with bigger, strong, taller sides. A kind of reverse argument on the playground classic of "my dad's bigger than your dad". Anyway, it was a view that caused a difference of opinion among talkSPORT's two fiery Scots, Alan Brazil and Jim White:

Brazil: I must admit, I'm backing Gordon to stay.

White: Why?

Brazil: Because I am. I think Gordon's as good as what there is out there at the moment.

White: I like Gordon Strachan a lot, I text him a lot, we chat a lot, but at the end of the day ... another failure. So, what happens in a situation like that? Change it. It has to be changed. "Genetics. We're not athletic enough. They're bigger than us. They jump higher than us. We don't jump higher than them." I'm sorry. I mean, I am sorry. I remember your time, when you played, 1982, 1986, I mean, fantastic players. Genetically we were OK. Gordon Strachan was genetically good enough to score against West Germany in the 1986 [World Cup] finals. Was Billy Bremner good enough?

Brazil: Yeah. Game's moved on, but yeah, you're right. Listen, I wouldn't have said what Gordon said about "we're too small", I wouldn't have done.

White: Here's a situation. We are not going to another major finals and we haven't done since 1998.

Brazil: We haven't got the players.

The discussion then moved on to the Scotland management job.

White: Listen, get the names in, Alan. This is what it should be about this morning. I'll tell you who sat in this studio the other day and off-mic said: "Yeah, but it would be a fantastic job, but I mean I don't know Scotland ..."

Brazil: Who?

White: Big Sam [Allardyce]

[Brazil snorts]

Barton: If, right, if Big Sam says: "I'll take it," would you swap Strachan for Big Sam?

Brazil: Umm ... if Sam ... [grunting noise]... I like Sam. I'm a big fan of Sam and I think Sam's an organiser and he will get it right.

White: Give us an answer: yes or no?

Brazil: I'm happy with Gordon at the moment.

White: OH MY GOD!

One man who did lose his job, in March 2019, was West Bromwich Albion manger Darren Moore, even though the Baggies were sitting fourth in the Championship at the time. And that prompted a furious Adrian Durham to air some very uncompromising views on the dismissal:

"I'm not saying anyone involved in making this decision is in any way racist. It's an issue that deserves deep thinking, not knee-jerk nonsense.

"I believe in their mind's eye, nobody could picture Darren Moore being so successful at West Brom because there are so few black managers who have been successful – because there are so few black managers in English football.

"All they see is white managers lifting trophies season after season, therefore there is a subliminal unconscious mindset that only white is successful.

"This is going to be a hard thing for a lot of people to take on board, but over the last ten years only two black managers have been successful in terms of promotion. The West Brom board's statement said Moore had 'failed to achieve consistency of form and results'. West Brom have won eight of their last ten away games! How can he be sacked with that run?

"They're talking rubbish. My opinion was they didn't want to appoint him in the first place, but he was so good at the end of last season that they had to appoint him. So at the first sign of someone moaning, they've sacked him, and they could not wait to sack him.

"Alan Pardew came in [after Pulis], didn't win any of his first eight games and oversaw a relentless charge towards relegation and took his players on a jolly to Spain when they nicked a taxi and got drunk until the early hours. There were all sorts of unprofessional allegations under Pardew and he STILL didn't get the sack after that.

"It took a run of eight defeats on the trot when they were ten points adrift [of safety] with six games left when they finally sacked Alan Pardew.

"And yet this guy, Darren Moore, the guy whose tactical brilliance saw them beat Spurs, win away at Manchester United, get a draw against a Liverpool side that was rampant at the time. His side beat Marcelo Bielsa's Leeds 4-1. They won at Norwich. They won at Sheffield United. They put seven past QPR. He's been sacked after two defeats and a draw.

"We will never know if West Brom would have got promoted under Darren Moore. It took months to sack the two white managers who were laying the foundations for CERTAIN relegation and yet the black manager who won more than half his league games in charge of West Brom is sacked after a run of two defeats and a draw. It's the most disgusting sacking of recent times. It's incredibly damaging to the fight for more respect and opportunity for black coaches and managers in English football and the decision makers at West Brom should be ashamed of themselves.

"The managerial revolving door does apply to everyone, I get that, but it does seem to speed up for black managers, doesn't it? Darren Moore's sacking is massively, massively out of order."

It's not only talkSPORT presenters who are passionate defenders of their views. Sometimes the sports stars being interviewed also feel they need to make their voice heard if they feel they've been treated unfairly, as was the case when Tony Bellew appeared on the Colin Murray show to talk about his upcoming fight with Nathan Cleverly. All was going well until boxing journalist and Murray's co-host on the day Steve Bunce chipped in:

Murray: Is it fair to say, while there would be fights after for the loser of this fight, that in terms of any real world-level ambition ...

Bellew: No, no, it's all over. It's done with.

Murray: That means it's everything, it's your whole career in one night.

Bellew: There you go, you just hit the nail on the head. Exactly that, that's where it's going.

Bunce: Well, Tony, what about if you beat ...

Bellew: Steve, in all honesty, mate, I'm not gonna answer your questions. All you've done is slate me since I left where I left, so I'll be totally honest with you, I'm not gonna answer your questions. What you said about me after the Stevenson fight was a disgrace. Someone who's known me since I was a kid wearing an amateur vest should have known better. Don't ask me questions, I've got no intentions of answering them. I should have told you when I saw you in Belfast but I didn't get the chance to get off the radio so I'm telling you now, don't you ask me a question cos you're gonna get an answer you don't like. You cannot call me. You said some things about me on the radio and on your stupid show about I'm willing to die in the ring. I'll say what I want, Steve, about boxing and do you know why I can? Because I fight. You talk about it and watch it. I do it, I fight. I drag myself off the floor, I get up from knockdowns, I'm the one who fights through cuts, through broken hands, not you, so don't call me personally on your stupid shows and the things you say. I've spoken enough to you.

Bunce: Well, I was going to ask a nice question.

Bellew: Yeah, well I'm not bothered about your nice question.

That was a case of something Bunce said that upset Bellew coming back to bite him and there are occasions, rare though they are, when talkSPORT's men behind the microphones probably wished they had kept their mouth shut. One such occasion occurred during the 2013/14 season and left Andy Goldstein and Jason Cundy feeling a bit light-headed.

The catalyst for this had been a call on the eve of the season when a gentleman rang in to promote Liverpool's chances of finishing in the top four. Now, given that they had finished seventh the previous season and it looked as though Luis Suárez would be leaving having been banned for ten matches for biting Chelsea's Branislav Ivanović, the *Sports Bar* duo were pretty confident in suggesting the Anfield club would fall short of that target. So confident, in fact, they agreed to have their heads shaved if the then Liverpool manager Brendan Rodgers confounded the odds.

And so it was in May 2014, with Liverpool having finished second, that Joanne Beckham, sister of former England captain David, arrived in the studio armed with a pair of clippers.

Cundy says: "As the season went on, we started to realise that we were in a bit of trouble. And we said whatever position Liverpool finish in, we'll cut our hair accordingly. Ideally, I wouldn't have had it done. I'm losing it as it is, so every little hair I have I treasure! But if there's one time of year to have that sort of haircut, it's the summer."

Goldstein, who at the time had a magnificent mane of hair, admitted it was the worst bet he'd ever lost. "I started growing a beard as I knew I was having it done. I had this weird thing where other people with skinheads were acknowledging me when I walked past them. I felt like I was part of a little group."

And to add insult to injury, Brendan Rodgers also joined them on air by phone as they had their haircuts.

The worst bust-ups on air are often between presenters and journalists. By definition, to be a journalist, or to be a talkSPORT presenter, you've probably got strong points of view and are not afraid to air them. And definitely not shy away from confrontation, which *The Sun*'s Neil Custis doesn't. He managed to get into a row on air with the mild-mannered Paul Hawksbee and Andy Jacobs when he was asked on the show to discuss the Louis van Gaal sacking shortly after Manchester United had won the FA Cup final. The sense was that there had been a concerted campaign from within Manchester United to brief against Van Gaal, with stories appearing highlighting things that had been going on within the club, seemingly in quick succession. A rather tetchy discussion ensued as Paul queried why these were all coming out now and Custis robustly defended what he put down to good journalism, going and getting stories:

Custis: This is all a myth. The idea that Man United briefed that LVG was getting the sack within minutes of lifting the cup is totally and utterly wrong. Nobody at Manchester United did this. One person put out a tweet saying he was set to be sacked. Now we've known that for five months. I've been reporting that for five months. So because somebody from the BBC said he was set to be sacked everyone's gone crazy and said Manchester United have been briefing this. How on earth could they do it? They didn't. They didn't. They simply didn't and Manchester United don't operate that way ...

Paul: [interrupting] So has everybody been sitting on this information, Neil?

Custis: No. No. No, let me finish. In the same way that with Davy Moyes when me and my colleagues announced that he was going to get the sack that was just journalists doing their job. It wasn't Manchester United briefing us that they were going to do that. You know people go out there and get stories and put them in newspapers. It doesn't mean that Manchester United are announcing this or being all Machiavellian or something like that, that's just what we do.

Paul: All this information that we've read in our papers today and in the last 36 hours everybody's been sitting on that until the moment everybody knew ...

Custis: No, no, no, no. Nobody's been sitting on anything because I and my colleagues have been reporting this for months. We've been saying LVG's on his way out. I've been saying that there was contact with Mourinho in December and he's been told to just sit tight, you know, don't accept another job, "You're going to get it".

Paul: OK, what about all these stories about players receiving emails they didn't read and would leave their phones on because there was some sort of check on whether they did and players who didn't know how to boil eggs. All this crackpot stuff that's suddenly come out in the last 36 hours. Where's that all come from in the last 36 hours.

Custis: Why do you call it crackpot?

Paul: Well you know they're odd stories. Whether Matteo Darmian or Marcus Rashford can cook an egg or not is neither here nor there. It's not necessarily LVG's fault.

Custis: So why's it not a story? Why are you asking me about it if it's not a story?

Paul: No. I'm not saying ... I'm not saying it isn't a story.

Custis: Why do you get journalists on your radio show and then criticise what they do?

Paul: I'm not criticising.

Andy: [stepping into the conversation] We're not criticising. That's a very strange attitude to take. I wasn't criticising you at all.

Custis: Why do you call it crackpot?"

Andy: Well, it's just a term. It's just a terminology. It's a funny story isn't it?

Custis: It's not a crackpot story.

Andy: It's a mad story isn't it?

Custis: It's a story ... It's a story ... It's a story.

Andy: What and stories can never have any description on them? They can't be called a mad story or a fun story or a crackpot story? It's just everything's just a story?

Custis: You called it crackpot to suggest that it's stupid to write it.

Andy & Paul: No that's not, it's not what it means.

Andy: Oh this conversation's pointless, really.

Paul: [exasperated] I don't know where we got to this stage.

Andy: It's ridiculous, I don't know why you've come on with this attitude. It's crazy.

Custis: I've not come on with ...

Andy: [to producer] Oh get rid of him.

The conversation continued though and Custis apologised "if I was stroppy earlier on" but explained that he was getting annoyed at criticism of the media in general for basically doing their jobs. Andy and Paul also made it clear that they'd been speculating as well and were part of the media. The conversation continued in a more 'amicable' fashion and ended on a laugh about a bet that Custis had with LVG. "That escalated quickly" said Paul at the end of the interview.

Alongside the rants and the arguments that happen among the presenters on air, there is also the brilliance when they, as fans, simply express and capture the mood of the nation, as Mark Saggers did as England exited Russia 2018.

'CLIPS OF THE WEEK'

The Top 20 All-Time Greats

#4

It's one thing talking on the radio, but it's an entirely different thing reading out things on the radio ... like emails. Here's Ronnie Irani having issues:

Irani: Got a great text here from Simon, saying I'm in Rotterdam at my ma and pa's house listening to your fantastic show ...

Brazil: No, really? Rotterdam?

Irani: Is there any chance you can give a discreet mention to Philip and Dorothy in Rotter ... oh no ... Rotherham.

Chapter 16

Hawksbee and Jacobs Take Vodka-Fuelled Night-Train Journey at Russia 2018

"There is no shame in this. There is absolutely no shame. You come back to England with your heads held high. You did more than we thought.

"We gave you the opportunity just to feel your way. You did brilliantly to come back and win it in the last minute against Tunisia, you put Panama away, which England sides in the past may not have done. You changed things for the Belgium game, which could have gone either way.

"You got rid of the penalty hoodoo when it came to Colombia and gave us a night none of us will ever forget. Then you did Sweden and it was comfortable, even though you were tired, to a man.

"Then you still find enough to come back here [to Moscow] and really worry this hardened Croatia team, to see [Kieran] Trippier score a magnificent free kick after just five minutes and for an hour to believe with everybody that we could reach a final against France.

"It wasn't to be and it might not be for some time. But there will be other chances and other opportunities as not just this young England squad grow and move forward, but those below them who are not only versed at the highest level of European and world football, but also winning at tournaments.

"John Stones has grown up at this tournament, Kieran Trippier is an outstanding player, Danny Rose, you just have to believe in yourself again. Danny, we're with you, you've never let anybody down. You came through cruel injury. It wasn't easy but you gave everything, particularly when you came on at two half-times of extra-time. And the rest of you, led by Harry Kane, well done. Jordan Pickford is an outstanding goalkeeper, Harry Maguire has basically got rid of any doubters, and it's not just the players on the pitch, it's the squad members as well.

"England are real once more. The fans are in tears, the team are in tears, but you've got everything to be proud of."

Those were the words of Mark Saggers as England bowed out of the World Cup in Russia in 2018. Two years after he eviscerated Roy Hodgson and his underperforming flops in Nice, the talkSPORT host was singing the praises of Gareth Southgate's young side that had won the hearts and minds of the nation.

"None of those rants I've done [at tournaments] have been thought out or planned," says Saggers. "They weren't written down, they were in the moment. What I've learned at talkSPORT is it goes back to my radio roots – a microphone and you. There might still be one more in me, but I don't know when."

It was a sad way for the tournament to end for the Three Lions, but it was one that had been memorable for talkSPORT in many ways. A little like Brazil four years earlier, there had been lots of scare stories in the build-up to the tournament, although understandably given the shocking violence that had been perpetrated by the Russian fans in France at Euro 2016. But the reality was things passed off largely without incident and the station produced brilliant content and superb match coverage.

"I went out twice to Russia and it was right up there. I really enjoyed it. Especially St Petersburg. For me it was absolutely sensational. The people were lovely, the whole place was good fun. It's what makes a tournament when the mix of people all get on," says Darren Gough.

As always, there were plenty of mix-ups and mishaps along the way, usually involving the 'holy trinity' – food, lodgings and transport. And, just as in Brazil in 2014 and France in 2016, Paul Hawksbee and Andy Jacobs were right in the thick of it.

Let's start with the grub. By now, it's been well established that Jacobs is unapologetically an enormous food snob and was generally less than impressed with the fare on offer in most places in Russia. But, as has also been established, he loves the recommendation of a guidebook and was confident he had found the perfect place to dine in Kaliningrad.

Insisting it was a mere 20-minute walk from where they were staying to the restaurant, he, Hawksbee and producer John Cadigan set off. Almost inevitably, 20 minutes became 30, and then 40, while the app they were using for directions claimed they were still another 40 minutes from their destination.

The heat was rising, not just from the boiling late-afternoon sun but also from Jacobs' slightly disgruntled and wearying colleagues. The fears were growing that this was turning into another 'Uruguayan sandwich'. Jacobs was insisting everything would be fine: "You're going to love it, it's on the river, the food's going to be fantastic." Hawksbee meanwhile was content "as long as I can have a cold beer when we get there".

They did eventually arrive and the place was indeed very grand, considerably more so than they had imagined, and they were seated in what could only be described as thrones. There was no one else in there apart from a couple of people who were in something called 'Fish Club', and what happens in Fish Club stays in Fish Club. But so far, so good.

The waitress duly arrived to take their drinks order and Andy chose a nice white wine, producer John was having a day off the booze so ordered a water and a thirsty Paul asked for a beer, only to be told: "No, we don't sell beer." At this point, Andy's face was a picture – a picture of horror, as for the final ten minutes or so of what had turned out to be a 70-minute walk Paul had been jokingly muttering, "I bet when we get there they won't even have beer". He was not best pleased to have been proved right.

And he wasn't overly chuffed when, having taken a while to peruse the extensive menu, he opted for scallops, only to be informed they didn't have any of those either! Add to the picture of doom the England fans who greeted them with 'Nescafe hand-shakes' having spotted them through the window sitting on their thrones and it made for an uncomfortable dining experience. On the plus side, however, the food was, by all accounts, the best they had in the country.

In terms of security, many of the pre-tournament safety brief-ings had involved topics such as being wary about using mobile phones in public and avoiding eye contact in the street in case you were attacked. But what no one had warned the talkSPORT team about was the appalling lack of road sense among the locals, so much so that people were living in constant fear of being involved in some kind of horrendous motor accident.

And that brings us to 'Lewis Warnock', talkSPORT's fixer and driver in Sochi, so named because he looked like Neil Warnock and drove like Lewis Hamilton. He looked like the kind of guy who would have been in the KGB 20 years ago. He could barely speak a word of English and he was a lunatic.

One day he was driving along a coastal road, weaving in and out of traffic as usual, with Hawksbee and Jacobs in the back along with producer John Cadigan, and football editor David Walker in the front. At one point they were in a tunnel and on one side was a massive articulated lorry, and on the other side was a very solid, very unforgiving concrete wall. And 'Lewis' spotted a gap. Walker says: "He just thought, 'I can make this' and he banged his foot down and went down the inside of this lorry. We were all thinking, 'Christ, we're not going to make it'. It was like something out of a Michael Bay movie.

"And then a few minutes later on the same journey, so we're already shaking, it was obvious he wasn't sure of the route. He'd put it into his satnav but was a bit confused and again he was trying to communicate with us by making a series of noises and pointing, and in the end he just pulled over on the hard shoulder on a blind corner. Cars were flying past us and we couldn't see anything behind us. Because he couldn't speak English, Andy was slating him the whole time. I actually wonder if he could understand a bit more than he let on and was doing it just to shut him up."

It wasn't only on the roads where there were fun and games; the trains were an experience, too. Although there was no fun to be had for one young producer the morning he derailed an early-morning trip from Moscow to Nizhny Novgorod.

The party was leaving at 7am to give them plenty of time to get to Nizhny for their match in the evening but with commentator Ian Danter and pundit Matt Holland waiting in the hotel reception at the appointed time, this young chap was still nowhere to be seen. As the clock ticked on, they tried ringing him with no luck before eventually Danter went up to his room and began pounding on the door, finally being met with the cheery words, "Ah, hello, Dants, come in," when it was eventually opened.

Less friendly was Danter's response and the worse-for-wear bleary-eyed producer very quickly realised he'd cocked up badly. He swiftly grabbed the broadcasting kit they needed and they were off. But now they were cutting it very fine, too fine as it turned out, because as they arrived at the station the train was pulling away. Trying to remain positive, the producer in question announced, more in hope than expectation: "It's alright lads, we can still make it." And it was at this point that Danter, normally one of the most mild-mannered men on tour, let rip. "What do you mean, we can still f*****g make it? It's gone. We're f****d."

Fortunately, if you can call a six-hour drive crammed into the back of a car fortunate, one of the local drivers, Slava (nicknamed 'Bobby Charlton' because of his terrible comb-over), was available to take them to Nizhny in time for the match, with one sheepish producer apologising profusely for much of the journey.

But he's not the first person to cause transport issues on tour down the years, with one senior member of staff once taking two high-profile presenters to the wrong airport during Euro 2016. Nor is he the first person on tour to regret a night out, with another senior member of staff once ending up with a very sizeable bill from a local gentlemen's club. It's all part of life's learning curve and, so long as nobody is hurt and nobody sulks, it just becomes another part of the 'talkSPORT on tour' folklore.

Those Russian trains were certainly an experience, though. Adrian Durham remembers one particularly arduous trip to Rostov from Sochi. "It was a distance of 340 miles, and it did seem odd that the journey time was 11 hours. We labelled the train 'The Rostov Trundler' and it couldn't have gone much slower had it tried. The guard on the train laughed and walked away when I asked if there was air conditioning, and with temperatures around 30 degrees Celsius, and five of us in one cabin sweating our wotsits off, it wasn't pretty. Add to that no running water, no food or drink, the filthiest toilet I've ever seen in my life, largely because there was no flush mechanism, and it added up to a situation where if you didn't laugh you would cry. So we laughed a lot. It ended in a wonderful singsong as we pulled into Rostov at around midnight."

So slow was the train, in fact, that at one station stop Matt Holland had time to actually get off and buy ice creams and beers for everyone. The other thing that was most memorable about that trip was the journey took place at the same time as hosts Russia were playing Spain in the last-16. So as the train rumbled slowly through the countryside, the talkSPORT team were receiving messages from colleagues elsewhere and were passing on the score updates to increasingly animated Russians on board the train as their country reached the quarter-finals thanks to a 4-3 penalty shoot-out win. The excitement levels certainly weren't helping to offset the lack of air-conditioning.

Meanwhile, on an overnight trip from Moscow to St Petersburg, Hawksbee and Jacobs were also having train issues. They couldn't find their beds at first and thought they were going to be sitting upright all night. Then a helpful woman came along and showed them how to release the catches to turn the seats into sleepers.

They had taken a bottle of vodka on board and, to help pass the time, had a few drinks and told each other ghost stories in the dark, thinking it might make for some good content on their show. Jacobs, not normally a big drinker, had a bit more than usual and was looking forward to a decent breakfast (there's that food snobbery again). But what greeted him at the table was a solitary and very unappetising buckwheat pancake.

So the transport was a bit hit and miss and undoubtedly required a fair deal of patience, but accommodation in Russia was, for the most part, pretty decent. There were one or two exceptions, however, with Hawksbee and Jacobs particularly unimpressed with what they found in Kaliningrad. "That was the worst hotel we stayed in," says Hawksbee. "Kaliningrad is like the Portsmouth of Russia but without the charm and the hotel was called The Navigator. It had a naval theme with ships' wheels and charts on the walls. It was right next to a petrol station, and you could smell petrol when you went to bed. It was an official FIFA hotel, but I'm pretty sure Gianni Infantino had never stayed there. There were gossamer-thin curtains you couldn't close at night, and there were bed bugs and mosquitos in the rooms."

Another lodging that failed to pass muster was the house talkSPORT used in Samara. It was a small log cabin on the Volga River, and was where Mark Saggers and his production team were staying on the night before England's clash with Sweden in the last eight. It was quite a way from town, and had extremely dodgy air conditioning. There was very little around so producer Sal Ahmad took it upon himself to head to the local shop to buy some ingredients for dinner. But despite his best *MasterChef* attempt, Saggs refused to eat it, claiming the chicken couldn't be trusted and, with a World Cup quarter-final the following day, he simply couldn't risk it. That food snobbery must have been spreading.

Any of the relatively minor issues the teams on the road were having with accommodation, however, were nothing compared to the situation facing the digital and social media team on one of the final nights on tour. There were four of them sharing an apartment in Moscow: producer Joe Aldridge; social media gurus Jamie Sanderson and David Williams; and YouTuber Hugh Wizzy, who was in Russia as part of his 'Mission to Moscow' series, which had aired on talkSPORT 2 in the six months or so leading up to the finals.

Aldridge, Sanderson and Williams had enjoyed a well-earned night out on a rare rest day but, on arriving back at the flat, they discovered Hugh Wizzy had double-locked the door from the inside. Attempts to wake him up failed miserably so the three of them had to sleep huddled together in the freezing, damp corridor of an ugly concrete grey apartment block.

That was to prove the straw that broke the camel's back in a relationship between the four that was already at breaking point, with Wizzy having done little to endear himself to the team.

One of the golden rules of touring is that everyone is in it together and one bad tourist can unsettle the whole thing. But Wizzy was erratic, just wanted to do his own thing, was always disappearing and was virtually impossible to pin down. Things had begun to take a turn for the worse almost immediately when he lost his immigration card and had to go to the immigration office to get a new one, and they didn't get much better. He would constantly complain of feeling tired so had to have a lie down in the afternoons. The Chinese whispers went into overdrive at that point with the more established presenters complaining (maybe jokingly, maybe not) that they had heard, "Hugh Wizzy has got two naps a day written into his contract". Well, you've got to laugh.

Mind you, no one was laughing the night Wizzy fell asleep after leaving a pizza in the oven resulting in the kitchen being engulfed in smoke. Maybe he'd missed his nap that afternoon?

Whether or not Wizzy will be part of talkSPORT's major tournament coverage moving forward remains to be seen, but one man who certainly will be is Adrian Durham. He is, after all, the only person to have covered every major tournament talkSPORT has been part of, right back to those early days in Amsterdam in 2000 in a hotel room with a TV and a lawyer! But that wasn't without drama of its own, even though there was no internal travel, no accreditation to take care of and no other accommodation to be booked. But talkSPORT still found a way to make it difficult for themselves – by sacking their main producer and engineer, the late Jim Brown, on day one of the tournament.

Brown had been asking for a bigger budget for the coverage but management kept refusing, to the point where Kelvin

MacKenzie sacked him shortly after the team had arrived in Amsterdam. And that was when Durham intervened. He says: "I rang Kelvin direct and told him we'd all get on with the job and do it to the best of our ability, but that I knew it would be so much better if Jim was there overseeing it. I put the phone down and within minutes Jim was reinstated. From that moment Kelvin knew I wasn't scared of losing my job – I was confident enough to know I would be able to work elsewhere – and he also knew I would stand up for what I believed in.

"That first tournament was special. That unofficial coverage of Euro 2000 led to a massive change when talkSPORT was allowed to win broadcasting rights for major tournaments. Previously we weren't even allowed to bid. It's the tournament where we started the fight to be taken seriously. We ripped up the sports broadcasting rulebook and rewrote it completely. You've no idea how satisfying that felt.

"We were not allowed to commentate on games in stadia in 2000. But a loophole was exploited, and when the bosses came to me and said: 'Do you want to go and work on the European Championships this summer? It will mean spending five weeks in a hotel in Amsterdam ...' I laughed out loud and accepted the challenge. We had a ball that month. Alvin Martin, Alan Parry, Jim Proudfoot and the rest – we absolutely loved it all. During the commentaries the BBC insisted we had to keep repeating this line, 'This is not the BBC'. We thought it was hilarious! They sent a lawyer to sit in the room with us, and he barely said a word. And he never ever bought a round."

So just how far has talkSPORT's tournament coverage come since those days in Amsterdam? In fairness, so far, it's virtually unrecognisable.

One clear sign that those bad old days were a thing of the dim and distant past came in France at Euro 2016 when Adrian Durham was stationed with the England team. He had discovered prior to the tournament that Joe Hart was a huge cricket fan and that, growing up, Darren Gough had been one of his heroes. The Football Association were not usually receptive to special requests for interviews during tournaments but, after several lunches, numerous emails back and forth and months of planning, Durham managed to arrange for Goughie and Hart to sit down for a special one-on-one interview. It turned out to be a brilliant chat, although it was almost scuppered at the last minute when Durham found out Goughie had booked a spa appointment for the same time! Fortunately, he was persuaded to postpone his pampering.

Goughie recalls: "I did the interview with Joe and I really enjoyed it. I've only been nervous in two interviews I've done working at talkSPORT. Joe Hart because it was actually at a major tournament and the other one was Anthony Joshua. I had 40 minutes on my own with him, up in Sheffield. I could have done another hour. It was the first time that we'd had him one-on-one.

"The relaxing thing with Joe Hart was that I'd played cricket and he actually is a decent cricketer himself. It helps being an ex-sportsman yourself, you actually get more out of them. I got stuff out of Joshua that I haven't heard since. He gave us everything on Dylan White, the Joseph Parker fight. He gave us so much stuff. I remember being interviewed myself and when it's someone you know or an ex-sportsman, you give them a bit more.

"It happened with Johnny Bairstow in Sri Lanka when he lost the plot having been left out and then he got a hundred in the Test match. And he came looking for us and he wanted to do the interview with me and he gave us gold, which didn't go down well with the ECB at the time. It was an amazing dig at the way he'd been treated and we played it out. I wanted to get something no one else had got."

That wasn't the only time Goughie nearly scuppered a broadcast in France, though. At the time the tournament was being staged, he was preparing to take part in *Tour de Celeb*, a Channel 5 show in which eight celebrities would train and then tackle the 75-mile Étape du Tour. So he was in training during the tournament and he set off one day for a bike ride. The problem was, he got lost.

"I'd rented a bike which was rubbish compared to mine. I'd set the Garmin on my phone to take me on a route which I'd put in at 80 miles. I ended up doing 120 miles that day! I just got lost. Didn't know where I was. I was literally in the middle of nowhere with no signal. So it was getting later and later and I didn't know what to do. When I asked people directions, they said 'Which part are you staying at?' and I didn't know that either, I just knew it was Chantilly."

After ages cycling aimlessly and with a live show to get back for, Goughie suddenly remembered the name of the hotel he was staying in. At this point his mobile signal kicked in and although no satnav tracking was coming through, he managed to call the hotel receptionist. "She asked me where I was and I said, 'I don't f*****g know'." Goughie stayed on the phone with the helpful receptionist on the other end of the line as he rode around trying to find landmarks she might recognise. Eventually, with just minutes to spare, he made it back to the hotel, dashed in, sweating profusely, to hear his rather mischievous producer opening the show by playing 'Bicycle Race' by Queen.

Durham reflects on how much talkSPORT's coverage has evolved: "There are obvious things like bigger budgets for each tournament, more staff, some great pundits, but the fundamentals have stayed the same from my point of view. Make no mistake, I still have that same feeling like a kid in a sweet shop when I'm on a plane heading to Russia or South Africa or Brazil. I'm genuinely excited about it. Perhaps a small number of the talkSPORT team complain too much without realising talkSPORT is a station that has to make its own money and its own programmes. We still have to fight for everything. I love those tournaments with talkSPORT. If you're prepared to put the work in, and do it with a smile remembering how great the job is, then they are memories to be cherished forever.

"I've loved all the tournaments I've worked at but Russia 2018 was my career high for many reasons. The football was fantastic, the country was spectacular, and I felt I did my best ever work at that tournament. From my point of view, as I rack up the tournaments, I've become more and more confident and that means my work is better because I worry less. The resources devoted to tournaments always increases and that makes things run far more smoothly. I think management has been far smarter in working out who's a good tourist and who isn't, and that makes a difference. I know that for one huge match at one particular tournament none of the team covering the game were speaking to each other. I'm thankful I wasn't working on that night.

"Doing the *Drive* show with Goughie live from the Luzhniki Stadium just before England's World Cup semi-final was special. For England to have got there was incredible, but to be hosting the show building up to that semi was mind-blowingly brilliant. I remember describing the scenes as the players arrived and walked out on to the pitch, and it suddenly hit me and I felt very emotional about the football, the World Cup, and how far I'd come in my own career to be where I was in that moment. My upbringing was pretty horrific, and at no point would the 12-year-old me have predicted I would be doing what I was doing that July day in Moscow 2018. What a wonderful world."

But while Russia 2018 may have been his favourite tournament so far, the most challenging one for Durham was undoubtedly Euro 2012. With all the dramas surrounding Matt Smith and the missing logistics, no one had any idea Durham was battling demons of his own.

He says: "In January that year I'd been diagnosed with depression. I was on medication, and in treatment. Life was in a bit of meltdown for several reasons. Depression has been within me for as long as I can remember. I was on medication for trauma as a child, but it wasn't properly diagnosed by a doctor as depression until January 2012.

"He immediately put me on medication, Fluoxetine, and offered to refer me to a therapist. In the hope of dealing with the situation as quickly as I could, I found my own therapist straight away.

"I instantly told my boss, Liam, who was very supportive and said if I needed time off that wouldn't be a problem. A couple of good friends at work also knew, and were always there for me which was brilliant.

"There were days when I wasn't right at all, lots of them. But radio is my love: some people get into radio as a stepping stone to TV, or because they couldn't quite make the grade in TV, but I wasn't like that: from a very young age I loved listening to the radio and it's what I always wanted to do. Consequently when the red light goes on and my microphone is live I feel totally relaxed and happy and at home. So as long as I could get through the morning, I knew my salvation was in sight. I also married my best friend and without her nothing positive would have been possible.

"I hear a lot of messages about men experiencing depression, about how they should talk about it and not bottle up feelings. But I think it's important they speak to the right people. Not everyone can handle receiving that information. And the right way forward is vital. So if anyone reading this suffers from depression, I can only share what happened to me and how I tackled it. Hopefully I can help others with this message.

"In Warsaw [at the 2012 Euros], I was sharing an apartment with Goughie for the first two weeks and he lifted me from a bad place. We went to the gym together every day, we cooked each other meals, we socialised and worked together and I was fine. Then Goughie went home, which was always the plan, and I was in the apartment alone. My descent was rapid, and one night in particular seemed impossible. As has always been the case, my release was working, so nobody would know what was really going on just by listening to the radio. But outside of those times it wasn't good for me. So I threw myself into my work, and got through it. Colleagues like Laurie Palacio and Mel Rudd turned out to be lifesavers without realising it. I'll always be grateful to those guys. Getting through those final weeks meant I came back more positive and ready to start again. It's not been perfect, I'm still in treatment, but I'm OK and it's been a lifesaver. I'm still working on the triggers, the causes and the tools to deal with depression days. It feels good, but it also feels like it will be a very long-term project."

Goughie comments: "I've known Adrian a long time now. I can see when it's approaching. I can lift people. It's the way I am as a personality. I'm not the man to be around when things are not going right, as in no hotel rooms booked or stuff like that. That's when I can lose it. All I ever ask for is 3 star. I'm happy, I don't give a s**t. I don't want a 5-star hotel, I'm from Barnsley. All I want is a pool, anywhere to sit down and relax and a gym. When you're away and you're doing stuff all the time, your mind plays tricks on you.

"That's why I got Adrian out of bed every day. Found us a gym and got him out and in there every day. He felt so much better. Even the last trip we did together in Porto, I didn't think he was at his best. I sense it. I feel it. So I'll go out of my way to make sure I'm with him. So I'll take him away for a drink together. When you know someone so well, you don't have to talk about it."

Russia 2018 certainly marked a turning point for the England national team, reaching the last four for only the second time on foreign soil, matching the success of Bobby Robson's team at Italia 90, and finally ending their penalty shoot-out hoodoo as they defeated Colombia in the quarter-finals.

But some things don't change, and one of those is Paul Hawksbee's indecision when it comes to buying gifts for friends and family.

In Brazil in 2014 Paul had a long list of people for whom he had to buy Havaianas and he, Andy Jacobs and their producer traipsed all over Rio in search of the specific pairs he needed, especially for his wife's friend, Mandy. Paul had also prevaricated in a similar fashion over buying a T-shirt when they visited the famous Corinthians Stadium in São Paulo. Jacobs says: "I walked in and saw a T-shirt I liked and something for my son and I bought them straight away. Paul was standing there for about half an hour looking through stuff and I said to him: 'You're never going to be in here again, it's twenty quid, just buy the T-shirt.'"

In Russia, Paul also wanted to get a World Cup T-shirt and they saw them in the airport in Kaliningrad but he decided against that because he wanted to buy it from the official shop in Moscow. So they went there, queued up for entry and the T-shirt was £10 more than it had been at the airport. He was determined not to be ripped off – so they left there in search of the Adidas shop which they finally located, but they didn't have the T-shirt he wanted. So it was back to the official shop, where they had to queue for another half hour to get back in. To pass the time while they waited, Jacobs was texting their former producer Tom Hughes with the words: "It's Mandy's flip-flops all over again."

Hawksbee, however, did eventually get his T-shirt and so, it would be fair to say, did Gareth Southgate, although he would probably have swapped it for a waistcoat. But he can certainly claim to have been there, done that and got the proverbial – and he undoubtedly brought the feel-good factor back and made the English public fall back in love with the England national team.

He even managed to get Saggers onside!

'CLIPS OF THE WEEK'

The Top 20 All-Time Greats

#3

Hell hath no fury like a talkSPORT listener wronged and they are very inventive in getting revenge. Here's Mike Graham reading out a listener's email at the time when the Greek debt crisis was in the news:

"Eric in Coventry says, 'Mr Graham, let the Greeks suffer. A few years ago I bought some expensive sunglasses from a shop in Crete. They broke as soon as I left the shop. I complained, but all I got was thrown out of the shop by three assistants. However, on my last night I superglued the locks to the shop door and had a poo in the doorway ... quality.' Well that's nice, Eric, I'm sure they'll be delighted to have you back."

Chapter 17 ⚽💬

The Legend of Alan Bernard Brazil

"**A**lan Brazil is a legend. There should be a special place in broadcast history for Alan, not just talkSPORT history. He's been sensational."

Those are the words Richard Keys uses to describe the man who has been getting up in the middle of the night for the past 20 years to kick-start the talkSPORT day. To say Alan Brazil is a phenomenon would not be an exaggeration. And when you consider his lifestyle, his longevity is even more remarkable. Pretty much everyone who works at talkSPORT is asked the same question on a regular basis: "What is Alan Brazil *really* like?" And the answer is he's exactly as people believe him to be – very much larger than life.

He lives life to the fullest, and is quite happy to share those life experiences with the listener. And that is a massive part of his charm and appeal. After all, how many blokes out there listening to talkSPORT on the way to work in the mornings can honestly say they haven't reported for duty worse for wear on the odd occasion?

"People are always asking me when I'm going to slow down and take it easy," Alan says. "But I don't see the point of slowing down. Why wouldn't you want to go out and enjoy yourself while you can? This is not a rehearsal."

Of course his high-octane lifestyle has occasionally landed him in the hottest of hot water with station bosses, but he always seems to come out the other side relatively unscathed.

History could have been very different, however, because even at the time he started working on the breakfast show he admits he was unaware of just what a prestigious time slot it is. And he wasn't too keen on the early mornings, either.

"I didn't even used to like getting up to go training, and we didn't start until 10am," says the former Ipswich Town, Tottenham Hotspur and Manchester United striker. "Mind you, at least I'm not running around in the cold any more and finishing work at 10am does have its upside." Yes, and we all know what that is, Al.

Having been forced to retire from football due to a back injury at the age of just 27, Brazil began his media career on local radio in Suffolk before spending much of the 1990s working as a co-commentator for Sky Sports on their Football League coverage. His first foray into national radio came in 1999 when he presented some evening shows on Talk Radio, which was soon to become talkSPORT.

He was actually persuaded to take over the breakfast show by former colleague James Whale who, after a few drinks in Canary Wharf, convinced him he was a natural for the role. And how right he was.

Also proving a natural fit alongside Brazil in those early days was Mike Parry. Their partnership began to take shape towards the end of talkSPORT's first year of broadcasting when Parry, who at the time was the station's Programme Director, would join Brazil in the studio to review the day's newspapers. At that stage, Brazil was the sole presenter, essentially opining on the issues and then throwing to audio clips. Parry felt a regular presence alongside the Scot would give the show a boost, and he knew just the man for the job ... himself. Well, he's never been backwards in pushing himself forward. The two of them had a real chemistry on air and this was buoyed by the fact that they would often warm up for their show by going into a small room and swearing at each other.

And so, in January 2001, Parry became the permanent co-host of *Sports Breakfast* and one of radio's great double acts was born. It was a non-stop barrage of banter, bickering and back and forth between two men who were equally passionate and opinionated. It was unmissable stuff and the audience loved it.

Steve Morgan, who was a producer at the time but would go on to became the station's Programme Director, says: "Anyone who sits behind a microphone for a living is slightly mad. Who imagines that anyone cares about what you have to say? There has to be an element of madness there, and it's all about how you harness that.

"Some of them verge on genius in their own way. Alan Brazil turns up at six o'clock if you're lucky and goes on air with a piece of paper that's been handed to him. He then delivers it with gusto, a sense of warmth and a real panache, like he's been rehearsing it for the past 12 hours. That takes not only consummate skill, but a real touch of genius, to make it sound as though he's in complete control when really he's only just walked in.

"And as for Parry, there is no one else like him and there's never been anyone like Parry. When you listen to Parry, you never go, 'Ah, it reminds me a bit of so and so,' or 'I can hear a bit of this person or that person'. He arrives on air as a completely unique entity and there's nobody else who sounds like him at all. There are plenty of people that have borrowed a little bit from here, or taken a bit from there, but not him. It sounds utterly unique and that's what makes him so special."

The pair struck up a strong rapport and the four hours each morning would simply fly by. And then the serious business began as the duo would often retire to one of their favourite watering holes to continue to put the world to rights, although Parry had to balance the post-show debrief with his 'day job' as the station's Programme Director. That he managed to achieve that so successfully was a remarkable feat, but it was a winning formula from the start, with Parry quite happy to have the mickey taken out of him by the former footballer.

"It was a laugh, we just had fun," says Brazil. "It helped that 'Porky' is so easy to wind up. He's so highly strung, whereas I'm much more laid back. I don't worry about things like he does. He was like my little puppet!"

Their quick-fire, quick-witted exchanges became the stuff of legend, with this being a typical example in the aftermath of a comfortable win for England's national team the night before:

Parry: Al, I was proud of the boys and proud to be English.

Brazil: English? But you're Welsh.

Parry: Al, when they gave out the geographical brains you must have been hiding behind the door. I think you'll find that Chester is indeed in England.

Brazil: Maybe, but look at you. All the signs say Celt. Short. Fat. Ginger.

Parry: Al, I'll have you know that I'm as English as fish and chips, as Yorkshire pudding, as the Royal Family ...

Brazil: The Royal Family? But she's German and he's Greek.

Parry: Your lack of education fails you, Alan. The Queen is as English as I am. We share many similarities.

Brazil: Aye, I'm sure she'll be thrilled about that!

Or this disagreement over the lifestyle choices of modern footballers:

Parry: Al, your only objective in being rich was to live a life of sloth. Young players now have different ambitions.

Brazil: Such as what?

Parry: Unlike your generation of players, they don't want to own pubs and play snooker all day. They want to make films and go to Hollywood. They want to rear animals and livestock.

Brazil: Animals and livestock? What are you on about now?

Parry: These are ambitious young people who want to use their wealth to fulfil proper ambitions.

Brazil: OK, so what are your ambitions then? Why do you work so hard to earn money?

Parry: In the hope, Al, that I'll get enough so I don't have to sit here every morning looking at your ugly mug.

Their partnership lasted four memorable years before ill health forced Parry off air. He was replaced by Graham 'Beeky' Beecroft before he returned to reporting duties in his native north-west in 2007 and Ronnie Irani arrived as Brazil's regular sidekick, which was a bit of a shock to the system of the former Essex and England all-rounder. "After the first show we had a drink at 10.15am," Ronnie said. "Having a Stella at that time was a real change for me!"

Another regular on the show for many years was sports news-reader Ian Abrahams, a man Brazil christened 'The Moose'. He was, and still is, unnaturally lively at the crack of dawn and on one particular morning when he was driving Brazil nuts about something or other, the big Scot turned around and snapped at him, "Will you just p*ss off? And do you know what? You look like a moose."

At the time, Abrahams, who has a thicker skin than a rhino never mind a moose, thought nothing of it. But he had a nasty surprise the next time he went on air to read his bulletin as Brazil introduced him with the words: "It's 6.30 and here with the news headlines is The Moose." And that was it, the name stuck.

Of course, Brazil isn't the only person The Moose annoys in the mornings. He has a particular habit of being over-friendly with presenters and guests on the station, especially if they are high-profile current or former sports stars. He loves nothing more than a bit of a chat and a photo with them, photos that come in particularly handy on their birthday when he tweets his best wishes to his "good friend" [insert name of person who has met him once here!]. He must have more pictures of sporting super-stars than Getty Images! To be fair to The Moose, however, there was one occasion when the commentary team were returning from a live broadcast and were sitting in an airport lounge when they noticed a bit of commotion going on a few yards away. It turned out to be Didier Drogba who was being asked by loads of fans for selfies. He was refusing them all, not wanting to be both-ered, but out of the corner of his eye spotted The Moose and came straight over with a big smile to hug him like a long-lost friend and have a chat.

Sometimes, however, his feeling of familiarity with people backfires on him, as it did spectacularly one morning when he was winding up breakfast co-host and "good friend" David Ginola. It was about the time the Newcastle United side, of which the Frenchman was a part, blew a seemingly insurmountable 12-point lead in the Premier League title race, eventually finishing runners-up to Manchester United. The Moose might have thought it was funny, but Ginola didn't. Indeed, so upset was he by the whole thing that The Moose was officially reprimanded and relieved of his news-reading duties for the remainder of the day.

Whilst The Moose is often the butt of Brazil's jokes, he is a tenacious football reporter who doesn't take no for an answer. He joined the station in 2003 and is terrific at getting the interviews the station needs with the players or managers, and prowls the media zones at the matches with zeal. The Moose has managed recently to upset Sean Dyche (never advisable) by suggesting his team's losing performance against Crystal Palace was "unacceptable"; to annoy Jürgen Klopp by suggesting Liverpool lack defensive cover after crashing out of the FA Cup to Wolves; to anger most Newcastle fans by saying they are not a "big club"; been told to "get off air" by Sam Allardyce who also called him a balloon for good measure and told producers not to put The Moose on with him again; and, perhaps his 'pièce de résistance', to elicit a response from an upset Rod Stewart after he slagged off Celtic following a European exit at the hands of AEK Athens.

If there was one saving grace from the Ginola incident, it was that at least The Moose had offended just one individual, rather than a whole nation as he did on the opening day of the 2010 World Cup in South Africa. That was when he was forced to apologise for on-air comments he made during the breakfast show, after saying he was afraid to venture into downtown Johannesburg. As Brazil would say, "What a numptie."

The radio marriage between Brazil and Irani lasted six and a half years before it was decided to completely revamp the show for the start of the 2013/14 season by utilising a roster of co-hosts including the likes of Ray Parlour, Brian Moore, Micky Quinn, Neil Warnock and the aforementioned David Ginola. The roster has continued to change and develop and newer names in the co-host hot seat alongside Ray Parlour include Lawrence Dallaglio, David Seaman and Ally McCoist.

But some things don't change, including Brazil's timekeeping, as Ally McCoist discovered on his first day in the co-host's seat.

The former Rangers and Scotland star says: "It was my first day at talkSPORT, and I was looking forward to it, genuinely looking forward to it, really excited. I've known Big Al for a long, long time prior to doing the show and obviously we're on air at six o'clock so I got myself into the office probably about five o'clock, keen as mustard. I was going through the newspapers and watching Sky Sports News, catching up with everything just so I was prepared. At 5.30am there was still no sign of Al but I wasn't really thinking anything of it, I knew he sometimes ran a bit late. I was still reading the newspapers – just out of interest, how did Glamorgan get on in the cricket yesterday? – the usual stuff I would never normally be interested in. It got to ten to six and [executive producer] Dave Richards was walking by and I said to him, 'Listen, none of my business really but ...', and I pointed up to the clock and shrugged my shoulders, 'What time do we start worrying?' And Dave looked at me as if I was from Mars and said, 'What are you worrying about? The news isn't even on yet.' Sure enough, as soon as the newsreader sat down and started reading the news, the door kicked open and what can only be described as a whirlwind stroke tornado came barrelling in.

"I was like, 'How are you?' And he was, 'Oof, I've been better, blah, blah, blah'. I'm like, 'We're on in about three minutes'. He's like, 'I know, no panic, no panic'. So we sat down and he was asking me what were the stories and I said, 'I think Glamorgan won at the cricket.' I was still thinking, 'What the ...' and the next thing Big Al was off. 'Good maaaarnin and welcome to ...' And again I was thinking, 'What the f*** just happened there ...?' The guy just switched on like that. It was, and is, remarkable.

"I have never had the pleasure of working with someone like Big Al before, but you've got to say, the man is an excellent broadcaster. He is extremely good at what he does. I know we have a laugh and a joke, but he's absolutely brilliant. You don't front a breakfast show for 19 years unless you're excellent. And that's what he is. I don't know if it's the Glasgow connection but he and I get on superbly well."

Of course, though, there is one very obvious difference between the two. "I don't think the green-and-white/blue-and-white divide will ever change," added McCoist. "In fact I'm fairly confident one or two things might change around here but him supporting Celtic and me supporting Rangers will never change. It's just not going to happen."

Another former Scotland favourite and ex-Rangers player offers a similarly glowing opinion of Brazil, despite his allegiance to the team in hoops across the city. "talkSPORT would not be talkSPORT without Alan Brazil," says Andy Gray. "I've known Alan for a long time – as a team-mate, as an opponent, as fellow broadcaster at Sky Sports, and for two years at talkSPORT, when I got to know him more than well as we took over from him every morning. It was a huge boost for us that Alan accepted us right away because he is the giant personality of talkSPORT, and if he had felt his nose was pushed out of joint it would have been difficult, but he wasn't. He was really welcoming and really supportive."

That warm and generous Brazil welcome was also felt by Laura Woods when she first joined the breakfast show crew.

She says: "When I was younger my dad was a massive talkSPORT listener so Alan's voice is one I have been very familiar with from quite a young age. So he represents a certain nostalgia for me. Whatever you watched or listened to when you were younger, if you saw it or heard it now you'd feel a little bit nostalgic. He resonates with me, and has done for a number of years.

"I first worked with him at the Sir Bobby Robson Celebrity Golf Classic, the year before I got the job at talkSPORT. I was so excited to meet him and work with him. He was next on the tee, driving up in a little buggy, and he knew he had to do an interview with us. The buggies all went past, all these famous faces, and then you saw Alan Brazil's come up. It pulled up really sharply, he got out of the buggy, walked over, and you could see the buggy was full of empty cans. It was probably about 10.30am, and it was boiling hot because it was in Portugal, and he walked over and his head was all red. I asked him if he needed some sun-tan lotion, and he just said, 'No, this I all I need,' holding up a can of beer in his hand.

"The following year the whole event culminated in a night at a bar on the beach. Alan was brilliant and he sat in a chair on the beach – Ray Parlour one side, me the other – and we sat there like kids listening to him. I just find him so welcoming and endear-ing, it doesn't matter who you are and he doesn't need to know who you are, he'll still welcome you and tell you a million stories that never grow old.

"I got the role doing the paper review on his show and I felt really comfortable going in there, and I've never looked back. We get on well and it's very easy working with him. From there the role developed so I probably owe him a lot. If you can work well with Alan and bounce off him, you're set really."

Of course, there are warm welcomes and warm welcomes, and all his co-hosts understand there can be perils attached, as McCoist, who co-hosts the breakfast show on Thursday and Friday each week, can attest.

"After about the third show we did together he decided to take me on what could only be described as a 'Brazil London Tour' of a number of West End premises. Niall Horan from One Direction was also with us, having been a guest on the show that morning. What could go wrong? As I looked at my watch at 11am I knew, I absolutely knew, I wasn't getting the 2pm flight from London City Airport to Glasgow. That's how confident I was that pro-ceedings were going to take a turn for the worse.

"So at 6.45pm I had a decision to make. Do I take the last flight to Glasgow? Do I take up Niall Horan's very kind invitation to sleep on his couch? Or do I go back with Brazil and sleep on his couch? And thankfully, in one of the best decisions I've ever made in my journalistic career, I got the last flight to Glasgow. I can remember all these punters who had obviously finished work in London for the week and were off home to Scotland looking at me knowingly and saying, 'Had a good day, Ally?' But I definitely did make the right decision.

"I cannot keep up with him, and I wouldn't even think of taking him on [in the drinking stakes]. But this is not like coming to work, this is not like a proper job. If you can't enjoy this, you can't enjoy anything. Every day you walk in and everyone is up for it. I mean we're talking about sport, and we love sport, so it's brilliant. But two days a week alongside Alan is enough. I'm not sure who would go first if we did any more, him or me. Two days a week is ample, with a capital A."

Working with Brazil certainly presents a unique challenge. "You don't manage Brazil, you manage the world around him," says former Programme Director Moz Dee. "When I first got to talkSPORT the news bulletins on the breakfast show would go on forever. I would get in to work in the morning and Alan would be dozing on the sofa during a news bulletin. So we cut those bulletins down to two minutes, so the listeners got more Alan Brazil. After all, that's who they were tuning in to hear.

"Having said that, in those days, for the first half hour of the show he was sometimes slower to warm up so we built a half-hour schedule peppered with guests and content that made sure he didn't have to speak a huge amount. That gave him time to get going and then you got him into it."

Those wise words of Dee's, "You don't manage Brazil," are words all his producers down the years will probably agree with. The current incumbent is Scott Richards, and he admits the job is unlike anything he's done before, and probably unlike anything he'll do again.

He says: "You never know what each show is going to be like. He turns up on a good day at about 5.55am, but the norm is about 5.58am. He has a quick flick through the papers and the Sky Sports channels and bases his opinion on what he's just read or seen. He's an absolute genius at it.

"During the show, he's like Ron Burgundy – whatever you give him he'll read. The amount of work that goes into creating a read or a cue for him is quite labour intensive, but he just picks it up, reads whatever is on the page in front of him – sometimes on air he's questioning what he's reading and will admit he doesn't agree with it even though he's just read it out.

"It's quite nice in a way because other presenters will have their own opinion on what they think the show should cover, and as producers we might disagree. But with Alan you know if we want to do this at this time we will do it, because he just follows what we tell him.

"I don't think I'll ever work with anyone like him again. I don't know how he's done this for nearly 20 years, and how he manages to go out with mates all day, eat very little, probably collapses into bed around 8–9pm (on a good day) and then gets back up and does it all again. It's unbelievable. He's not real."

These sentiments are echoed by current breakfast show co-presenter Ray Parlour, who says:

"Working with Alan is brilliant. I'll always remember my first day on my first show. I was a bit nervous. Obviously you're going to be for your first show. And between 6 and 6.15 he'd had a sleeve of biscuits. Not just one or two, but, the whole lot. Then at 8 o'clock he's organising where we're going to go after the show! So he's been brilliant to work with. He's got a lot of fans out there. When I'm doing after-dinner speaking, everyone's saying, 'Where's Alan? Where's Alan Brazil? Is he really like that?' The biggest compliment I can pay him is that no one asks me about Denis Bergkamp or Thierry Henry, they ask me about Alan Brazil."

Dean Saunders has exactly the same experience. "People used to ask me in the street, 'What's that Gareth Bale like? What's Ryan Giggs like? What's Ian Rush like? What's Mark Hughes like?' Now, every person to a man asks me, 'What's that Alan Brazil like?' Everybody likes him. If I'm doing an after-dinner speech, and I mention his name, everybody laughs."

Brazil's habit of cutting it fine before going to air is well established and in the early days 'Barman Dave' Richards also had another producer, Andy Clarke, to ensure Brazil got to the show in time. One freezing cold winter's morning, having phoned and phoned Brazil's mobile repeatedly, Clarke was dispatched across Blackfriars Bridge half an hour before the show was due to start, to go and knock Alan up from the apartment he was staying at. Clarke knocked, and knocked and knocked, but to no avail. Resigned to a management bollocking for failing to deliver Brazil, Clarke walked back over the bridge and into the studios to find Brazil sitting on the couch outside the studio having a cup of tea. A mischievous Brazil said with a grin, "Ah, Clarkey, I just drove past you in the cab. I thought it was weird you were walking over the bridge at that time in the morning." Sometimes, however, getting him into the studio requires the craft and guile of Henry Kissinger. Certainly David Walker, now the station's Football Editor, will never forget the day he first produced *The Alan Brazil Sports Breakfast*.

They were set to have Mark Bosnich as co-presenter for the first time. The former Aston Villa and Manchester United goalkeeper had been a regular guest on the show from Australia, but he was in the country so it was decided to get him into the studio for the whole show. It was a pretty big deal, as the pair were always talking about how they needed to get together and have a beer, although Alan probably would have preferred to do it in Sydney.

Of course it was the usual story with Brazil, one all of his producers over the past two decades have got to know all too well. If he's not arrived at ten to six they're not too worried, five to six and they're still thinking it will be fine. But when it gets to 5.59am and there's still no sign of him they begin to fret ever so slightly. So at 6am breakfast-show debutant Walker was staring down the barrel when a call came into the control room from reception to tell them Alan was outside. That was the good news. The bad news was ... he wanted to go home. Reception was told not to let him go under any circumstances as Walker ran down the stairs. Meanwhile, the show was starting, the newsreaders were going through the morning headlines and the overnight presenter was having to stay on air to fill in for Brazil.

Walker got downstairs and outside the building where he found Brazil hanging half out of a cab in the road, leaning forward into the gutter where it appeared he was about to be sick. Walker says: "He looked up at me, his eyes were so red, and he said: 'Dave, I don't know ... seafood yesterday ... I'm not sure ... I've eaten something ... dodgy seafood ... I can't do the show ... no way.' And we knew he'd been out all day the day before because he'd been talking about it on the show. I said to him: 'Al, Bosnich is here.' And he went: 'Oh, for f***'s sake, I forgot about Bossie. Fine, OK, I'll do it.' We got him upstairs, but we couldn't put him on air straight away. We had to sit him down in the control room, and the image I always liken it to is when there's a whale on the beach and people are just spraying it with a hosepipe to try to revive it. So we were feeding him loads of water and coffee, but he was just sitting there. We finally got him on air at around 6.15am but the show was a bit of a shambles. I was thinking to myself, well, what if he goes home? This is the first time I've produced the show and I'll have Mark Bosnich on his own for four hours."

As so often happens with Brazil, disaster was averted, however narrowly. He always seems to find a way. He has also found his way to some memorable destinations over the years, although it would be fair to say some trips have been more successful than others.

One early overseas jaunt saw Brazil and Parry take to the skies to the USA in January 2004, in an idea that was off the wall even for talkSPORT. British Airways Flight 223 from London to Washington had been grounded for two days amid the threat of a terror attack and Brazil convinced himself he and Parry needed to be on board once it finally departed to send a message to the potential terrorists that they could not win. The plan was then to present the breakfast show from Washington before returning home the following day.

British Airways loved the idea and agreed to fly the pair first class free of charge. But as they prepared for take-off on day three, a delay left Brazil and Parry sitting on board a near-empty plane on the tarmac for a little over three hours. But no matter, that just meant extra drinking time to get through as much free Champagne as possible. And so successful were they in that mission that the cabin crew actually had to send out for more bubbly before they could eventually take off.

That set the tone for the entire trip as the pair proceeded to enjoy BA's hospitality throughout the flight before sampling the delights of a Celtic Supporters' Club in Washington and then a local piano bar. The revelry was paused for a few hours at 2am local time as the fun-loving duo presented *Weekend Sports Breakfast*, still having not slept since they left London. Five hours later, once they were off air, both men were ready for some shut-eye but, within three hours, were back in tandem at the hotel bar as neither had been able to sleep. And with their return flight not due to leave until 4am the following morning, well, what else was there to do but continue the party?

Seven months prior to that Washington adventure it had certainly been party time for Brazil when he was dispatched to Seville to present the breakfast show on the morning of the UEFA Cup final between Porto and his beloved Celtic. The trip was not without its problems, starting with the fact they could not find their way into the city having landed at an airport several hours from Seville. Sound engineer Phil von Oppen was the man tasked with driving Brazil and Parry from the airport but they ended up hopelessly lost. At one point, they even crossed the border into Portugal! Having finally made their way to the city, Brazil was taking no more chances, so hopped out of the hire car and flagged down a passing taxi for the final stretch to their hotel.

With the final taking place the following evening, Brazil joined a number of his fellow Celtic fans for a few drinks that night, with Parry naturally along for the ride. But he bailed out of proceedings relatively early leaving Brazil to create havoc. Brazil picks up the story: "I'd met a mate of mine in Seville who was with an old guy that had never previously been on a plane before. Never been out the country before but had flown out for the game. Massive Celtic fan but he didn't have a ticket. So I said to him, 'You're not going to get one, there's about 100,000 people here. Bugger it, you can have my ticket. In fact you can have Mike Parry's as well.' So I gave them both our tickets.

"But I didn't tell Parry. So on the day of the game we're having a few drinks and Mike's going, 'Come on, Al, we've got to go, we'll miss the start of the game'. And I'm saying, 'I've got something to tell you, Mike … we don't have any tickets.' 'Of course you've got tickets,' he says. 'We've got tickets.' I said, 'No, I've given them away'. Parry was laughing now and I said, 'No it's not a joke, I gave them away. And to make matters worse, we've not got a bed tonight either. They had no bed so I've given them our beds.' He said, 'You're joking'. But I said, 'No I'm not, we'll just stay up all night!' Parry wouldn't talk to me for ages saying he didn't mind the tickets but not the bed. Anyway we ended up watching the game in a bar and staying up through the night."

Brazil would have gone to that match but, as has been mentioned previously, he has regularly turned his back on major sporting events.

One such occurrence was the Ricky Hatton–Floyd Mayweather fight in December 2007 when, on arrival at Las Vegas airport with Manchester United fan and breakfast show co-host Ronnie Irani, and being a former United player himself, Brazil found himself the subject of plenty of stick from Hatton's army of mainly Manchester City supporting fans. That was enough for the big man, who immediately decided he had better things to do than spend his Saturday night in an arena full of boozed-up Mancunians abusing him, good naturedly or otherwise.

At this point Irani was still confident he could persuade his buddy that, having flown halfway around the world, they really should, maybe, perhaps, actually attend the fight. But Brazil would not be swayed and instead was quite content to amuse himself by drinking and gambling on the Strip.

In his own way, Brazil does enjoy these overseas trips, but in a way most ordinary folk would probably struggle to understand. For instance, he spent a week in Rio de Janeiro at the start of the 2014 World Cup. But other than to present the breakfast show between 2am and 6am each morning and fulfil his obligations to a well-known electronics company who were paying him handsomely for his time, he spent all day, every day sitting next to a massive generator by the swimming pool supping lager. This despite the fact that one of the world's most famous and iconic beaches, the Copacabana, was literally across the road.

Another prime example of the weird and wonderful world of Alan Brazil on tour was his week-long trip to Brisbane for the first Ashes Test in 2017. It was a late call by his talkSPORT bosses to allow him to travel Down Under and, by the time the decision had been made, the cost of his first-class ticket was a whopping £11,000. Of course, he couldn't go alone as someone would have to make sure he was able to broadcast his show each day from the other side of the world, so producers Tom Hughes and Scott Richards were dispatched along with him. Clearly, however, their tickets in economy didn't quite cost as much as the presenter's luxury travel arrangements.

So luxurious, in fact, that he had basically been allotted his own cabin on the flight. It wasn't merely a nice comfortable flat bed, it was actually a room complete with his own shower. So when Hughes and Richards arrived in baggage reclaim to meet him, they were somewhat surprised to find him sitting there, bright red in the face, sweating and looking as though he had run a marathon. It seems he had enjoyed other things in first class, but not the bed or shower.

Brazil tells the story: "We came via Singapore and I was travelling first class and the boys were behind me. I was on this Napa Valley red. It was magnificent. And the attendant kept saying to me, 'Shall I make your bed, sir?' And I'm saying, 'No, no, no. I'm fine.' And she's saying, 'But you look tired,' and I'm saying, 'No I'm watching the movies'. I had *The Godfather* films on. I said to her, 'The only thing you need to look out for is when my glass is empty. Eventually, we were approaching the airport for landing and she says, 'Can I get you anything? We might be here for another 20 minutes circling as it's very busy.' So I said, 'Well, I'll have another glass of red'. She went away coming back a few minutes later saying, 'Sir, you can't. You've drunk all four bottles. We've run out.'"

They did the show each day from a pub in Brisbane, often with members of the Barmy Army in attendance, but with no actual guests – they were all back in the studio in London. Brazil went to the first hour of the first day of the first Test and other than that, when he wasn't on air, spent the rest of the trip in his hotel room. Even now no one really knows why he wanted to fly all the way to Brisbane to spend a week jet lagged in a hotel room, but to him it made sense.

At least on that trip he was happy to be there, but there are times when he is less thrilled with his surroundings. One such venture was to Rome in April 2018 for Liverpool's Champions League semi-final. He was accompanied by co-presenter and former Liverpool and Aston Villa striker Dean Saunders. But the trip got off to a sticky start.

"The whole trip was funny," says Saunders. "On the way to the airport, Alan said we should get a taxi to Heathrow. I'm thinking, 'Not the Heathrow Express? It's only about a 20-minute trip.' Alan said, 'No, Billy the Cab will take us'. So we get in the cab but it's taking us ages and we're stuck in traffic and Alan is saying, 'This is a mistake this, Deano, it's a mistake. It's a mistake going this way. So this was how the day had started out."

"Then we got to the airport and Alan got his ticket out and said: 'We're in economy. We're only in economy, you know? Unbelievable. I'm going to ring Dave [Richards].' But Dave's not answering so he's leaving messages saying, 'Dave, Dave, we're in economy, it's not on. It's not on.'

"So then The Moose turns up and The Moose is only sitting further up the plane than Alan and we were at the back. So Alan's on the plane and raging. The Moose is all comfy and snoring and we can hear him from the back of the plane. Alan had also turned to his producer and said: 'We'd better not be far from the hotel when we get there.'" Luckily for Barman Dave, they weren't.

Everything started going swimmingly on the day of the game, as Brazil and Saunders presented the breakfast show from a lovely rooftop terrace bar above the famous Spanish Steps. This location had the added benefit of allowing them to get stuck in to the post-show refreshments as soon as they were off air.

Saunders continues: "The show finished at 10. Alan orders a bottle of Champagne and we had a few drinks, sat outside on the restaurant table on the terrace. Some Liverpool fans turn up and they were on the balcony above. There were other people coming in. This woman came in and sat to the side of us with her 16-year-old son."

The pair enjoyed the bubbly and continued into the afternoon, with Saunders manfully trying to keep up with his partner. At around 3pm in the afternoon, with neither having even been to the toilet, Saunders announced he needed to go and headed off to find the facilities. When he returned some 45 minutes later he looked extremely fragile and pale. Producer Hughes asked him if he was alright, adding a knowing pat on the leg for good measure. Saunders had been well and truly 'Brazilled'.

But that wasn't even the worst of it because shortly afterwards some Liverpool fans who were drinking on the terrace just above them threw a water bomb down at the talkSPORT table, and it exploded everywhere.

Saunders continues: "One of the lads up above on the roof, got a bag of water, tied it in a knot, and threw it over the top and it bounced right in front of Alan. It just missed me but it hit Alan and the woman and it's gone all over her. We didn't know what it was at the time. It could have been anything – piss, lager, wine – we didn't know.

"We had signed autographs for some of the lads that did it and they had been talking to Alan. They'd been nice. It was one person who thought it was funny. Apparently he does it as a prank all the time."

Brazil recalls: "We'd been chatting away, having a few pictures then someone throws a bag of water from the balcony. The poor woman next to me got the fright of her life. I thought she was going to have a heart attack. My first worry was that it was piss but it wasn't, it was water. We just left it and sat there. If it had been piss I'd have run up there but would probably have got battered as there was about 30 of them."

To add to his displeasure, the Liverpool fans had filmed it, and the breakfast boys, sensing an opportunity, took the footage and published it on the show's Twitter feed. Alan hadn't seen this and was clearly not best pleased. Normally, Alan is up for a laugh as much as anyone at the station, but on this one he became angry at giving the guy any notoriety and refused to come down from his hotel room to do the show the following morning. That resulted in The Moose having to take up presentation duties with Saunders before Brazil arrived about 40 minutes in, sat down and broadcast as normal. The audience was told he'd 'got stuck in traffic'. Saunders says, "I asked Alan if he'd watched the game, to which he said, 'No, I listened to it on the radio'. And I said, 'What, in Italian?'"

During the short trip, Brazil had ventured no further than the bar and the hotel. So imagine the surprise of the producers, who had managed to catch a few sights, when Brazil announced as they headed back to the airport in a cab, "Nah, Rome, it's not for me."

It's certainly never dull when people are overseas with the big man.

But when his mind is made up, it's made up, and often no amount of persuasion will convince him to change it. That was certainly the case in 2018 when he flat out refused to go to Russia for the World Cup, despite repeated attempts to get him there. Even after England had beaten Colombia in the last 16 and he was hearing so many positive stories about Russia from the likes of Ally McCoist, Ray Parlour and Adrian Durham, he simply stood his ground and made it clear he was more than happy to remain in London. "I don't know why everyone was making such a fuss," he said. "I just didn't want to go. And it wasn't like Scotland were playing."

Of course that stubbornness can be an advantage in a broadcaster, particularly when they are having to back up their views. But sometimes they can say things that go very much against public opinion, and Brazil has certainly found himself in that category a few times over the years. Not that he tends to care too much whether people agree with him or not.

After all, not too many people would have described the suicide of comedian and actor Robin Williams as "diabolical" and added they were "really annoyed about it". Brazil had also mentioned that initially his wife had told him that it was Robbie Williams who had died rather than Robin, but said, "Oh, OK. It didn't hit me hard like if it had have been Robbie, and thank

God it wasn't." Even with his co-host Brian Moore arguing against those views, Brazil would not be swayed, insisting his only sympathies lay with Williams's family. He added: "I believe he's got a daughter as well, what's she feeling like this morning? Now she's got to sort out the arrangements. I think it's just shocking, I really do. I don't have a lot of sympathy, I'm sorry."

Sympathy was also in short supply in January 2019 when he laid into Andy Murray after the tennis ace's tearful retirement speech on the eve of the Australia Open when he broke down in front of the media. It may have had housewives the length and breadth of the UK sobbing, but Brazil was having none of it.

He said: "I don't do blubbing. He's playing tennis for God's sake, I'm not having the bubbles, the tears. The pain, the pain, the pain. What were the tears? I don't recall Djokovic or Federer crying their eyes out. I admire what he has done, but I don't want tears. If he's in pain, go to a proper specialist and get it sorted. I'm not having this. Anyone can play tennis. I'm more mobile than he will ever be. Don't get married and don't have a kid if you want to be a sportsman. I'm putting this down to being a father. Having a kid changes your life. I'm being serious, I think Andy's got a bit of a problem to be honest. He's got to be a little bit careful. I don't like to see a grown man break down like that. I had people kicking me, not Slazenger balls hitting me."

Even co-host All McCoist branded him a "cold-hearted man", while Jim White went a touch further, claiming his fellow Scot was "talking utter tripe".

Former England manager Sam Allardyce joined the breakfast show in a co-hosting role in 2017 alongside Alan Brazil. Allardyce says: "I used to listen to Brazil and occasionally later on the day, e.g. Keys and Gray. They were fantastic – gave a lot of credibility to the station. Alan is legendary – not just as a presenter – but watching him working from 5.55am or usually 6.05am! He's very generous and times when he brings you in. It flows so well and 90 minutes can fly by. Sometimes at 6am you think, 'Four hours, what are we going to talk about? [But it] goes so quick. Alan always puts his hand into pocket for the breakfast, never lets me pay, and we occasionally share a few drinks after a show. I know my limits now. Younger days I would have carried on.

"I joined on the basis of airing a manager's point of view compared to other presenters and pundits relating some stories from my career ... promotion, relegation, transfers, etc. [It's a] nice platform – unedited, completely live – which really appeals. It's good to be involved and have so many people listening. Maybe I've upset one or two but generally [they] have been OK. My judgement has always been what people say to me in the street, not what the media say about you. Now I get stopped very regularly by people in the street saying, 'I like listening to you on talkSPORT,' more than you'd imagine.

"As a manager, you are not well liked. [I] don't listen much but at times the press officer tells you what they are saying about you. I accept what you have to do [talkSPORT] and can see that's helped grow the station to what it is today. In the earlier days sometimes saying things for effect. Used to sound manufactured! The station is now more successful than anyone else doing sports radio. My advice to managers and ex-players thinking of going on is, 'Give it a go and see how you feel'. A few more managers would be great on talkSPORT, it's a fantastic opportunity."

One story involving Brazil which will live on in the memory was the night that, not long after being acquired by News UK, a get-together party was arranged in The Shard. News UK had made a couple of acquisitions so this was a chance for all the staff in the companies to get together and get to know each other. It was a meeting of minds and ... er ... culture. There were canapés, vol-au-vents, things on cocktail sticks and some fine wines and plenty of beers and Prosecco. The great and the good from the company were there. All of the senior management, editors from *The Times*, *The Sunday Times* and *The Sun*, feature writers from the 'Style' fashion section, writers from *The Sun*'s weekly 'Fabulous' magazine, bookish writers from *The Times Literary Supplement*, political editors and analysts. Chief Executive Scott Taunton, perhaps mindful at what might unfold given the track record of the talkSPORT team, issued a three-line whip. Everyone to be there on time. Everyone to behave. And everyone to mix and mingle. That message got through to most with the exception of Alan Bernard Brazil, Mr Michael Quinn and Mr Raymond Parlour who arrived late for the event. Clearly having had some refreshments during the day and clearly very merry.

Parlour says: "We had a little livener beforehand. Me, Mick and Alan but I got there late. I came in from Essex on the train and I met Micky and Alan in another bar in The Shard. I don't know how long they'd been there. I think Alan had been there for most of the day. We ended up going to the do that night and it was quite 'lively'."

While they proceeded to help drink the house dry, Brazil was due for a 'roll-call' photo with Rebekah Brooks and top *Times* sports writer Henry Winter. Winter is a dapper man but on this occasion and a good 11 hours after finishing his show, that's not a description that would have applied to Alan who by now looked like he'd just come out of the rainforest having been mauled by an orangutan. The assembled throng was entertained to a photo of Brooks and Winter both looking exceptionally smart with a sweating Brazil perched on the end of the photograph. It sort of summed up that cultural divide. Brazil did the photo, turned to leave the building and promptly fell down the flight of stairs.

Brazil recalls the ending slightly differently: "We'd been in The Shard on the top floor during the day but it was my knee that went on me. I was on the escalator and my knee just buckled underneath me. It was when I was having big problems with it."

Parlour, who had been with him during the day, 'sort of' agrees, saying: "I remember Alan couldn't get down the stairs. He tried to get down that last step but he had to hold on to the rail. He put it down to the fact that his 'knees locked' although I don't know how many bottles of wine he'd had that day."

Despite a lifestyle that would finish off lesser mortals, Alan Brazil is now one of the longest-serving breakfast-show presenters in British radio. His contribution to radio was recognised on

4 December 2014, when he was inducted into the Radio Academy's Hall of Fame – a very prestigious award and one that cements his legendary status. The Radio Academy is the industry body for the sector and as well as helping people get into radio, runs a series of festivals and events as well the Hall of Fame induction which honours those who have made a significant contribution to radio. Alan was inducted at a lunch at London's Savoy Hotel in front of a star-studded guest list with everyone who's anyone in British radio attending.

Brazil was pleased with the award. "There's all these different awards for radio but the BBC seem to win everything. It was a big surprise but great because my kids came, and Jill came. What was really nice about it, apart from being in the Hall of Fame, was the other presenters who came up to me. Jo Whiley told me her dad listens every day and Trevor Nelson said he was a big listener. You think, 'wow' that's great, other presenters listen. I'll have done 20 years in December [2019]. It's a long time so it was nice to get a bit of recognition."

In being honoured this way, Alan's name now sits alongside many other famous names from British radio including Sir Jimmy Young, Richard Dimbleby, the Goons, Terry Wogan, Kenny Everett, Tony Hancock, Kenneth Williams and Arthur Askey.

Not bad for a boy from Castlemilk.

He celebrated his 60th birthday in June 2019 with a live Friday morning broadcast from his local pub followed by a get-together near his home in Suffolk the following day. He's been getting up before the crack of dawn and presenting a four-hour sports radio show every weekday for the last 19 years and he's brilliant at it. And he shows no signs of stopping just yet.

'CLIPS OF THE WEEK'

The Top 20 All-Time Greats
#2

Here's 'Beeky' getting ever so slightly confused giving a score update:

"OK, Mansfield 1, Northampton 0 in that, er ... other play-off. Er, sorry, Mansfield 0, Northampton 1 ... Mansfield 0, Northampton 1 ... er ... Day getting the goal after 14 minutes played ... Er, Northampton 0, Mansfield 1 ... I beg your pardon, let me get it right.

Northampton 0, Mansfield 1 in that other play-off semi-final which is going on today. That's a Division Three play-off semi-final so it's Mansfield 0, er, Northampton ... sorry it's Mans ... Northampton 0, Mansfield 1 ... let me get it absolutely right in that other play-off semi-final that's going on today ..."

Chapter 18 ⚽

Three New Stations Launch and Media Mogul Murdoch Gets on Board

alkSPORT has seen huge changes over the years, rising from the madcap early days under Kelvin MacKenzie's stewardship to its current place as the world's largest sports radio broadcaster.

There have been plenty of bumps in the road along the way, but there has never been a more turbulent period than the 18 months between January 2015 and June 2016. By the end of it all, nothing would ever be the same again.

In that time period, UTV Media, (the then owners of talk-SPORT) launched and then sold a new TV station in the Republic of Ireland; created three new national radio stations in the UK; and were taken over by one of the largest media organisations in the world. It was quite the wild ride.

UTV (Ulster Television) had existed for more than 50 years where it owned the regional ITV franchise to broadcast in Northern Ireland. It also had a signal overspill into the Republic of Ireland, where it could be picked up on cable systems and by Irish rooftop aerials in areas around the border. That meant that although TV3, which was the ITV equivalent in the Republic, also held the rights to broadcast big ITV programmes such as *Coronation Street*, lots of people in the Republic watched on UTV because that's where they always had.

So UTV knew that there were a reasonable number of viewers who watched their programming in preference to TV3 in the Republic. They took the view that if they approached the market in the Republic properly and acquired the necessary broadcast and distribution rights, they could grow and monetise those viewers. So plans were formulated and a brand new TV station, called UTV Ireland, was to be launched from offices in Dublin in direct competition against TV3.

Through UTV's position as a regional franchise holder in the ITV network, they had approached ITV's in-house production team to do direct deals to broadcast programmes such as *Coronation Street*, *Emmerdale*, *The Jeremy Kyle Show* and *Ant & Dec's Saturday Night Takeaway* on the new Dublin-based station.

But it wasn't all plain sailing. Whilst UTV Ireland had bought the rights to *The Jeremy Kyle Show*, it was only for the current series. Their rivals TV3 still held the rights to re-runs of the old *Kyle* shows – and so they broadcast them head to head against the programmes UTV Ireland had just acquired. TV3 also already had the rights to big blockbusting ITV programmes which were produced outside of ITV's in-house production team, by independent production companies, including one of the hottest shows at the time, *Britain's Got Talent*.

In short, from day one of launch in January 2015, in the face of a very aggressive scheduling from TV3 and viewer criticism of the overall programme content and the amount of repeat shows, it became apparent very quickly that UTV Ireland wasn't going to attract the audiences it needed in order to be sustainable. The audiences weren't on target. And therefore the vital advertising revenue was not flowing in at the rate required. So losses were mounting at the new TV station.

All of which put a huge financial strain on the overall UTV Media group and for talkSPORT the knock-on effect was keenly felt. Although the station was doing really well, there was not going to be significant investment while the focus of the business was on fighting a battle in the TV market in Ireland.

Scott Taunton, who had by now been named as UTV Media's Chief Operating Officer, says: "With radio, even if you think you've got it right, you don't get the audience numbers until months after programmes have been broadcast due to the audience measurement system. But with TV, you get overnight ratings. You know the next day. You know from day one what the numbers are.

"Had we been launching a new national radio station in January 2015 no one would have panicked until much later in the year because of the audience measurement method."

As it was, within months of the launch of UTV Ireland, negotiations began between the UTV board and ITV to sell the television assets to ITV, which took place in October 2015. Subsequently, ITV went on to sell UTV Ireland to TV3.

The UTV name was also sold to ITV as part of that deal, meaning the radio group needed a new identity, and it was eventually decided to revert to being called Wireless Group (as it had been when talkSPORT first launched back in 2000). While this drama was playing out across the Irish Sea, there were also major changes afoot within talkSPORT Towers.

An opportunity had come up to bid for a new set of digital radio licences in the UK and, as part of a joint venture consortium, UTV Media (Wireless Group) had won the licence.

That was announced in March 2015 but, with all the uncertainty surrounding UTV Ireland, and the financial strain that was causing, Taunton remembers thinking the board might not actually be too pleased they had been successful, when at any other time they would all have been doing cartwheels.

Whatever the thinking, it was too late to back out. It now meant that, having been awarded the frequency, they had 12 months to deliver the new stations they had promised as part of the winning consortium – talkSPORT 2, talkRADIO and Virgin Radio.

So it was a ridiculously tight timeline and, of course, as was the talkSPORT way – maximum ambition, minimum budget – they would be doing it on effectively a shoestring. There was just £1 million of capital expenditure to build all the new studios required and anything that went alongside them – desks, chairs, computers, any other IT equipment, the whole shooting match. It all had to be done for less than £1 million.

And no one was really sure where the new studios would go, or where any of the people sitting at the desks and operating the computers to create the shows would be housed. This was in a building already creaking at the seams and with multi-lingual instructions pleading with people not to block the bogs!

Indeed, so tight was the space that Taunton had to give up his management office in order for it to be rebuilt as a studio for Virgin! More presenters and producers were turning up daily as the new stations headed towards launch.

Ex-Radio 1, Radio 6 and Capital FM presenter Edith Bowman was brought in to host the *Virgin Radio Breakfast Show*. *The Sun* film critic Jamie East covered mid-mornings. The first ever female winner of *Big Brother*, Kate Lawler, joined from Kerrang! Radio to present the afternoon show and comedian Matt Richardson took on the drive-time slot. On talkRADIO, Paul Ross was on the breakfast show, with Julia Hartley-Brewer, Jon Holmes and Sam Delaney covering the other shows throughout the day and with Ian Lee on the late-night slot. At weekends on talkRADIO there was an eclectic line-up of presenters for launch including *Homes Under the Hammer* presenter Martin Roberts, TV presenter Penny Smith, Eamonn Holmes, Bob Mills and Howard Hughes with his *The Unexplained* show. Also finding its way on to the schedule was a show called the *The Two Mikes*, featuring talkSPORT's Mike Parry and Mike Graham's weekly battles. And talkSPORT 2 added to the melee with a raft of new producers brought in to get the live sport from Cheltenham and the World T20 to air.

The new stations also meant talkSPORT would lose some of its stalwarts, people who had worked tirelessly down the years to help build the station into what it had now become, often in the most trying of circumstances. Mike Bovill was named as Managing Editor of talkSPORT 2, Dennie Morris took up the same role at talkRADIO, while Lauren Webster was named Production Manager of that station.

There was a lot of upheaval and a huge amount of work that went in to launching the three new stations in less than 12 months. It was a massive achievement by all involved, although it's hard to believe they pulled it off.

On 16 March 2016, talkSPORT 2 was the first to launch. Unlike talkSPORT's frenetic launch back in 2000 when the desks were still being screwed together as the station went live, talkSPORT 2 was in much better shape, but the usual teething problems were prevalent. Nothing was quite fully ready. The studios didn't quite work properly and there were lots of things still unfinished. Bovill was not allowed to employ any full-time staff, everyone had to be freelance, and no one could start before 1 March. So Bovill had just two weeks to get his team – a number of whom were kids straight out of college – trained and ready to launch a national sports radio station. And somehow they did it. The pressure around the launch was compounded by the fact that rather than do the easy thing and launch from the studios, it was decided to go on location and launch from the Cheltenham Festival which started that day.

As a complementary service to talkSPORT, the second station made perfect sense and would allow for the broadcast of more than one sporting event at any given time; football on one station, cricket on the other, for example.

National Controller Liam Fisher says: "talkSPORT 2 was born out of the fact that on a linear channel like talkSPORT you can only broadcast one thing at a time. So when two sporting events we want to cover are on at the same time we have to make a choice as to which one to broadcast. Invariably that is Premier League football, which meant a lot of other things were getting overlooked, things like the English Football League (EFL), rugby world cups, golf events and international cricket. It gave us the opportunity to pursue these rights now we had the additional channel."

The perfect example of this was the deal talkSPORT 2 struck with the EFL. Fisher added: "From the EFL's point of view, they had the situation where the BBC owned the rights but didn't broadcast as many matches as the EFL would like, perhaps due to other scheduling clashes. So we said to them [the EFL] we want the rights, and not only that but we will broadcast those games. If you give us 110 games a season we will broadcast 110 games, we won't just broadcast 45. We'll do the whole lot. So they are getting exposure for their clubs. We're treating these teams the way we would treat Premier League clubs. We're giving them national exposure and giving people the opportunity to hear their club matches, particularly for fans who can't attend when their team is playing away from home."

As noted earlier, the new station launched live from the Cheltenham Festival, a staple of the talkSPORT calendar for a number of years – and at the eleventh hour they had also managed to pull off something of a coup and secure rights to the ICC World T20, which started on the day of launch.

So they went straight from the launch at Cheltenham into live commentary of international cricket. That evening they had live Champions League football followed by overnight coverage of the ATP Masters tennis event in Indian Wells. By anyone's standards, that was a very strong start.

Unfortunately, not making such a strong start was Andy Murray. Following the euphoria, and relief, of the launch, the normally mild-mannered Bovill was relaxing in a hotel bar in Cheltenham when, in the early hours of the morning, he shocked a packed crowd by loudly exclaiming, "Argh, you ****!" as he discovered Murray, then the world's No1 ranked male player and at the top of his game, and one of the pillars of the planned coverage for the first week of the new station, had been beaten in Indian Wells. At that point, it's fair to say the pressure was probably getting to him. That's Bovill, not Murray. Whilst you can plan for lots of things, one thing you can't plan for is sporting success.

But from those difficult early days, talkSPORT 2 has developed into a destination for sports fans and continues to deliver top-quality coverage of Premier League football, Champions League football, exclusive Football League and Carabao Cup commentaries, as well as live Premiership and international rugby union, and live international cricket, including England's winter tours to Sri Lanka and the West Indies in 2018/19.

And some of the kids who started there in early 2016 have even grown into adults.

Incredibly, however, the unveiling of the three new national radio stations – including the extraordinary feat of launching Virgin Radio from a moving train travelling between Manchester and London – was not to be the biggest story of 2016.

At around the same time as the new stations came into being, talks were beginning that would change the landscape for talk-SPORT and its new sister stations forever.

Early discussions to sell Wireless Group had begun with Rupert Murdoch's News Corp, but at that stage there was a big gap in valuation expectations and the two parties were nowhere near agreeing a deal. Within three months, however, they were.

Taunton says: "A lot of people would not necessarily have thought News Corp would be the natural buyer for a group of radio stations and I think even myself and other members of the board would not necessarily have assumed News Corp would be interested in these assets. But once you hear it, it makes perfect sense.

"As we worked our way through the process I was convinced it would be a good thing for talkSPORT, for the wider Wireless Group and for the people within it. Not least because News Corp is happy to take a long-term view on business, and to invest for the future. You don't get criticised for big ideas and aspirations. That's exactly what our national stations have needed."

Even after the £220 million deal was agreed, however, there was one more potential stumbling block – Brexit.

"I remember meeting David Dinsmore (Chief Operating Officer at News UK) and Chris Longcroft (Chief Financial Officer) on the Friday before the Brexit referendum and the conversations had gone well and the general view was we were basically there on the deal," added Taunton.

"Sensibly everyone wanted to wait until after the referendum to see what state the markets were in and no one was keener than me to stay up and watch proceedings, pretty much expecting the deal to be announced the following day.

"The result took the advisers by surprise, although some members of News were expecting it, and the markets took a turn.

There was an expectation that it might be a while before Britain was open for business again.

"But what I really respected about News Corp is they took a couple of days to reflect on their position and then came back and said they wanted to continue on the same terms and that they were backing Britain. I think that was the first acquisition of a public company post the referendum."

What followed was a period of integration that eventually saw the radio stations move, after 19 years, from the rather dilapidated talkSPORT Towers to purpose-built, multi-million pound, state-of-the-art studios overlooking the River Thames in News UK's London Bridge headquarters.

This time there were no engineers under the desk to greet them. And Adrian Durham had a chair to sit on. But the move from the South Bank to London Bridge did mean the end of an era, and the end of talkSPORT's time at Hatfields, which had been the station's home since its inception in January 2000.

The building had seen a lot of changes over the years since talkSPORT's launch. Graham Norton and his production company So Television occupied the ground floor for a number of years before being booted out to make way for the new radio stations. The infamous canteen had been built and then rebuilt. In the latter stages there were far too many people in the building for the plumbing to cope and the four production-floor toilets – affectionately named Tevez, Radcliffe, Ennis and Ronaldo – were frequently closed as they often resembled a crime scene. The two showers in the basement took a battering every Wednesday lunchtime as the weekly five-a-sides took place on the council pitches opposite. It wasn't unusual when taking clients on a tour of the building to arrive in the lift in the basement to the sight of a dozen sweaty blokes wandering around in their underpants and towels waiting to get washed.

As the stations and staff moved in stages across to the current London Bridge premises, there were a few clusters of staff left in the building which came to be known as 'Precinct 13' – the forgotten outpost. There was a genuine fondness for the place among the staff, but in the end there were precious few tears when it came time to say farewell particularly with the revelation that there were maggots discovered under the carpet tiles as the removal men stepped in.

This is how Jim White described Hatfields the first time he visited. "I thought it was a s**thole, an absolute dump. And then it didn't even live up to that billing." Anyone who worked there will know he had a point. There's no doubt it had a unique feel to it.

At various times down the years exterminators or fumigators were called in to deal with infestations of mice, fruit flies and any number of bugs, the toilets would block on an almost daily basis and the kitchen on the building's second floor, which is where the studios were housed, should probably have been condemned. But the place had a sense of nostalgia about it and the cramped production floor led to a real vibrancy.

The tightness of the team and the often 'backs to the wall' mentality meant that for many of the ex-players coming in to do shows, it was the closest thing they had to replicating the dressing-room feel.

Ray Parlour says: "Yeah definitely. The guys behind the scenes do such a great job but people don't see that. You know, all the producers, they run the show. And it's a little bit like that footballer banter in between the ad breaks. I'm very lucky to get the opportunity at talkSPORT and I've loved every minute of it. And as much as Alan [Brazil] would moan, he loves it as well."

Dean Saunders comments: "I got two bits of advice when I started doing this. One was from Alan saying, 'Don't ever try and pretend you were at a game when you weren't, because you'll get stuck'. And the other bit of advice from Liam Fisher was, 'What we want is that when people are on their way home from work and listening to the show and stop outside their house – they stay in the car because they want to carry on listening'. So we try and talk like we're sat down the road. If we go down the pub afterwards or for lunch, we carry on the conversation. You wouldn't even know we were on the radio. People wonder what we talk about in the breaks. We carry on talking in the breaks as if we were on the air."

For all its faults, the building at Hatfields holds a place in the hearts of many that worked there given it had hosted some of the biggest names in UK sporting history (and other professions) over the last 20 years. Some now gone but mostly living. These included: Alan Shearer, Alex 'Hurricane' Higgins, Frank Lampard, Gary Neville, Gene Simmons, George Best, Don King, Hulk Hogan, Harry Redknapp, Gordon Brown, Alastair Cook, Ant & Dec, Joe Root, John Barnes, Graeme Souness, Joe Frazier, Jedward, Ian Botham, Anthony Joshua, Boris Johnson, Brian Clough, Courtney Walsh, George Foreman, Bradley Wiggins, Frank Bruno, David Cameron, Evander Holyfield, Greg Rutherford, Kevin Keegan, Meatloaf, John Cleese, Glenn Hoddle, Jonny Wilkinson, Kenny Dalglish, Kevin Pietersen, Michael Palin, Noel Gallagher, Liam Gallagher, Mike Tyson, Michael Parkinson, Ledley King, Mark Cavendish, Paolo Di Canio, Paul Gascoigne, Ronnie O'Sullivan, Stephen Hendry, Shane Warne, Roy Hodgson, Sugar Ray Leonard, Terry Venables, Prince Naseem Hamed, Rebecca Adlington, Niall Horan, Olly Murs, Russell Brand, Simon Cowell, Tim Henman, Tom Hardy, Richie McCaw, Tyson Fury, Wayne Rooney, Gary Oldman, Vitali and Vladimir Klitschko, David Haye, Jimmy Anderson ... and many, many more. George Best actually did his last ever interview in the talkSPORT studios. Alex 'Hurricane' Higgins was a gaunt figure when he arrived. And when Prime Minister Gordon Brown paid a visit, he was presented with the iconic photo showing the extraordinary half-time score in the UEFA Cup tie in 1995 of Raith Rovers 1, Bayern Munich 0.

The man with the biggest fan mob was Hulk Hogan who stopped the traffic both inside and outside the building; the best-smelling man was, apparently, Paulo Di Canio; George Foreman set his best-selling grill up in the studios to give a demonstration while Paul Hawksbee and Andy Jacobs had their hands covering the fire alarm; and Mike Tyson arrived with 15 minders that you'd never want to meet in a dark alley.

In no particular order, in Hatfields, the coffee machine didn't work; the kettle was full of limescale so anything that came out of there was disgusting; the bins were overflowing; the fridges were a health and safety hazard; and the dishwasher was full of dirty dishes that no one wanted to deal with.

Jim White comments: "You'd walk in and you were delighted if you could get some of the cheese out of the mousetrap, and if nothing bit you on the backside when you were on the throne in the morning. But the building had character, it was a production line, and had an atmosphere all of its own. Certain individuals I invited in had a look around and they were like, 'Really, you're telling me this is a studio'."

Andy Gray recalls: "I spent many a happy morning when I got in around 8.30am washing up cups because at that time of the morning there would be an awful lot of cups in the sink that needed washing. There was a dishwasher but I opened that one day and it was even dirtier than the sink! Keysie used to spend the break between Alan's show and our show hoovering the studio, tidying the desk, throwing out all the papers. When Alan was finished, the studio could look like anything."

Gray was not the only one to view the kitchen facilities with a healthy degree of suspicion. When Sir Alan Sugar (he was not yet a Lord) came in to be a guest on the *Hawksbee and Jacobs* show, he graciously turned down the offer of a cup of tea after noticing that the guide dog belonging to a visually impaired producer had been sick on the floor by the sink. Meanwhile, Neil Warnock had his own reasons for bringing his own mug to the studios. On his first week co-presenting the *Sunday Exclusive* show, he had used a talkSPORT mug and had been ill for the rest of the week. After that, he insisted he wasn't taking any more chances.

Another man who arrived prepared was world snooker champion Ronnie O'Sullivan, who turned up one day to be a co-host with Colin Murray and brought his own packed lunch with him. Brilliantly, he also washed up a few cups and gave the kitchen a bit of a rub-down. He was always welcomed back.

Slightly less welcome were singing twins Jedward, who were right at the top of the charts when it came to being among the strangest guests ever to appear on talkSPORT. While waiting to go on air, they walked around the production floor opening drawers in people's desks – even while people were sitting there – and also opened all the cupboard doors in the kitchen and had a rummage around the fridges. It was certainly unusual behaviour, and also foolhardy. Most of the people who worked there wouldn't go near the fridges.

The big problem was that the building really wasn't big enough for four national radio stations, with talkSPORT and talkRADIO having to share office and studio space on the second floor, with talkSPORT 2 one floor below and Virgin Radio on the ground floor. And the presence of a music radio station in among their speech radio brethren certainly caused the odd issue, the biggest of which was when Virgin had a band in playing a live session the noise would often bleed through the floor and the talkSPORT 2 studios would shake. On the day Virgin launched, Reef played a live gig on the ground floor in front of an excited audience of staff and clients and almost took talkSPORT 2 off air.

And the other bugbear for the staff was that Hatfields also had a rather 'unfortunate' car park at the rear of the building. There was a very narrow ramp from the street down, lots of poles to navigate and a very tight bend. In the morning three or four cars would signal 'car park full'. What felt like virtually every day, someone would have to go and move their car as they'd be blocking Alan Brazil in – more often than not Danny Kelly's big Jeep. Whilst Brazil would be sitting waiting in reception, some poor young producer would be sent to ask Danny to move his car. Which he normally couldn't as he'd be in the middle of his live show so he just used to throw the keys to them and ask them to move it. But given the aforementioned tight squeeze in the car park, for a 21-year-old fresh out of college, trying to reverse £50,000 worth of car up the ramp was nerve racking. It got to the stage that the producers would run and hide rather than have to move the presenters' cars. There was also an ongoing argument over space with the law-firm neighbours. It would be a frequent occurrence that they'd be asking for talkSPORT cars to be moved out of their space.

In the end they got a pop-up bollard working which would prevent any non-registered cars from parking in their space.

But unfortunately through malfunction or otherwise, the bollard managed to pop up twice to rip out the underside of Simon Jordan's Maserati and did a similar damage job to Mike Graham's Jaguar F Pace. Graham explains: "I didn't realise that Simon Jordan's car had been hit by the same bollard three days earlier. Anyway, I'd just finished my late-night show, jumped in the car to reverse out when the bollard popped up and ripped out the underside of the car, puncturing the petrol system as well. Needless to say when the insurance company asked, "Could I smell petrol," the answer was "Yes". They advised evacuating the area but I wanted to get home so waited two hours for the breakdown services to arrive. The bigger problem as it happened was that Ian Lee was following me out but my car was blocking him in and was still there the next day! All in all it took a month for the car to get fixed."

All of that is now in the past, however, with the new offices and studios a thing of beauty. The WiFi works, the chairs all have arms *and* legs, each desk has a fully functioning computer that doesn't take 15 minutes to boot up, there are automated video cameras in the studios, state-of-the-art coffee machines and clean toilets that don't block twice a day.

'CLIPS OF THE WEEK'

The Top 20 All-Time Greats

#1

Here is the unforgettable breakfast-show chat, and our top clip of all time, between Alan Brazil, Mike Parry and TV critic Garry Bushell:

Bushell: I feel a bit of a fraud today.
Brazil: Why?

Bushell: Because I wasn't watching any TV last night. I was at the filming of the BAFTA tribute for Bob Monkhouse over at the BBC.

Parry: Bet that was a lot of fun?

Bushell: Oh, there were some really nice contributions from some great people, including some of the best of the younger comics around now, like Jimmy Carr, Jack Dee and Steve Coogan. And the clips were absolutely sensational, they had all of his greatest one-liners, his acting roles, nostalgia by the bucket load. I mean, you forget he was in things like *Carry On Sergeant*.

Parry: Well, Garry, many people forget that he was one of the greatest stand-up comedians you've ever seen. I saw him years ago when I was a reporter in Chester and at the time we only knew him as the host of *The Golden Shot*.

Brazil: I tell you what, he can do a blue version as well which is meant to be fantastic.

Bushell: Oh yes, you can get those on DVD probably now. This tribute show goes out the weekend after next on BBC One. And you're right, you're left in no doubt that Monkhouse was a giant.

Brazil: Garry, what about Bob's health now?

[Silence]

Bushell: Er ... he died at Christmas.

[More silence]

Parry: I think Mr Brazil was, erm, just ... just looking a little back there rather than forward ...

Brazil: I see. I heard two different versions of it, to be honest. Two different versions I was told.

You do have to wonder who told him the *other* version.

Chapter 19 ⚽

Shiny Happy People

The new talkSPORT studios at News UK HQ in London Bridge were officially opened on 7 March 2019, a star-studded day so far removed from the very first day of broadcast almost 20 years previously that it could have been a different station. And in many ways, of course, it was.

There was certainly something different in the air when Alan Brazil turned up at the studios at 5.23am, quite probably his earliest arrival since records began! This truly was a new dawn.

He was joined on air by Ally McCoist and Dean Saunders with the pair both keen to have their say on their new surroundings. Saunders insisted: "This place [the studio] is like a spaceship. The last one looked like a scene out of *Shameless*."

But for all the joy and good cheer, McCoist did have a genuine concern about a potential issue with their palatial new home high up in the London skyline. "What if, Al, somewhere down the line there is a problem with the lifts? I don't see you getting up the full 17 floors!" Some of the regulars on the station do indeed do this 17-floor climb every day, including former Crystal Palace player Clinton Morrison.

But that was a worry for another time with everyone determined nothing would spoil the party, to which some huge names had been invited. The guest list read like a Who's Who, including England manager Gareth Southgate, England Lionesses manager Phil Neville, pop superstar Olly Murs, England Rugby

World Cup winner Lawrence Dallaglio, former world super middleweight champion George Groves, cycling legends Sir Bradley Wiggins and Mark Cavendish, former England wicket-keeper Matt Prior, celebrity chef Michel Roux Jr, and legendary commentator and now station regular John Motson. Not bad for a first day.

Chris Evans also popped in for a chat and a glass of bubbly, having earlier had Brazil on his own breakfast show on Virgin Radio just a couple of floors below, while News UK's Chief Executive Rebekah Brooks and Wireless Group CEO Scott Taunton joined Brazil to cut the ribbon and officially open the new studios following talkSPORT 2's relocation there the week previously.

Taunton said to staff at the launch party: "talkSPORT and talkSPORT 2 are in a good place editorially, commercially and now physically too – occupying the best radio studios in the country. This is a truly exciting time for Wireless and the opportunities that will come to work ever closer with our colleagues at *The Sun*, *The Times* and *The Sunday Times*.

"Today is a landmark day. Our leading media brands are already collaborating. Alan [Brazil] joining Chris Evans on air this morning is just the beginning. The future's bright, with the best brains and broadcasters now in The News Building."

It was left to Rebekah Brooks and Alan Brazil to cut the cake in front of the assembled crowd. As they joined hands and slid the knife in, someone shouted, "You need to make a wish!"

Brooks smiled and said, "I wish Alan would turn up every day". To which Brazil quipped, "So do I!"

Ray Parlour captures the change perfectly: "It's been a different level. It's like going from a relegation battle into Champions League football. That's how I'd sum it up. The building itself, the class of the place, the studios. Just everything involved in this building has been absolutely superb."

And the station also has a new boss, with Lee Clayton, formerly the Head of Sport at the *Daily Mail*, recruited as Head of talkSPORT at the end of 2018. It completes something of a full circle for Clayton, who presented the Sunday breakfast show on the station for three years in the mid-noughties. And he has now returned to his first love – radio.

"I had very little radio experience, certainly no presenting experience, but Kelvin MacKenzie had some kind of idea that I might be able to do it. I was thrust into it but I had a brilliant producer, Russell D'Albertanson, who showed me the ropes."

Clayton's first co-host was Tony Cascarino and, as life would have it, Cascarino is back on the station co-hosting *Weekend Sports Breakfast* under Clayton's management. During one show, Cascarino's false teeth fell out live on air, leaving Clayton in a fit of giggles. That didn't seem to particularly bother Cascarino at the time, but he was less than impressed when his ex-mother-in-law also started laughing at him in the supermarket having heard Clayton winding him up about it on the show. Clayton says that Cascarino actually took him into a cupboard in the old talk-SPORT studios and told him if he laughed at him again on air he was going to hit him. "I thought he was joking," says Clayton, "but he was deadly serious. I really thought he might whack me but eventually he calmed down."

Clayton has retained his love for talkSPORT ever since those days, and was thrilled to be asked to take the helm at the station. He says: "I'd been at the *Mail* for 14 years as Head of Sport and I had lots of opportunities to leave and go elsewhere. I had spoken to my wife about it and when she asked me if I were to leave there and do something else what would I like to do, I said I'd like to go and run talkSPORT. So when I was offered the chance to do that it was an opportunity I couldn't refuse."

talkSPORT has long been viewed as the 'noisy neighbour' but since its acquisition by News UK it is now clearly a major player. As the station turns 20 years old and is now settled in its new London Bridge studios, what next? After broadcasting the FIFA Women's World Cup in summer 2019, the station has now acquired more live Premier League matches than ever before for seasons 2019/20 to 2021/22 – with over 115 live matches every season across the talkSPORT network on Saturdays from mid-day through until the early evening. It is a massive coup for the station which allows them to really get behind Saturdays

– the traditional home of live football. Despite all of the movement of games to suit TV schedulers, Saturday remains 'game day' when the bulk of games happen and everyone keeps an eye on the scores up and down the leagues.

The station is already preparing for its coverage of Euro 2020 which uniquely and excitingly will be hosted at various countries rather than having one host nation. Following that will be Qatar 2022 (assuming it remains there!) and, in between, England cricket tours of South Africa and India. So the live sport keeps on coming and Alan Brazil keeps on creating the magic every weekday morning on the station.

As Brazil says: "Here is different class compared to Hatfields. Now it's a joy to get out the car and walk up into that [News UK] building. It's an absolute joy. You feel good and you feel you're part of an organisation that is going places. I've done nearly 20 years now and this has been worth it. It's different class."

Oh yes, talkSPORT really has come a long, long way in the past two decades, but you get the sense that this is only the beginning. There are big plans and big ambitions, and in many ways it feels as though the journey is only just starting.

Happy birthday, talkSPORT! Here's to the next 20 years …

ABOUT THE AUTHOR

 **Ian Cruise** (50) was born in Luton and is a fan of his hometown club. He worked for talkSPORT between 2010–2017, managing all digital editorial content for the station. He covered three major football tournaments during his time at talkSPORT, the European Championship finals in Poland and Ukraine in 2012, and France in 2016, as well as the World Cup finals in Brazil in 2014. With more than 30 years' experience in sports media, both digital and print, his previous clubs include MirrorFootball, Football365 and *Shoot* magazine (he still has his League Ladders!). He is the author of sporting biographies on Peter Crouch and Fernando Torres, and has contributed to a host of publications.